Principles of Islamic Ethics for Contemporary Workplaces

Abdus Sattar Abbasi
COMSATS University Islamabad, Lahore Campus, Pakistan

Razaq Raj
Leeds Beckett University, UK

IGI Global
PUBLISHER of TIMELY KNOWLEDGE

A volume in the Advances in Human Resources Management and Organizational Development (AHRMOD) Book Series

Published in the United States of America by
IGI Global
Business Science Reference (an imprint of IGI Global)
701 E. Chocolate Avenue
Hershey PA, USA 17033
Tel: 717-533-8845
Fax: 717-533-8661
E-mail: cust@igi-global.com
Web site: http://www.igi-global.com

Library of Congress Cataloging-in-Publication Data

Names: Abbasi, Abdus Sattar, 1970- author. | Raj, Razaq, 1968- author.
Title: Principles of Islamic ethics for contemporary workplaces / by Abdus Sattar Abbasi and Razaq Raj.
Description: Hershey : Business Science Reference, 2020. | Includes bibliographical references and index. | Summary: "This book explores principles of Islamic ethics for contemporary workplaces"-- Provided by publisher.
Identifiers: LCCN 2020001193 (print) | LCCN 2020001194 (ebook) | ISBN 9781799852957 (hardcover) | ISBN 9781799852964 (paperback) | ISBN 9781799852971 (ebook)
Subjects: LCSH: Business--Religious aspects--Islam. | Social responsibility of business. | Work environment.
Classification: LCC HF5388 .A23 2020 (print) | LCC HF5388 (ebook) | DDC 297.5/64--dc23
LC record available at https://lccn.loc.gov/2020001193
LC ebook record available at https://lccn.loc.gov/2020001194

This book is published in the IGI Global book series Advances in Human Resources Management and Organizational Development (AHRMOD) (ISSN: 2327-3372; eISSN: 2327-3380)

British Cataloguing in Publication Data
A Cataloguing in Publication record for this book is available from the British Library.

Advances in Human Resources Management and Organizational Development (AHRMOD) Book Series

ISSN:2327-3372
EISSN:2327-3380

Editor-in-Chief: Patricia Ordóñez de Pablos, Universidad de Oviedo, Spain

MISSION

A solid foundation is essential to the development and success of any organization and can be accomplished through the effective and careful management of an organization's human capital. Research in human resources management and organizational development is necessary in providing business leaders with the tools and methodologies which will assist in the development and maintenance of their organizational structure.

The **Advances in Human Resources Management and Organizational Development (AHRMOD) Book Series** aims to publish the latest research on all aspects of human resources as well as the latest methodologies, tools, and theories regarding organizational development and sustainability. The **AHRMOD Book Series** intends to provide business professionals, managers, researchers, and students with the necessary resources to effectively develop and implement organizational strategies.

COVERAGE

- Diversity in the Workplace
- Strategic HRM
- Personnel Retention
- Employee Relations
- Corporate Governance
- Worker Behavior and Engagement
- Personnel Policies
- Human Relations Movement
- Organizational Behavior
- Job Enrichment

The Advances in Human Resources Management and Organizational Development (AHRMOD) Book Series (ISSN 2327-3372) is published by IGI Global, 701 E. Chocolate Avenue, Hershey, PA 17033-1240, USA, www.igi-global.com. This series is composed of titles available for purchase individually; each title is edited to be contextually exclusive from any other title within the series. For pricing and ordering information please visit http://www.igi-global.com/book-series/advances-human-resources-management-organizational/73670. Postmaster: Send all address changes to above address.

Titles in this Series

For a list of additional titles in this series, please visit:
https://www.igi-global.com/book-series/advances-human-resources-management-organizational/73670

Youth Work in a Digital Society
Zeinab Zaremohzzabieh (Universiti Putra Malaysia, Malaysia) Seyedali Ahrari (Universiti Putra Malaysia, Malaysia) Steven Eric Krauss (Universiti Putra Malaysia, Malaysia) Asnarulkhadi Abu Samah (Universiti Putra Malaysia, Malaysia) and Siti Zobidah Omar (Universiti Putra Malaysia, alaysia)
Business Science Reference • © 2020 • 301pp • H/C (ISBN: 9781799829560) • US $295.00

Appreciative Inquiry Approaches to Organizational Transformation
Sudipto Bhattacharya (Vellore Institute of Technology, India) and Tanusree Chakraborty (Rajalakshmi School of Business, India)
Business Science Reference • © 2020 • 277pp • H/C (ISBN: 9781522596752) • US $225.00

Innovative Management and Business Practices in Asia
Patricia Ordoñez de Pablos (The University of Oviedo, Spain) Xi Zhang (Tianjin University, China) and Kwok Tai Chui (The Open University of Hong Kong, Hong Kong)
Business Science Reference • © 2020 • 365pp • H/C (ISBN: 9781799815662) • US $225.00

Stress Analysis and Disparities Among Men and Women in the Outsourcing Industry Emerging Research and Opportunities
Sonal Pathak (Manav Rachna International Institute of Research and Studies, India)
Business Science Reference • © 2020 • 150pp • H/C (ISBN: 9781799820239) • US $145.00

Strategies for Attracting, Maintaining, and Balancing a Mature Workforce
Claretha Hughes (University of Arkansas, USA)
Business Science Reference • © 2020 • 338pp • H/C (ISBN: 9781799822776) • US $215.00

Management Control Systems and Tools for Internationalization Success
Nuno Miguel Teixeira (Instituto Politécnico de Setúbal, Portugal) Joaquim Silva Ribeiro (Instituto Politécnico de Setúbal, Portugal) Ana Bela Teixeira (Instituto Politécnico de Setúbal, Portugal) and Teresa Godinho (Instituto Politécnico de Setúbal, Portugal)
Business Science Reference • © 2020 • 270pp • H/C (ISBN: 9781799820079) • US $245.00

IGI Global
PUBLISHER of TIMELY KNOWLEDGE

701 East Chocolate Avenue, Hershey, PA 17033, USA
Tel: 717-533-8845 x100 • Fax: 717-533-8661
E-Mail: cust@igi-global.com • www.igi-global.com

Table of Contents

Preface

Contemporary workplaces are subject to numerous challenges from absolute technological transformation to real-time globalised working platforms. Significant developments have brought human life in today's age of robotics and androids. However, still, there is a huge thirst for workplaces where people trust each other unconditionally; employees have absolute belief in their top management, shareholders look at financial statements without a shadow of doubt, and society considers business organisations as their partners. Scholars are working tirelessly to achieve this objective for decades. Standardisations and certifications have brought significant improvement in overall confidence in contemporary organisations. But, suddenly an incidence of any breach of trust anywhere on this planet shatters the confidence of masses on business organisations.

Our focus on training and development somehow fails to sustain pressures and temptations. People do cross lines where they find opportunity to settle pressure or address both spontaneous and chronic temptations.

One way of approaching this challenge is to connect contemporary workplaces to the belief system. This book is designed to provide a framework of Islam work ethics for contemporary workplaces to approach issues and challenges of today's workplace in a manner which remains rewarding for both lives, here and hereafter. This unique motivation will probably facilitate people to develop aspiring workplaces in modern organisations where besides achieving material objectives people attain spiritual satisfaction through their routine of daily activities both at office and home.

This Book addresses key aspects of contemporary workplaces; however, there might be numeral aspects which our good readers may think should be the part of coming editions. We are looking forward to your valuable feedback to improve our work (In Sha Allah).

ORGANISATION OF THE BOOK

The book is organised into 12 chapters. A brief description of each of the chapters follows:

Chapter 1 discusses and critically evaluates the conceptual, theoretical and principles of Islamic ethics of workplace and playing a critical role in developing the individual person and the whole society. Islamic ethics is based on the al-Qur'ān and Hadith and the whole process of business dealing is based on the eyes of faith. The chapter reveals that in today's competitive environment it is imperative for the corporate world to find a management paradigm to execute strategic policies in true spirit for effective and efficient performance of organisations to achieve optimal outcomes. The Islamic teachings advocate that Islamic ethics are founded on the concept that certain absolute truths apply everywhere. Islamic ethics do aspire for people to consider developing a standard that speak for right or wrong.

Chapter 2 establishes the importance of Islamic work ethics plays very imperative part for companies to develop standards and business dealings based on honesty. The overall aim of the chapter is to discusses the ethical issues were not properly addressed by the businesses for better economic transparency toward key stakeholders. The ethical issues were not followed by businesses and perform economic transparency toward key stakeholders. The ethical issues are not being followed by businesses and shows economic transparency to key stakeholders. The Qur'ān declares that pursuance of safe and high-quality ideals as one aspect of actualising safe and reliable products and services for the customers. Islam encourages the business contractors and suppliers to conduct activities according to Islamic ethical guidelines.

Chapter 3 examines and evaluate the fundamental beliefs of the Islamic ethical system that there to serve and develop good morality and avoid indecency and immoral conducts within business dealings. The ethic policies within multinational companies can cause long term complications and conflicts for people with different backgrounds and religion. The overall aim of the chapter is to consider ethics of multinational companies (MNCs) activities and for their workforces. The Islamic ethics system helps and enhance businesses, workforce and customers to operate in honest and transparent manner. More importantly the Islamic ethics system emphasis that our personal and business dealing should be according to commandment of Allah and ethical behaviour to be part of the faith. This chapter has developed some key insights into the interactions between the Islamic ethics and multinational companies (MNCs) activities and their workforces.

Chapter 4 reviews the principles of corporate governance codes and explain how to create approachable system to support individual businesses. Also, provide examination for customers and businesses to understand and provide clear-cut accounting terms for principles of Shari'ah developed Islamic Finance. The chapter further suggest that Corporate governance plays important role in economic performance because it provides mechanisms which affect returns on investment. Multinational companies need a set of institutional and market mechanisms that allow managers and board members to maximise the value of the residual cash flows to the shareholders. Particularly, adopting the rules and principles when implementing weight and measures, fair trading rules, checking business, frauds and auditing illegal contracts.

Chapter 5 demonstrates that Information Technologies has rapidly grown and changed the global communication networks ways of sharing and exchanging the information. The new technology has completely changed businesses communication format with customers. It is very difficult for ordinary individual to understand and realise that how much technologies have been changed which will impact on daily life of individual customers. Immense development of new technologies has been the focus of debate regarding ethical guidelines for their application. The chapter further analyse information technology has radically changed the way businesses communicate with their customers and how ethics is being undermined in the business industry. Islamic workplace ethics believe that confidentiality sharing of information should only be given to limited and relevant stakeholders in the business.

Chapter 6 provides insights into Islamic ethics a fine balance between shareholders' interest and value for other stakeholders of the society. Injustice in Islam seen as an obstruction to the human welfare, deepen social unrest and dissatisfaction among society in general. In Islam, the role of the state includes the administration of a social security system in which the religiously decreed zakat assumes a central position. Chapter also argued that management of an organisation must work toward achieving Islamic ethics through just and equitable means. Illegal ways and means are considered to spoil the whole system of corporate organisation.

Chapter 7 addresses the conceptual implications of companies planning to engage the Muslim customers, employees and other stakeholders. Islam sees business as an essential pillar of society and before the noble prophet Mohammad (PBUH) commencement his mission, he was very successful businessman with his honesty, reliability and trustworthiness towards his customers. Chapter further examined the organisations operating in Muslim communities need to know fundamental beliefs that drive the behaviour of Muslim customers. Today organisations are embracing multiculturalism as business pragmatism. Awareness about permissibilities can facilitate consumptions on macro level. The Islamic ethics make it very clear to manufacturers and traders not to make false promises, false hopes and deception is any of the promotional activity. The prophet Mohammad (PBUH) set the standards for business dealing even before he declared the prophethood that traders should follow honesty, reliability and trustworthiness towards his customers.

Chapter 8 focuses on reviewing development of Islamic banking vs. Conventional banking. Islamic finance over the last few decades is one of the fastest growing area in the world. Leading Muslim countries started to adopt the Islamic finance as a key and important financial transaction tool for trading. The Islamic ethics in finance support the economic monetary system that is designed to operate according to Quran and Sunna of Prophet Muhammad (PBUH). The Islamic Finance is comparable system to conventional banking that sets up capital markets, banks, investment and insurance companies. It is essential for Islamic banks and financial institutions to follow Shari'ah compliant financial system. The growth of ethical banking is believed to have given a boost to Islamic banking

Chapter 9 explores how Islamic ethics and corporate social responsibility (CSR) two compatible concepts. chapter further discuss that corporate social responsibility (CSR) is an idea that has been constantly evolving as business firms are continually more aware of the community around them. CSR encompasses a business firm's obligation to society beyond simply maximising its profits. Islam in the light of the holy Qur'ān and Hadith suggests that there seems to be congruence between the ideals of social responsibility and justice and business transactions in Islam that has a character with prevailing notions of corporate social responsibility (CSR). Corporate social responsibility (CSR) since early 1990 has attracted worldwide attention and acquired a new reverberation in the global economy.

Chapter 10 discusses impact of religion and religiosity at the workplace cannot be ignored in almost aspect of management; it takes even more importance when it comes to develop conflict management strategies. Chapter further argues the holistic approach of Islamic work ethics for effective conflict management approaches ranging from parties in the conflict to others surrounding the situation to discharge their responsibilities according to the guiding principles of Islam. The conflict itself is neither negative nor positive but a natural state of human interactions. The religious interventions to be leveraged to create effective strategies for conflict management. The teaching of Prophet Muhammad has encouraged his followers to remain steadfast in the aspect of conflict with leadership and when a person felt oppressed.

Chapter 11 provides an understanding of the Maqasid al-Shari'ah and discuss the essential objectives of Maqasid al-Shari'ah for whole society within Islamic al-Shari'ah. However, understanding the concept of the Maqasid al-Shari'ah is essential part of the faith. Chapter further suggests that Maqasid al-Shari'ah is essential part of the faith and set out clear goals for business community to follow when dealing with business transactions. The justice and moral values of individuals are based on faith as a central point when dealing with people and society. Protection of every one's property is an important element in Islamic ethics. Therefore, Islamic ethics paves the way for organisational environment that ensures welfare and protection of all stakeholders of the organisation.

Chapter 12 analyses and discusses diversity management as an inclusive concept, encompassing a broader focus than employment equity. Chapter further developed logical argument how diversity through Islamic ethics can be achieved and management at modern contemporary workplace. The management of diversity is important factor for senior management to consider employees backgrounds as a fundamental principle for individual and business community to overcome challenges facing modern workforce. Islamic ethics value diversity as a key principle in development of human resources management and improve productivity modern workplace. Islamic ethics keep concept is to develop human organisations according to Qur'an.

Abdus Sattar Abbasi
COMSATS University Islamabad, Lahore Campus, Pakistan

Razaq Raj
Leeds Beckett University, UK

Acknowledgment

We would like to thank Allah (God), the most glorified, the most beneficent, with his Grace, and Beneficial Guidance we have finished this book.

We would like to express our deepest gratitude to all our family members and all our friends around the world for their love and support.

Chapter 1
Overview of Islamic Ethics

ABSTRACT

This chapter critically evaluates the conceptual, theoretical, and principles of Islamic ethics of workplace and presents various themes and critical discourses that underpin the sections within this chapter. History of business progression over several centuries suggests unprecedented improvements and creativeness during the journey to embark on the current status of scientific modernism. From barter, the only form of business transactions, to the digital economy of the 21st century, from mere farmhouses to today's digitalised multinational corporations (MNCs), from grain economy to internet of things (IoT), the transformation of the business world remained unbelievably overwhelming. Ethics is a subject of diverse views, opinions, and theories. However, the study of Islamic teachings suggests that Islamic ethics are founded on the concept that certain absolute truths apply everywhere. Universal values do transcend cultures to determine what is good or bad and right or wrong.

INTRODUCTION

Despite all these glaring attainments, the corporate world needs to promptly respond to the fundamental concerns of contemporary workplaces regarding behavioural aspects of the workforce towards ethical standards and norms of organisations (Abbasi, 2008). Islamic ethics is based on the al-Qur'ān and Hadith and the whole process of business dealing is based on the eyes of faith. This chapter will offer a distinctive in its philosophy and link the concept of Islamic ethics through workplace as a notion of identity for both individual and organisation.

DOI: 10.4018/978-1-7998-5295-7.ch001

Islamic Ethics at modern-day workplace is increasingly becoming an important factor for the industry in the Muslim world. The major problem for managers is lack of understanding of organisational behaviour related to Islamic values, beliefs, and work ethics. Islam is a complete way of life for individual to follow work ethics set out by the Qur'an and Hadith. The one who follows Islamic way of life intends to follow organisational settings and workplace requirements as been stated by Ahmad and Owoyemi (2012, pp.117)

Islam lays great emphasis on work. In many places in the Qur'an and Hadith, it has been made clear that time should not be wasted. In the Qur'an, Allah draws attention to all the magnificent creations as an indication of the proper planning that leads to wonderful results—for Muslims believe that He creates nothing haphazardly.

Abbasi (2008, p.1) further argues that:

seventy per cent of organisations that have formulated strategies failed to execute them. A Fortune Magazine study has shown that 7 out of 10 CEOs, who fail, do so not because of bad strategy, but because of bad execution. In another study of Times-1000-Companies, 80% of directors said that they had the right strategies but only 14% thought they were implementing them well. Only 1 in 3 companies, in their own assessment, were achieving significant strategic success.

Statistics such as these are under our common observation with variations of some extents from sector to sector, country to country or over the time in the same society suggesting that "all that glitters is not gold". The importance of effective implementation of a carefully articulated strategy is indeed fundamental to attain strategic success. However, there are variety of debates about how an organisation can guarantee realisation of strategies efficiently and effectively for long-term sustainability. Contemporary workplaces are subject to frequent ethical dilemmas. As it is too early to probe into a discourse on solutions, let us first consider some implications of the subject at hand.

Ethical behaviour of employees is a challenge around the world for contemporary organisations, and it is hard to disagree that, despite significant research still institutions are subject to substantial difficulties to manage ethical issues. According to Beekun (1997), in a survey of three hundred organisations from around the world over eighty-five percent of senior executives suggested that the following issues were among their top ethical concerns:

a. Employee conflict of interest
b. Inappropriate gifts
c. Sexual harassment
d. Unauthorised payments

Fiorina (2001) stated the Islamic ethical legacy in these words,

Islamic civilisation created continental super-state, within its dominion lived hundreds of millions of people, of different creeds and ethnic origins. Islam created an enlightened leadership that nurtured culture, sustainability, diversity and courage that led to 800 years of invention and prosperity. The reach of their commerce extended from Latin America to China, and everywhere in between. In today 's ethical crisis we must affirm our commitment to building organisations that aspire to Islamic ethical values.

This chapter further discusses the importance of ethics in the workplace and playing a critical role in developing the individual person and the whole society. Development The development of ethical policies will enhance community cohesion, unity and efficiency within the workplace and society in large. In many places in Qur'an and Hadith states that ethics needs to implement within society. The Qur'an states that:

Let there arise out a group of people inviting to all that is good enjoining what is right and forbidding what is wrong. They are the ones who attained success (al-Qur'ān 5:44)

The Qur'an makes very clear in the above verse, call people for good deeds and inform what is right and inform them what is wrong. The message from this verse is to implement good ethical beliefs and principles in individual life and society as a whole and live life according to Qur'an and Hadith.

Islamic Ethics for Globalised Diverse Workplace

Islamic teachings acknowledge diversity thus appreciate and respect individual differences. Islamic work ethics consider all creeds, races, and ethnicities equal, while reward is based solely on performance:

Indeed, the most noble of you in the sight of Allah is the most righteous of you (al-Qur'ān 49:13)

Islamic work ethics focus on managing diversity and provide a reliable framework to work in today's globalised diverse workforce through following teachings of being merciful among themselves:

merciful among themselves (al-Qur'ān 48:29)

Islamic work ethics emphasise mutual consultations:

and whose affair is [determined by] consultation among themselves (al-Qur'ān 42:38)

The last sermon of the holy Prophet (PBUH) underscores that Islamic ethics are based on equality, equity and performance (Last Sermon, n.d.):

All mankind is from Adam and Eve, an Arab has no superiority over a non-Arab nor a non-Arab has any superiority over an Arab; also, a white has no superiority over a black nor a black has any superiority over a white except by piety (taqwa) and good action.

There are several verses of the Qur'ān and sayings of the last Prophet Muhammad (PBUH) about the diverse and multicultural nature of human society.

Had Allah willed, He would have made you one nation [united in religion], but [He intended] to test you in what He has given you (al-Qur'ān 5:48)

The creation and existence of human beings on this planet are reflective of immense diversity. However, there is equal emphasis in Islamic ethics on the unity and brotherhood of mankind. Islamic ethics ensure that this innate diversity does not lead to conflicts and disharmony as mentioned in the following verse:

O mankind fear your Lord, who created you from one soul and created from it its mate and dispersed from both of them many men and women (al-Qur'ān 4:1)

The above verse educates people that they belong to a couple that was created from one soul, to inculcate respect among them for each other. The following verse also emphasises the same aspect and suggests promoting brotherhood among people.

O mankind, indeed, We have created you from male and female and made you peoples and tribes that you may know one another (al-Qur'ān 49:13)

Human diversities are the beauty of the society, as mentioned in the following verse alongside the creation of heavens and the earth about the variety of languages and the skins.

And of His signs is the creation of the heavens and the earth and the diversity of your languages and your colours. Indeed, in that are signs for those of knowledge (al-Qur'ān 30:22)

Islamic Ethics and Ethical Theories

There are three categories of ethical theories that businesses need to follow in the workplace according to the Qur'an and Hadith.

- First is the set of theories that looks at the process or the means of a decision; that is, how do we arrive at the decision?
- Second, are the theories that address what is good and bad by looking at likely outcomes or consequences of a decision.
- The third is a set of theories that looks at the caring aspects of decisions.

These three categories remind us that the assumptions upon which ethical claims can be made may vary widely. These distinctive categories of ethical theories and correlation of these approaches with the three virtues of faith, hope, and charity are an added benefit as we think about the possible ethical bases for the contemporary workplace.

The theories also need to be considered whether they are universal in nature, for all times and all places, or, depending on the context. The cultural context in which workplace ethics are considered may well affect the shared understanding of what ethical means. A short example of the results of different assumptions about what is ethical may be found in the consideration of the Japanese, North American or Pakistani approach of examining the background of employees' spouses. The Japanese culture is homogeneous, and the introduction of difference is generally not seen as good. In fact, families and the individual's company used to conduct a background investigation of an employee's potential spouse to make certain he or she is purely Japanese and not from an outcast group such as the *burakumin.* Such activity is still seen in western Japan as fulfilling an ethical responsibility. In North America, especially on the part of the employer, such an investigation would likely be regarded not as a moral duty but as an immoral action, on the grounds of both privacy and racial prejudice (Harvey and Allard, 2009). In Pakistan, it is almost inconceivable to attempt such investigation. People will retaliate even before any legal proceeding against such an employer considering it against cultural or religious norms and values.

In cultures that measure high on the universalism dimension, such as the United States, Switzerland, Australia, and Canada, rules are seen to apply to all equally. In particularistic cultures such as China, Japan, Venezuela, Greece, and India, rules are more variable, depending on the context and the actors.

Islamic ethics emphasises that people should feel for others according to one's own preferences. The last Prophet Muhammad (SAW) stated:

"The Messenger of Allah (PBUH) said: 'None of you truly believes until he loves for his brother" or he said, "for his neighbor, what he loves for himself" (Sunan Ibn Majah, Book 1, Hadith 69)

Deontological theories are also based on the same concept of duties and moral obligations. The most well-known deontological theory is Emmanuel Kant's categorical imperative "Do unto others as you would have them do unto you". Deontological theories are based on duties, rules, and obligations that lie outside the person. Religious practice tends to rest on a deontological approach to ethics. For example, table 1 illustrates the five obligatory duties of a Muslim person:

Table 1. Five Obligatory Religious Duties of Muslims

1. Faith on Tawhid and Finality of Prophethood of Muhammad (PBUH)
2. To Establish Daily Five Congregational Obligatory Prayers
3. To Pay Zakat (Obligatory Charity)
4. To Observe Fast During the Month of Ramadan
5. To Perform Hajj (Pilgrimage to Makkah) If Applicable

There is another example of deontological ethics in the workplace when we consider the ethics codes of different organisations. Ethics codes are rule-based and suggest that the corporate citizen is bound by duty to follow the rules.

Islamic ethics are based on the concept of accumulation of good or bad deeds:

Then as for one whose scales are heavy [with good deeds], he will be in a pleasant life. But as for one whose scales are light; his refuge will be an abyss (al-Qur'ān, 101:6-9)

Teleological ethical theories consider the good that comes from a focus on the ends achieved by a contemplated action (the Greek *lelos* means end). This approach holds that decisions are right or good if they produce a desired goodness and bad if they produce some undesirable state (badness or pain). Therefore, teleological approaches are action-based, connected with implementation — while deontological approaches concern the process. Utilitarianism, the greatest good for the greatest number, illustrates such an action-based, results-oriented approach. A business example is found in cost-benefit analysis, through which the benefit is weighed against its cost. The decision is then made to follow the path that provides the greatest overall gain for the least cost.

For example, a manager might structure a layoff list with the least trained and newest members of the organisation as the first to face cuts, on the basis that keeping people with seniority will lead to the retention of higher levels of knowledge, which, in turn, may lead to better results for a larger number of people.

Distributive justice, concerned with fair and equitable outcomes, is another ethical theory within the teleological category. Distributive justice suggests that ethical decisions are those that lead to a fair distribution of goods. Ethical justice would be measured by the capacity of the decision to enhance cooperation among all by its fairness. Because these theories rely on outcomes that depend on actions, but we do not know the outcomes of an action often until well after it is completed, that's why these approaches are connected to hope.

Utilitarianism, in its assertion that a good or ethical decision is one that produces the greatest good for the greatest number, seems on first examination to be business friendly. If we take diversity as an example, a utilitarian approach might argue that valuing differences would lead to behaviours that would be likely to lead to better results for the company's stakeholders, through a diverse workforce that is, perhaps, better at decision making and that possesses increased creativity, better knowledge of markets, and increased communication abilities. Such a work team would be likely to produce better results for a broader array of people, the various stakeholders.

An example of the distributive justice theory in human resource processes that rest on principles of fairness and justice: all employees- regardless of level and type of contract (part time/temporary) would receive medical and other benefits, profit sharing, retirement contributions, and bonuses. Selection, compensation, and promotion systems might also offer examples of distributive justice, utilitarianism and teleology. The ethical rationale would be that we make this decision because it is the right thing to do in order to produce equity, not that we make this decision because it will be good for business. These are all examples of universal application.

Teleological theories in a particularistic context would be theories that apply to differences among people and consider the ends or outcomes in order to judge the ethical nature of a decision. Self-actualisation might be an example here, that we have a moral duty to fully develop our skills and talents, and that organisational decisions that lead in that direction (support for education, training programs, mentoring systems) are ethical ones.

Islamic ethics are centered on mutual care, as mentioned in following saying of holy Prophet (SAW);

Ibn 'Abbas told Ibn Az-Zubayr, "I heard the Prophet, may Allah bless him and grant him peace, say, 'A man is not a believer who fills his stomach while his neighbour is hungry (Al-Adab Al-Mufrad 112)

Caring unlike deontology and teleology is a non-rational emotional claim. These are the theories that come, neither from a reasoned sense of duty nor from desired outcomes, but, because they are psychological and emotional in nature, "from an interpersonal connectedness" an ethic of charity.

Philanthropy comes to mind readily: belief systems that value a love for humanity, for example, Edhi Foundation, Alkhidmat Foundation, Chhipa Welfare Association who a sole love for humanity. People who join other organisations for volunteer work in a specific setting or who pursue community volunteer work in a specific effort might offer us examples of particularised caring ethics.

The last sermon of the Prophet Muhammad (PBUH) is the epitome of caring ethics. After praising and thanking Allah (SWT) he said:

...O people, just as you regard this month, this day, this city as sacred, so regard the life and property of every Muslim as a sacred trust. Return the goods entrusted to you to their rightful owners. Hurt no one so that no one may hurt you. Remember that you will indeed meet your Lord, and that He will indeed reckon your deeds. Allah has forbidden you to take usury (interest), therefore all interest obligation shall henceforth be waived. Your capital, however, is yours to keep. You will neither inflict nor suffer any inequity.....

All mankind is from Adam and Eve, an Arab has no superiority over a non-Arab nor a non-Arab has any superiority over an Arab; also, a white has no superiority over black nor does a black has any superiority over white except by piety (taqwa) and good action. Learn that every Muslim is a brother to every Muslim and that the Muslims constitute one brotherhood. Nothing shall be legitimate to a Muslim which belongs to a fellow Muslim unless it was given freely and willingly. Do not, therefore, do injustice to yourselves... (Last Sermon, n.d.)

Convergence and Divergence of Global Ethical Beliefs

Islamic ethics do aspire for greatest good for greatest number of people but do not consider it a standard for right or wrong. An aspect which is declared as wrong is believed that it carries something bad in the long run even if it apparently seems attractive for greater number of people e.g. usury.

Although Islamic ethics do protect individual rights, they do not consider one's long-term self-interest as a primary objective of every activity. Islamic teachings consider all believers a body as mentioned in the following saying of the holy Prophet (PBUH).

Nu'man Ibn Bashir reported Allah's Messenger (PBUH) as saying: The similitude of believers in regard to mutual love, affection, fellow-feeling is that of one body; when any limb of it aches, the whole body aches, because of sleeplessness and fever (Sahih Muslim 2586 a)

Islamic ethics do respect the fundamental rights of all people but do not believe in "when in Rome, do as the Romans do". Justice is the founding stone of Islamic ethics including procedural, distributive and interactional justice. Fair and impartial treatment of people according to legal rules and standards is deeply rooted in Islamic ethics.

Despite the increasingly multinational nature of the workplace, there have been few studies of the convergence and divergence in beliefs about ethics across cultures. In a study spanned three continents, six themes emerged to determine convergence and divergence in beliefs about ethics.

Here are two invaluable quotes to understand the convergence of beliefs about ethics:

1. Moral excellence comes about as a result of habit. We become just by doing just acts, temperate by doing temperate acts, brave by doing brave acts (Aristotle, 350 BCE).
2. Lead them with virtue and regulate them by the rules of propriety, and they will have a sense of shame and, moreover, set themselves right (Confucius, 551-479 BC)

Divergence in beliefs about ethics across societies on this planet can manifest in terms of the degree of importance or prevalence of any dimension of ethical or unethical behaviour at the workplace. Nevertheless, we cannot find 180-degree views about ethical or unethical beliefs, because the survival of human societies is subject to relatively dominant good in the social fabric. The dominance of evil cannot prevail in the society; however, varying degrees of immoralities are fact of life. Corporate scandals worldwide have raised awareness of and attention to ethics. In today's global environment ethical issues confront several cultural boundaries. Therefore, organisations are increasingly facing the challenges of convergence and divergence of ethical norms in their operations usually beyond borders. Societal cultures do influence beliefs about ethics and understanding these differences is critical for an appropriate workplace. Societal cultures do influence sensitivities to ethical issues. However, despite the increase in multinational nature of the workplace, there have been few studies of cross-cultural convergence and divergence in beliefs about ethics.

According to Resick, et. al. (2011) six main themes for both ethical and unethical behavior at the workplace have been identified. The first theme of ethics is a character which includes demonstrating honesty, trustworthiness, and integrity. The second theme is accountability means complying with laws and regulations, taking personal accountability and holding others answerable. Third includes consideration and respect for others, treating others with dignity and respect, remain approachable, compassionate and considerate at workplace. Fourth is fairness and no-discriminatory approach at the workplace leading to fair, just and objective decisions. The fifth dimension is organisational and social collectiveness meaning thereby putting organisational and collective interest ahead of personal interest, focusing on sustainability and long-term success of all stakeholders including society and the environment. The sixth ethical aspect is openness and flexibility toward inclusion, respecting diversity and accommodating all voices. On contrary, table 2 shows six themes of unethical behaviour at the workplace across societies.

Table 2. Unethical Behaviour at Workplace across Societies

1	Acting in self-interest, misusing power, pushing blame onto others
2	Deception, dishonesty, collusion, and corruption
3	Lack of Accountability, compliance, and transparency
4	Lack of personal values and moral code
5	Incivility including bullying, exploiting, vindictive behaviour and harassment
6	Narrow and short-term focus on profit and short-term interest, avoiding or ignoring social and environmental issues, a win at any cost attitude

Character remained universal dominated ethical theme across societies in Asia, Europe, and America. Social relationships, consideration and respect for others remained dominated in Asian and European societies while accountability dominates in America.

Acting in self-interest and misusing power are considered unethical across societies. Incivility is considered as second most agreed unethical aspect at workplace while deception and dishonesty are considered as second most agreed unethical practices in America.

This gives a worldview of convergence and divergence about ethical practices at contemporary workplace. Teachings of Islam about ethics are aware of diverse nature of human societies, therefore, do address these and several other dimensions of convergence and divergence of ethics across societies.

Five Myths About Islamic Work Ethics

Intention

It has been noticed that Muslims in their communities emphasise that intentions to perform a task or achieve an objective are important aspect and there is no doubt that intentions shape almost a half of the landscape of any activity. But, somehow, too much emphasis on appropriateness of intentions has undermined focus on final outcomes or achievements. It has been observed, by and large that practicing Muslims particularly in Muslim majority countries utilise this aspect of 'good intentions' as an excuse of their low performance. They usually suggest that we had good intentions to work & perform, we came to the workplace, we performed our tasks as much as we could; we are not responsible if still targets are not achieved. It is indeed a misleading interpretation of famous saying:

Verily actions are only dependent on intentions....

Actions are certainly dependent on intentions, but intentions are however not actions, one has to convert intentions into productive actions.

Efforts

People also argue that, we have done all what we can with our given abilities; however, results are subject to approvals and provisions from the Almighty, which is undoubtedly correct. However, we should not forget that there are clear commandments as follows:

"Then shall anyone who has done an atom's weight of good, see it! And anyone who has done an atom's weight of evil, shall see it" (al-Qur'ān 99:7-8

Islamic work ethics are founded on the concept that even atom's weight of good or bad will not go vain.

Results

In Muslim societies generally success and failure are considered as something already destined in individual's life. Whereas teachings are indicative of the fact that one gets what one strives for.

And that there is not for man except that [good] for which he strives (al-Qur'ān 53:39)

Scope of achievements is far beyond the boundaries of earth and skies. One can aspire to achieve knowledge even beyond existing limitations of space explorations.

O company of jinn and mankind, if you are able to pass beyond the regions of the heavens and the earth, then pass. You will not pass except by authority [from Allah] (al-Qur'ān 55:33)

This signifies the ability and capacity of mankind to achieve beyond boundaries of earth and heavens.

Accomplishment

In majority of Muslim population those who punctually offer prayers and perform other mandatory rituals *('ibadah)* are considered pious *('abideen)* and accomplished. However, Islam clearly states that only abiding with mandatory rituals is not an indication of accomplishment; rather it is required to disperse to explore unlimited opportunities provided by the Almighty to seek blessings of Allah (SWT) for prosperity and happiness.

And when the prayer has been concluded, disperse within the land and seek from the bounty of Allah, and remember Allah often that you may succeed (al-Qur'ān 62:10)

Flawed concept of accomplishment led many educated people to give priority to 'ibadah commitments over their professional obligations which is indeed against the spirit of Islamic work ethics.

Success

It has been noticed that Muslim colleagues satisfy their lack of success in professional careers as being rewarded in hereafter. Many of such mates eventually marginalise themselves from the mainstream with the view of short-lived worldly affairs. Islamic teachings give equal importance to the success in this life and life hereafter.

But among them is he who says, "Our Lord, give us in this world [that which is] good and in the Hereafter [that which is] good and protect us from the punishment of the Fire" (al-Qur'ān 2:201)

It gives clear indication to pursue success in this world and in hereafter too. It means attainments in hereafter are not the only aspect of Islamic teachings.

Work Ethics in Today's Visibility

Privacy is not just an individual or religious affair; rather it is a right of every individual at the contemporary workplaces that must be respected by the state, the government and the corporate employers. One of the companions of the Holy Prophet reported:

Hazrat Umar Bin Khattab, the second caliph, was roaming in the city one night when he heard shouting and cursing coming from a residence; he then peeked over the perimeter and started admonishing the man: 'You, the sinner, do you think that God will ignore your sins, as you're sinning against him?' The man replied: 'Woe, commander of the faithful, do not rush to judgment; if I sinned once, you sinned three times. God has forbidden you to look into someone's fault, and you have done otherwise. God has commanded you to enter peoples' homes through the front door, and you have intruded over the fence. And you have approached me without salutation, and God has commanded you not to enter into other peoples' homes without their permission, and without saying 'greetings' (Salam) when you enter their premises. (Hayat, 2007)

O ye who believe! Avoid suspicion as much (as possible): for suspicion in some cases is a sin: and spy not on each other, nor speak ill of each-other behind their backs. Would any of you like to eat the flesh of his dead brother? Nay, you would abhor it . . . but fear Allah: for Allah is Oft-Returning, most Merciful. (al-Qur'ān 49:12)

Those who desire that scandal should spread among the Muslims, for them is the painful torment in this world and the Hereafter and Allah knows and you know not. (al-Qur'ān 24:19)

The last Prophet Muhammad (PBUH) said:

A ruler who seeks to expose the faults of its subjects is bound to drive them to falter (Kadivar, 2005)

It is an individual's sole privilege to determine the boundaries of the personal life, the personal information and the personal affairs; no one including the state and the government has any authority to breach those boundaries (Hayat, 2007). However, matters of public interest and the common good certainly need intervention when they are subject to visible threat by individual actions. There is no ambiguity in Islamic ethics on the demarcation of personal and collective domains of the society.

CONCLUSION

This chapter has examined the conceptual, theoretical and principles dimensions of Islamic ethics of workplace. The Islamic Ethics at workplace plays important role for employees and senior management to understand organisational behaviour in relation to Islamic values, beliefs and work ethics. The Islam is complete way of life for individual to follow work ethics set out by the Qur'an and Hadith. Ethical behaviour of employees is a challenge for managers, and they are facing significant problems to manage ethical issues within their workforce.

The chapter reveals that in today's competitive environment it is imperative for the corporate world to find a management paradigm to execute strategic policies in true spirit for effective and efficient performance of organisations to achieve optimal outcomes. The Islamic teachings advocate that Islamic ethics are founded on the concept that certain absolute truths apply everywhere. Islamic ethics do aspire for people to consider developing a standard that speak for right or wrong. Islamic ethics do protect individual rights, but they do not consider one's long-term self-interest as primary objective of every activity. Islamic teachings are based on the saying of holy Prophet (PBUH). Islamic ethics is based on procedural, distributive and interactional justice. Fair and impartial treatment of people according to legal rules and standards is deeply rooted in Islamic ethics. Despite the increasingly multinational nature of the workplace, there have been few studies of the convergence and divergence in beliefs about ethics across cultures.

Discussion Questions

1. Examine and evaluate the principles of Islamic ethics at workplace?
2. Discuss and analyse fair and impartial treatment of people according to Islamic ethics?
3. What are Five Myths about Islamic Work Ethics?
4. Critical analyse the organisational behaviour in relation to Islamic values, beliefs and work ethics.

REFERENCES

Abbasi, A. S. (2008). *Role of Islamic Leadership in Value Based Corporate Management* (PhD Thesis). NUML Islamabad, Pakistan.

Ahmad, S., & Owoyemi, M.Y. (2012). The Concept of Islamic Work Ethic: An Analysis of Some Salient Points in the Prophetic Tradition. *International Journal of Business and Social Science, 3*(20), 116-123.

Aristotle. (384-322 BC). *In justice is all virtues*. Retrieved July 18, 2008 from: http://www.wisdomquotes.com/cat_justice.html

Beekun, R. I. (1997). *Islamic Business Ethics*. The International Institute of Islamic Thought.

Confucius. (400 BC). *Without truth I know not how man can live*. Retrieved July 9, 2008 from: http://www.freerepublic.com/focus/news/685635/posts

Fiorina, C. (2001). *Technology, Business and Our Way of Life: What's Next?* Retrieved June 23, 2008 from: http://www.hp.com/hpinfo/execteam/speeches/fiorina/ minnesota01.html

Harvey, C. P., & Allard, M. J. (2009). *Understanding and Managing Diversity – Readings, Cases and Exercises* (4th ed.). PHI Learning Private Limited.

Hayat, M. A. (2007). Privacy and Islam: From the Quran to data protection in Pakistan. *Information & Communications Technology Law, 16*(2), 137–148. doi:10.1080/13600830701532043

Kadivar, M. (2005). *An Introduction to the Public & Private Debate in the Islamic Culture*. Retrieved on November 03, 2019 from: https://nawaat.org/portail/2005/02/05/an-introduction-to-the-public-private-debate-in-the-islamic-culture/

Last Sermon of the Holy Prophet Muhammad (PBUH). (n.d.). Retrieved on November 03, 2019 from http://www.fja.gov.pk/last_sermon.php

Muhtada, D. (2012). Managing workforce diversity: An Islamic perspective. *Indonesian Journal of Islam and Muslim Societies, 2*(1), 79–108. doi:10.18326/ijims.v2i1.78-108

Resick, C. J., Martin, G. S., Keating, A., Dickson, M. W., Kwan, H. K., & Peng, C. (2011). What Ethical Leadership Means to Me: Asian, American, and European Perspectives. *Journal of Business Ethics, 101*(3), 435–457. doi:10.100710551-010-0730-8

Chapter 2
Islamic Ethics and Stakeholder Management

ABSTRACT

The company is an important part of society and plays a critical role in developing the economic activities of community based on honest and ethical obligations. Over the last three decades, company structure has been changed due to increased customer demands for goods and services. The chapter highlights that the importance of moral and ethical belief has been evaded due to mass production and greed, which has caused the company to neglect to look after the interests of stakeholders and society. Islamic work ethics encourages the company and individual to own company and make a profit based on Islamic ethos to boost prosperity within the community and show professionalism in increasing economic wealth and avoid oppression. Islamic ethics plays a critical role to address the stakeholder's responsibilities to meet the obligations to society and develop economic transparency to avoid financial crisis.

INTRODUCTION

This chapter highlights the importance of Islamic work ethics plays very imperative part for companies to develop standards and business dealings based on honesty. Prophet Muhammad (PBUH) after marrying Khadijah (RA) started travelling the Arabia for business trips. Whole Makkah and Arabian region were amazed by his honesty and kind customer dealing, because he

DOI: 10.4018/978-1-7998-5295-7.ch002

followed the business ethics by showing respect to customers and clients. His impressive and remarkable personality has taught us the how to deal with business and economic principles. Prophet Muhammad (PBUH) said:

The truthful and honest merchant is associated with the Prophets, the upright and the martyrs (Al-Tirmidhi).

At the beginning of the new millennium several businesses such as Enron, WorldCom, Tyco and Lehman Brothers terribly collapsed. However corporate scandals continued to make headlines around the globe.

The chapter discusses the ethical issues were not properly addressed by the businesses for better economic transparency toward key stakeholders. Legislations such as Sarbanes-Oxley Act (SOX) 2002 and following initiatives are conscious efforts to keep corporate world safer and stronger to handle ethical challenges. Al-Aidros et al (2013, p.2) stated that,

This circumstance goes with the fact that the existing ethical issues are not always clear and understandable. To identify whether a behaviour or decision is ethically performed, there are several ethical theories to explain what is right and what is wrong.

According to the Freeman (2002), "The list of companies who have been in trouble for ethical scandals is impressive. In response to these scandals, the American President (Bush) has exclaimed, that we have got to be ethical in big businesses. As terrible as these scandals have been, there is absolutely nothing new about any of them. Worse, absolutely nothing has been fixed. The main problem is not the recurrent waves of scandals; it is rather the idea that what good management is hijacked by a view that says management's only obligation is to maximise shareholder's value, is a very narrow sense of that term. Corporate world has to return to the basics of what good management is. To do that, corporate leaders have to stop separating business from ethics"

Myths About Contemporary Business Ethics

There are different views about the role of ethics for contemporary workplaces and businesses. The main principle of business ethics for workplace is to help individuals with virtuous values and beliefs that meet the business values outlined by the management. The ethical values should ensure that behaviours are aligned with corporate management views and beliefs. The major problematic myth of business ethics is management having very slender and unsophisticated views of ethical issues within organisation. Abbasi (2008) argued that:

ethics are the key to bring value in corporate management. All corporate scandals stem from ethical dilemma. There are many myths about business ethics; these myths are usually presented as excuse to avoid ethics in business. First myth holds a view that ethics is a personal and individual affair, not a public or debatable matter. But individuals are integral parts of organisational culture, who have norms, values, rules of conduct, and standards to govern what is acceptable and what is unacceptable. Therefore, to argue that ethics related to business issues is only or mainly a matter of personal or individual choice is to depreciate the role of organisations in shaping and influencing members' attitudes, perceptions and behaviours.

The key issue facing organisations is that by not following the ethical values within workplace and act in act in socially negligent ways, which leads the managers to show unethical behaviour. Therefore, it is critical for multinational corporations (MNC) to incorporate business ethics at workplace before making decisions on profitability and avoid failures and future calamities. The multinational corporations (MNC) should improve the strategic development to enhance the ethical values and maximise the corporate profitability for the future. Abbasi (2008) further discussed that:

Business and ethics do not mix is the second myth. But Business is a human activity therefore can be evaluated from a moral perspective. If everyone in business acted amorally or immorally the business would collapse. Employees would openly steel from employers; employers would recklessly fire employees at their will; contractors would arrogantly violate obligations; and chaos would prevail. Third myth is that ethics in business is relative. This is one of the more popular myths, and it holds that no right or wrong way of believing or acting exists. Right and wrong are in the eye of the beholder. This myth paves the way for much confusion in business practices. If ethical relativism is applied to its logical extreme, no one would argue or disagree with any one about moral issues, since each person's values would be right and true for him or her.

The board of directors and managers are not involved in developing the business ethics strategies and trusts that business ethics will automatically fits within movement and running an organisation. The multinational corporations (MNC) management believe that business ethics is a complicated and philosophical debate for religiously believed workforce. The management believes further that ethics are not essential programme or strategy for organisation to develop in depth. According to Abbasi (2008) that:

last myth holds the view that information and computing are neither moral nor immoral, but are amoral, i.e., they are in a grey zone. But one cannot view business information without human beings. Disinformation, misleading information, inaccuracy in computing are all offence while truth and accuracy in disseminating the information are always regarded as goodness.

Work Ethics in Islam

Islamic ethics provide clear guidance for business managers to adopt and implement the importance of ethics within organisation structure in the interest of workforce moral and wellbeing. There are numerous Qur'anic verses and hadiths which discuss the principle of ethics and inviting people towards goods and forbidding people from wrong doings as a society and individual. According to Abbasi (2008)

ethics may be defined as a set of moral principles that distinguish what is right from what is wrong. It is a normative field because it prescribes what one should do or abstain from doing; the term most closely related to ethics in the al-Qur'ān is Khuluq. The al-Qur'ān also uses a whole array of terms to describe the concept: Khayr (goodness), birr (righteousness), adl (justice), haqq (truth and right), taqwā (piety) and so on.

According to a hadith, "You are not better than people with red or black skins unless you excel them in piety"

Once a Bedouin asked the Prophet Muhammad (PBUH) "When would the Hour (Doomsday) take place?" Prophet Muhammad (PBUH) replied, "When honesty is lost, then wait for the Hour (Doomsday)". Bedouin said, "How will that be lost" Prophet Muhammad (PBUH) said, "When the power or authority comes in the hands of unfit persons, then wait for the Hour (Doomsday)" (Beekun, 1997).

In Islamic work ethics no businessman is allowed to do dishonesty. In it is mentioned that

Give just measures and cause no loss (to others by fraud). And weigh with scales true and upright. And withhold not things justly due to men (al-Qur'ān, 26:181-183)

Islamic ethics normally do not prefer to interfere in the open market and encourage market forces to regulate dynamics of sales and purchase. However, in Islamic ethics it is prohibited to manipulate the market through hording of other interventions. According to a hadith:

He who hoards is a sinner

Deception in sales and purchase is also a sin in Islamic work ethics. Traders are cautioned to be engaged in any kind of cheating, false oaths to generate sales are prohibited in Islamic work ethics. According to a hadith, "The swearing (by the seller) may persuade the buyer to purchase the goods but that will be deprived of Allah 's blessing (Beekun, 1997)"

Deliberate sale and Purchase of stolen goods is prohibited in Islamic ethics. According to a hadith "He who buys the stolen property, with the knowledge that it was stolen, shares in the sin and shame of steeling (Beekun, 1997)"

It is just obvious that Islamic work ethics inspire workplaces which are free from any kind of swindle, deceit, influence, steeling, cheating, or any kind of misconducts. Every business on this planet also has the same desire, therefore it makes a lot of sense for business practitioners and academics to utilise underlying spirit of Islamic ethics for the benefit of corporate organisations.

Ethics are Corporate DNA

Alsop (2004) declared ethics as corporate DNA to enhance the corporate reputation; based on his discussions Abbasi (2008, p. 15) further argued that "ethics must become an entrenched part of the culture. Ethics are not just the fashion of the day. Academic studies of some of America 's largest companies have shown that a strong reputation for ethical behaviour pays off financially, too. Curtis Verschoor, an accounting professor at DePaul University in Chicago, found that companies expressing a strong commitment to their ethic code performed better than others on measures such as investment return, sales and profit growth, and return on equity. Ideally ethics and values should be integrated into performance appraisals and compensation plans. Companies should reward employees who abide by their standards and punish offenders. It's very disconcerting when employees see their colleagues skirting or violating standards but still receiving pay raise and promotions. The ethical code then looks hollow, and employees no longer have much incentive to abide by it"

Islamic Work Ethics and Customers

According to Saeed *et. al* (2001), "International marketing practices, embedded in a strong ethical doctrine, can play a vital role in raising the standards of business conduct worldwide, while in no way compromising the quality of services or products offered to customers, or surrendering the profit margins of businesses. Adherence to such ethical practices can help to elevate the standards of behaviour and thus of living, of traders and consumers alike"

The quality of the production process is of a paramount concern in Islamic ethics. The Qur'ān declares that pursuance of safe and high-quality ideals as one aspect of actualising safe and reliable products and services for the customers.

O you who have believed, eat from the good things which We have provided for you and be grateful to Allah if it is [indeed] Him that you worship (al-Qur'ān 2:172)

And We divided them into twelve descendant tribes [as distinct] nations. And We inspired to Moses when his people implored him for water, "Strike with your staff the stone," and there gushed forth from it twelve springs. Every people knew its watering place. And We shaded them with clouds and sent down upon them manna and quails, [saying], "Eat from the good things with which We have provided you" And they wronged Us not, but they were [only] wronging themselves (al-Qur'ān 7:160)

[Saying], Eat from the good things with which We have provided you and do not transgress [or oppress others] therein, lest My anger should descend upon you. And he upon whom My anger descends has certainly fallen (al-Qur'ān 20:81)

O mankind eat from whatever is on earth [that is] lawful and good and do not follow the footsteps of Satan. Indeed, he is to you a clear enemy (al-Qur'ān 2:168)

And eat of what Allah has provided for you [which is] lawful and good. And fear Allah, in whom you are believers (al-Qur'ān 5:88)

Then eat of what Allah has provided for you [which is] lawful and good. And be grateful for the favour of Allah, if it is [indeed] Him that you worship (al-Qur'ān 16:114)

[Allah said], "O messengers, eat from the good foods and work righteousness. Indeed, I, of what you do, am Knowing (al-Qur'ān 23:51)

They ask you, [O Muhammad], what has been made lawful for them. Say, "Lawful for you are [all] good foods and [game caught by] what you have trained of hunting animals which you train as Allah has taught you. So, eat of what they catch for you, and mention the name of Allah upon it, and fear Allah". Indeed, Allah is swift in account (al-Qur'ān 5:4)

This day [all] good foods have been made lawful, ... (al-Qur'ān 5:5)

According to (Saeed *et. al.*, 2001),

in some of these Qur'anic verses the phrase 'Eat pure things', precedes 'do righteous deeds. One can simply deduct from the sequence of these phrases, which are probably meant to impress and emphasise the principle, that righteous deeds are meaningless without purity in matters pertaining to production, consumption, and marketing of pure and lawful products and services.

According to Islam, the promotional techniques must not use sexual appeal, emotional appeal, fear appeal, false testimonies and pseudo research appeal, or contribute to the dullness of the mind and/or encourage extravagance. Within the Islamic framework, these methods are unethical since they are utilised purely to exploit the basic instinct of consumers worldwide with a view to gain profits and greater market share. Furthermore, Islamic ethics strictly prohibits stereotyping of women in advertising, excessive use of fantasy, the use of suggestive language and behaviour, and the use of women as objects to lure and attract customers. These Islamic principles of promotional behaviour are not mere ideals, but practicable everyday actions as in Saudi advertising guidelines and sales trainings and as shown by the Prophet (PBUH) and his disciples. For example, a famous disciple, "Jarir (RA) always pointed out to customers the flaws in his goods. When told that his business was bound to collapse, he replied, we promised the Prophet (PBUH) to deal honestly (in our marketing activities)" (Saeed *et. al.*, 2001).

According to the Islamic principles marketers are expected not to ignite unrestricted exploitation of consumer sentiments through extensive exaggeration, deception or other means. Islamic ethics demand protection of consumer rights to enable them for free and independent judgment and choice. Consumers have the right to access available and known information about the product or service to be able to make an informed decision. In Islamic ethics access to such information is the right of the customer. Any transaction concluded under constraints or coercion is prohibited since the ability to think rationally while making any decision is a prerequisite in Islamic law (Saeed *et. al.*, 2001).

It is a moral duty of the business to ensure that customer is aware of all features of the product, implicit or explicit, including defects and hazards. "Al-Ghazali goes into an elaborate description on the necessity of faithfully serving the customer in this regard: One who conceals defects is an oppressor, deceit and a fraud. Deceit is unlawful ... it becomes easy to seek good of the people if one knows that the profit in the next world is better than the wealth and treasures of the world and that these will end with the end of life, but his sins and virtues will remain" (Sidani and Ariss, 2015). It is important to be truthful in terms of meeting the specifications required, in today's business environment ISO certification is a manifestation of Islamic work ethics to deliver declared quality to customers. In terms of weight and measurement e.g. food and construction items it is essential that customer gets what has been declared. This hints at an early awareness that products should faithfully meet the customers' expectations. The business should maintain a fair price and not a higher one when approached by a buyer who is not aware of the standard price of the commodity. False bidding is also prohibited, when a seller can raise the price by creating a hypothetical second buyer. This specific practical advice is related to profit maximisation through deceptive techniques. Islamic work ethics significantly emphasise transparent and obvious pricing for uninformed customers (Sidani and Ariss, 2015).

Islamic Work Ethics and Employees

The basic necessities of an employer and employee should be the same. A more classical definition of what is "basic" can be found with Abu Ishaq al-

Shatibi's useful division of goods into "necessities", "wants", and "luxuries". He suggested that necessities are what are needed for subsistence and are "indispensable" for human survival. Wants are things that improve one's "quality of life" while removing "bearable hardship and difficulty". Finally, luxuries are products that "add beauty" to one's life. According to Possumah, *et al.* (2013),

the employer-employee relationship is considered quite important for the overall functioning of society. Although Islam recognises that social divisions are going to exist in any community, these divisions should not be used to exploit other groups. It has been suggested that an employer should consider their employees as members of their own family.

International Labour Organisation defines basic needs to include "minimum requirements of a family for private consumption", notably food, shelter and clothing, and "essential services" provided by and for the community at large, such as safe drinking water, sanitation, public transportation, and health and education facilities. Although this seems a bit of an extreme interpretation of the Islamic principles, it suggests the fact that an underlying egalitarian ethic is present. Likewise, some basis for setting minimum requirements exists within Islamic law by generally mandating Muslims to pay the *zakat* the poor-due or poor-tax but exempting all those whose net worth does not reach a minimum level (*nisab*).

About the amount of "real wages" in a Muslim society, Islamic juristic discourses suggest that it should be "at least at a level that would enable employees to fulfil all their and their families' essential needs in a humane manner".

One mechanism that has been encouraged under Islamic law is that of mudaraba (also spelled muzaribat or mudarabah) or "profit sharing". The basic principle at work is that "every firm should be required to establish a profit-sharing scheme for its employees" (Chapra 1992). In other words, this is a situation where one person invests while the other person works and "through mutual consent" they divide the profit. How this would work is that an "agreed proportion of the firm's net profit" would be set aside annually to be partly distributed among the employees as a "profit-sharing bonus" and partly utilised to improve their benefits. According to Syed and Ali (2010),

both the Qur'anic teachings and the sayings of the Prophet Muhammad (PBUH) emphasise the virtue of hiring competent people and to avoid nepotism and discrimination" For example, the Qur'an advises (28: 26), "Truly, the best of people for thee to employee is one who is competent and trustworthy.

Interestingly, the Prophet (PBUH) recognised that those who hire unqualified individuals do disservice to their community and faith. Prophet (PBUH) stated,

He who is in a leadership position and appointed knowingly a person who is not qualified to manage others, then he violates the command of God and His messenger" and "when a person assumes an authority over people and promotes one of them because of personal preferences, God will curse him for ever.

Furthermore, the second Caliph, sayyidi Omar (RA), who was known for his administrative skills, underscored the importance of behavioural and moral aspects along with performance potential in selecting employees for jobs. He said, "When a person is in charge of Muslim affairs and appointed for reasons of favouritism or kinship relationship [nepotism], then he cheats God, the Prophet, and the community"

Shareholders and Islamic Work Ethics

In any business activity protecting shareholders' interest is the prime duty of employees and other relevant stakeholders, because owner of the capital has a primary role in any economic or commercial activity. Economic conditions cannot flourish in any society where owners of capital don't find conducive environment. Therefore, Islam gives explicit teachings to discharge the trust faithfully.

And if one of you deposits a thing on trust with another, let the trustee (faithfully) discharge his trust, and let him fear his Lord. (al - Qur'ān 2:283)

Islamic teaching is much explicit than several latest developments in the field of corporate governance. According to Tricker (1984) "corporate governance is giving overall direction to the enterprise, with overseeing and controlling executive actions of management and with satisfying legitimate expectations of accountability and regulation by interests beyond the corporate boundaries". Cannon (1994) contends that "corporate governance tries to sum all those activities that makeup the internal regulations of the business in compliance with the obligations placed on the firm by legislation, ownership and control. It incorporates the trusteeship of assets, their management and their deployment (Cannon, 1994)". Corporate governance acts as a bridge between shareholders and the corporate management and facilitates their interaction to encourage best practices.

Islamic work ethics not only emphasise truly delivering the trust but also educate to not eat up assets of each other.

O ye who believe! eat not up your property among yourselves in vanities: but let there be amongst you traffic and trade by mutual good-will: nor kill (or destroy) yourselves: for verily Allah hath been to you Most Merciful! (al - Qur'ān 4:29)

Islamic Work Ethics and Environment

Abbasi (2008) argued that "Islamic teachings are quite explicit to protect the environment. Cleanliness is one of the important requirements to be a Muslim. Islamic ethics ensures that every member of organisation adopts and practices cleanliness and purity".

For Allah loves those who turn to Him constantly and He loves those who keep themselves pure and clean. (al - Qur'ān 2:222)

A hadith "cleanliness is half the Faith" endorses the importance of cleanliness in Islamic work ethics. The holy Prophet (PBUH) said,

If the last hour strikes and finds you carrying a nursling tree to the grove for planting go ahead and plant it.

The ethics is essential in organisations to protect the environment and individuals from all calamities and improve the clean settings for workforce. According to Abbasi (2008)

Islamic ethics emphasise cleanliness and purity and expect from all of the followers to practice and promote cleanliness in everyday life to make the surrounding environment free from all kinds of pollutions. One can address today's popular issue of environmental pollution through practicing Islamic values in the life. It is one of the important responsibilities of Islamic leadership to protect the environment within and outside the organisation from all hazards, and to improve it even further for healthy and clean life of all stakeholders. Emphasis on plantation is an indication of deep concern for protection of environment and keenness for the healthy living of people, because plants contribute to the world's environmental stability.

Islamic Work Ethics and Suppliers/Contractors

The holy Prophet (PBUH) prohibited using religion as a tool in transactions to increase sales. This is the very reason that oaths in transactions are banned. Islamic ethics require that market players should have fair access to market information. The holy prophet Muhammad (PBUH) outlawed meeting suppliers before they arrived at the market for fear that they might not know the current market price. According to a hadith:

Do not go to meet the caravans on the way (in other words, buying their goods without letting them know the market price) (Abbas and al-Aali, 2015).

Islamic Work Ethics and the Community

According to Possumah, *et al.* (2013), "Islam emphasises distributive justice and incorporates in its system a programme for redistribution of income and wealth so that every individual is guaranteed a standard of living that is humane and respectable and in harmony with the regard for the dignity of man inherent in the teachings of Islam. A Muslim society that fails to guarantee such a humane standard is not worthy of the name". As the last Prophet (PBUH) declared, "He is not a true Muslim who eats his fill when his next-door neighbour is hungry".

'Umar, the second Caliph, explaining the redistributive justice in Islam, emphasised in one of his public addresses that "everyone had an equal right in the wealth of the community, that no one, not even he himself, enjoyed a greater right in it than anyone else, and that if he were to live longer, he would see to it that even a shepherd on the Mount Sana'a received his share from his wealth". The Caliph 'Ali is reported to have stressed that "God has made it obligatory on the rich to provide the poor with what is adequately for them; if the poor are hungry or naked or troubled it is because the rich have deprived them (of their right), and it will be proper for God to account them for it and to punish them". The jurists have almost unanimously held the position that it is the duty of the whole Muslim society in general and of its rich to take care of the basic needs of the poor and if the well-to-do not fulfil this responsibility in spite of their ability to do so the state can and should compel them, to assume their responsibility.

CONCLUSION

This chapter has discussed and measured a range of theoretical perspectives on Islamic Ethics and Stakeholders' Management. At start of the new millennium several businesses have collapsed, and several was involved in corporate scandals throughout the world, likes of Enron, WorldCom, Tyco and Lehman Brothers. The ethical issues were not followed by businesses and perform economic transparency toward key stakeholders. The ethical issues are not being followed by businesses and shows economic transparency to key stakeholders. Ethics are the key to bring value in corporate management and businesses. All corporate scandals stem from ethical dilemma, due to businesses not following the ethical belief has been described the teaching of Prophet Muhammad (PBUH). The Islamic ethics principles has stated that companies and individuals should follow robust and valid ethical framework to help businesses to achieve a profitable success in business activities.

Chapter also discuss the importance of quality of the production process is of a principal concern in Islamic ethics. The Qur'ān declares that pursuance of safe and high-quality ideals as one aspect of actualising safe and reliable products and services for the customers. Islam encourages the business contractors and suppliers to conduct activities according to Islamic ethical guidelines. Islamic ethics states that companies should have fair access to market information. The holy prophet Muhammad (PBUH) outlawed meeting suppliers before they arrived at the market for fear that they might not know the current market price. It is a moral duty of the business to ensure that customer is aware of all features of the product, implicit or explicit, including defects and hazards.

Chapter further discuss the Islamic ethics stress that cleanliness and purity and expect from all the followers to practice and promote cleanliness in everyday life to make the surrounding environment free from all kinds of pollutions. The holy Prophet (PBUH) prohibited using religion as a tool in transactions to increase sales.

Discussion Questions

1. Critically discuss and evaluate the limitations of Islamic Work Ethics?
2. Analyse and discuss the substantial evidence suggests that moral and ethical belief has been evaded due to mass productions and greed has neglected company to look after the interests of stakeholders and society as a whole?
3. Islamic ethics in business is very important for companies to develop standards and business dealings based on honesty? Discuss
4. Critically evaluate the role of Islamic Work Ethics within Suppliers/ Contractors?

REFERENCES

Abbas J. A., & al-Aali A. (2015). Marketing and Ethics: What Islamic Ethics Have Contributed and the Challenges Ahead. *Journal of Business Ethics, 129*(4), 833-845.

Al-Aidros, A., Shamsudin, F. M., & Idris, K. I. (2013). Ethics and Ethical Theories from an Islamic Perspective. *International Journal of Islamic Thought, 4*, 1-13.

Alsop, R. J. (2004). *The 18 Immutable Laws of Corporate Reputation*. Kogan Page.

Azid, T., Asutay, M., & Burki, U. (2007). Theory of the firm, management and stakeholders: An Islamic perspective. *Islamic Economic Studies, 15*(1), 1–30.

Beekun, R. I. (1997). *Islamic Business Ethics*. The International Institute of Islamic Thought. doi:10.2307/j.ctvk8w1zv

Cannon, T. (1994). *Corporate Responsibility. A Textbook on Business Ethics, Governance, Environment: Roles and Responsibilities*. Pitman.

Chapra, M. U. (1992). *Islam and the economic challenge*. The Islamic Foundation.

Freeman, E. R. (2002). *Fixing the Ethics Crisis in Corporate America*. Retrieved December 12, 2005 from: https://www.darden.virginia.edu/olsson

Possumah, B. T., Abdul Ghafar Ismail, A. G., & Shahimi, S. (2013). Bringing Work Back in Islamic Ethics. *Journal of Business Ethics, 112*(2), 257–270. doi:10.100710551-012-1246-1

Saeed, M., Ahmed, Z. U., & Mukhtar, S. M. (2001). International Marketing Ethics from an Islamic Perspective: A Value-Maximisation Approach. *Journal of Business Ethics, 32*(2), 127–142. doi:10.1023/A:1010718817155

Sidani, Y., & Al Ariss, A. (2015). New Conceptual Foundations for Islamic Business Ethics: The Contributions of Abu-Hamid Al-Ghazali. *Journal of Business Ethics, 129*(4), 847–857. doi:10.100710551-014-2136-5

Syed, J., & Ali, A. J. (2010). Principles of employment relations in Islam: A normative view. *Employee Relations, 32*(5), 454–469. doi:10.1108/01425451011061630

Tricker, R. I. (1984). *Corporate Governance: Practices, Procedures and Powers in British Companies and Their Boards of Directors*. Gower Press.

Weiss, J. W. (2003). *Business Ethics*. Thomson South-Western.

Chapter 3
Islamic Ethics and Crisis Management

ABSTRACT

The Islamic ethical system is unique and respects the rights of individuals. The Islamic codes and principals are based on the attitudes, morals, virtues, and obligations of the individual and whole civilisation. In multinational companies (MNC), ethical codes and principals are undermined in terms of human feeling, values, and beliefs. The Prophet Muhammad (PBUH) stated that the aim of his mission is to enhance good morals and values among my ummah and individual people. The chapter examines and evaluates the fundamental belief that the Islamic ethical system is there to serve and develop good morality and avoid indecency and immoral conducts within business dealings.

INTRODUCTION

The ethics is integral part of the multinational companies (MNCs) activities and for their workforces. The ethic policies within multinational companies can cause long term complications and conflicts for people with different backgrounds and religion. Most of the multinational companies faces challenge how to adopt ethic policies which can meet the need of the workforces with different cultural background and religions. Hadisi (2014, p.34) states that:

DOI: 10.4018/978-1-7998-5295-7.ch003

Islam refers to business as a sine qua non of human life. It is such an essential factor that before the prophet Mohammad's mission inception, God guided him to become a successful merchant in the first place.

The Islamic ethics system is designed to help the traders and customers to operate in honest miner. More importantly the Islamic ethics system emphasis that our personal and business dealing should be according to commandment of Allah and ethical behaviour to be part of the faith. It is essential to understand that according to Islam business activities should be conducted as part of the worship and obedience to Allah. Prophet Muhammad (PBUH) stated that:

The truthful merchant is rewarded (by being ranked) on the Day of Resurrection with prophets, veracious souls, martyrs and pious people (Hadith- Tirmidhi)

The trade was one of the most essential tools in the time of Prophet Muhammad (PBUH) and his companions that played part in spreading Islam, because following specific Islamic principles and codes of practice according Quran and Hadith. This chapter will critically analyse and evaluate the business ethics codes and principles for multinational companies in accordance to Islamic ethics code of conduct.

Ethical Codes and Principals

Therefore, Islamic ethical system gives very clear guidelines to individuals, businesses and whole society to respect and follow ethical codes and principals. In addition, common problem with ethical principals in 21st century managers are not being honest to their employees, showing nepotism and favouritism, undermining employee by taking credit for their work. The business managers and employees taking and offering kickbacks for unfair advantage over other competitors are also serious concerns. Jackson (2013, p.5) suggested following ten basic principles for multinational companies.

1. Support and respect of international human rights declarations remain the responsibility of business organisations.
2. Organisations have to show zero tolerance for abuses of human rights.
3. Organisations have to support the freedom of association and facilitate collective bargaining initiatives.
4. Forced and compulsory labour has to be considered by business organisations as gross violation of ethics

5. Elimination of child labour should be top on agenda for business organisations.
6. Organisations have to work towards abolition of all types of employment discriminations in all relevant professions.
7. A special attention towards environmental issues is expected from business organisations.
8. Proactive strategies towards environmental responsibilities are expected from business organisations.
9. Development and promotion of environmentally friendly practices have to be encouraged by business organisations.
10. It is expected from business organisations to work toward eradicating all types of corruptions including bribery and coercion.

History of ethical crisis continues over decades, according to Abbasi (2008) hundred and forty-eight company secretaries who worked for Fortune 1000 CEOs declared that forty-seven per cent had been asked to lie at some time by their bosses. Some key segments including government employees, sales representatives and law practitioners are graded as top three areas for their unethical behaviour. It is not less than a surprise that government which is guardian of millions of people is at the top. Media was reported at number four. In a survey of two hundred sales managers showed that forty-nine per cent of their representatives did lie during their sales negotiations. Workplace theft has been estimated to cost United States business dollar forty billion each year. A poll in 2002 found that thirty-three per cent of Americans had hardly any confidence in the executives of big companies.

In a survey by Hill & Knowlton of nearly six hundred corporate executives, it was proved that forty-two per cent of them were concerned about unethical corporate behaviour. Subsequent studies reported later in this chapter suggest that despite extensive global efforts still ethical issues remain the core concern for business practitioners, academicians and researchers. Legislation, revamping curricula in business schools, campaigning all around business operations and even severe punishments nothing worked to eliminate the ethical crises from the corridors of business organisations. Table 1 illustrate corporate reputation threats to organisations.

Employee engagement and loyalty historically remained a challenge for corporate sector. According to a report published in 2011, seventy-six per cent of employees, although not looking actively for a new job, however, intend to leave their current organisation anytime if the right opportunity knocks

Table 1. Threats to Corporate Reputation

Criticism of the company or its products in print or broadcast media	49%
Unethical corporate behaviour	42%
A disaster that disrupts operations	36%
Litigation or adverse court judgments	35%
Allegation about product safety problems by a special-interest group or customers	29%
Allegation about product safety problems by government officials	24%
Criticism of the company or its products on the Internet	13%

Source: The 18 Immutable Laws of Corporate Reputation, Alsop (2004).

their door. Some other studies suggest that organisations lose their 20% to 50% of their employee base annually (Declining, 2012).

A recent study reported that forty-nine per cent employees are not satisfied with their existing jobs and employers proclaiming that they have not been given appropriate development opportunities. Thirty-five per cent American employees have been reported unsatisfied with their jobs during 2018. Only thirty-six per cent of employees showed satisfaction about their career growth and workload (Loyalty, 2019). Today employee loyalty at some companies is even lower. Employees are more cynical and less trusting because of all the recent cases of accounting abuse and executive greed. Table 2 highlights employee's loyalty within corporate organisations.

Table 2. Employees' Loyalty

True loyalty and desire to stay with their employer's for at least two more years	24%
Proud to work at their companies	64%
Strong Attachment	45%
Believe their employer deserves loyalty	43%

Source: The 18 Immutable Laws of Corporate Reputation, Alsop (2004).

Islamic Ethics

In Islam, the duty of every Muslim is to obey value system of Qur'ān and Sunnah. People groomed through value system of Qur'ān and Sunnah exhibit these qualities in their personal and professional lives. Islamic ethical system (IES) provides comprehensive pattern of management which protects all stakeholders of the organisation. Islamic ethical system focuses moral development of human beings, thereby making sure that people follow the rule of law through their own will, not through fear or force. IES stipulates tested principles of value building among members of organisation. In subsequent pages the reader will observe the impact of these values in managing people effectively and efficiently. Aim of HRD experts has always remained to build a group of people that is trustworthy, committed and proficient. But the main problem with today's HRD expert is that he separates an individual's professional life from his/her personal life (first myth about business ethics). On the other hand, in IES, individual is an entity, who behaves in the same manner in both personal and professional lives. It is not possible that an individual is dishonest in personal life but honest in professional life or vice versa.

IES starts working from the core of issue and educates the person to adopt all those ethical values which time are tested. IES inculcates total value-based culture among people, and every group member starts facilitating others to follow and practice values which ensure prosperity for both the individual and the organisation".

Therefore, the Almighty says in the Qur'an:

Let there arise out of you a band of people inviting to all that is good, enjoining what is right, and forbidding what is wrong (al-Qur'ān 3:104)

An issue is a condition or pressure, either internal or external to an organisation that, if it continues, will have a significant effect on the functioning of the organisation or its future interests (Brown, 1979). A crisis, on the other hand, is defined as any unplanned event that can cause death or significant injuries to employees, customers, or the public; shut down the business; disrupt operations; cause physical or environmental damage; or threaten the facility's financial standing or public image (Clark 1995/1996).

A sequence of tasks or procedures to recognise, study and predict the crisis and provide specific course of action to enable an organisation to avoid or handle the crisis issues is called crisis management. Crisis management is more effective if the organisation is proactively prepared to cope with emergencies (Darling *et al.*, 1996).

Islamic conception of universe is based on perfection of its creation. Islam is a complete and genuine school of thought with prime objective to address and respond every enquiry pertaining to human requirements including social, spiritual, emotional, intellectual, collective or individual in this life or in the life hereafter (Ashtiany, 2009).

Identification of Crisis and Preparedness

The whole life in Islam moves around the preparedness for the life hereafter, 'the unseen'. To be prepared for the unseen is exactly according to the teachings, norms and centuries of practices of followers of Islamic way of life. Identifying what can lead to bitter outcomes in the life hereafter spreads over entire body of teachings in Islam. Therefore, to identify factors which can exacerbate the experience during the times of crisis are aligned with the spirit of Islamic ethics. Then, being prepared with all known aspects and resources to handle the crisis is the essence of teachings on Islamic work ethics for contemporary workplace. In dynamic environment of today's businesses, despite all the efforts a company puts forth to scan the environmental issues, crises can occur and have to be managed. Acknowledging a crisis and communicating with the stakeholders are as important as planning the prevention, diagnosis, and intervention to solve crisis situations (Kash and Darling, 1998).

Teachings of al-Qur'ān are comprehensive and applied with multidimensional interpretations valid for all human communities with diverse requirements and all times till the Last Day to address needs of human beings. Teachings of al-Qur'ān are applicable to all matters related to human life on this planet (Ashtiany, 2009).

We have revealed to you the book which clarifies every matter (al-Qur'ān 16:89)

Hundreds of years before the recent developments in earth sciences al-Qur'ān guided the mankind about the concept of plate tectonics through following verse, probably with the objective of educating human beings to learn about the catastrophes of earthquake by the possible movements of earth plates. This knowledge naturally would have led to the developments in construction capabilities to avoid disasters. However, there had been little progress among Muslims for effective crisis management in the wake of earthquake.

And in the Earth are neighbouring pieces (al-Qur'ān 13:4)

Above verse clearly suggested the need of safe construction and avoiding even small mistakes while developing the infrastructure to avoid crises thus saving extremely valuable creature on the earth.

The Qur'an stated in Chapter 99 (1-9).

In the name of Allah, the Beneficent, the Merciful:
When the earth is shaken with its [final] earthquake
And the earth discharges its burdens
And man says, "What is [wrong] with it?" –
That Day, it will report its news
Because your Lord has commanded it.
That Day, the people will depart separated [into categories] to be shown [the result of] their deeds.
So, whoever does an atom's weight of good will see it,
And whoever does an atom's weight of evil will see it.

With the reference of the first verse most interpretations relate this chapter with the earthquake of the Day of Resurrection. However, a simple interpretation suggests the occurrence of an earthquake event. Ashtiany (2009, p. 7) stated that:

With this view, Verse 6 can refer to the time when humans see the results of their deeds on what they have done in terms of building works. People who have constructed well shall see its safe results and those who have violated the principles of safe building will be in sorrow to see the collapse and other unhappy results. This verse is followed by Verses 7 and 8, which can be interpreted as signifying that even a very small good deed in respect of earthquake safety and safe construction and development would lead to positive results. On the other hand, even a very small violation or attempt to ignore safety will produce devastating results.

The same concept has been described in the following verse of the Qur'ān as:

Whoever does good, the reward to him is better than his deed, and whoever do bad shall not be rewarded, or shall be punished [to the extent] of their deeds (al-Qur'ān 28:84)

Mitigation and Prevention of Crisis

Surely the Qur'an guides one to that which is most upright and gives good news to the believers who do good so that they shall have a great reward (al-Qur'ān 17:9)

Business organisation during their day-to-day operations cannot predict every unseen aspect of operations. Management of unforeseen issues which usually lead to a crisis is mostly missing in number of organisations around the world. Sometimes, despite appropriate measure, crisis surprises organisations with new and unique dimensions. Therefore, experience curve has its place in the literature of strategic planning and management about learning from mistakes made during organisational processes. Managerial activities such as scenario analysis, contingency planning and focusing on the negatives of risk managements to bring balance through surprise management have evolved in contemporary business studies (Kash and Darling, 1998). The Qur'ān also educates that:

O you who have believed, persevere and endure and remain stationed and fear Allah that you may be successful (al-Qur'ān 3:200)

Minimising the risk and zero tolerance for violation of codes needs good management and governance practices with wide-ranging command and control systems for people with authority to develop communities efficiently. Teachings of *Amr-bil-maruf* (inviting for good) and *Nahye-anil-Munkar* (forbidding wrong) can be used to encourage participation of communities in the in the management and governance practices. Both these key concepts of Islamic work ethics can facilitate effective implementation of risk reduction at contemporary workplaces (Ashtiany, 2009). Teachings of al-Qur'ān about these notions are given below:

And from among you there should be a party which invites one to do to good and enjoins what is right and forbids the wrong, and this it is that shall be successful (al-Qur'ān 3:104)

Ye are the best of peoples, evolved for mankind, enjoining what is right, forbidding what is wrong, and believing in Allah. If only the People of the Book had faith, it would be best for them: among them are some who have faith, but most of them are perverted transgressors. (al-Qur'ān 3:110)

The use of this key concept in Islamic societies can enhance community participation and supervision, which would be very useful as a means of mitigation and prevention of issues and crises at workplace.

Response and Monitoring

Today businesses are prone to sudden and extensive crises due to extended operations and technological vulnerabilities. Nowadays it is not about if an organisation will experience a crisis, instead it is about when and what types of crisis an organisation is expected to face. It is equally important that contemporary workplaces have to ensure regular evaluation to determine organisational preparations to deal with probable devastations such as earthquake, floods, tempering, accidents, or strikes (Mitroff, *et. al.*, 1996).

That is because your Lord would not destroy the cities for wrongdoing while their people were unaware (al-Qur'ān 6:131)

According to Ashtiany (2009, p.)

in the chapter of the Qur'an entitled 'Ankaboot' (Spider), verse 40, and in the 'Nisa' (women) chapter, verses 78 and 79, and in relation to human actions and responses, sin and bad deeds emphasise that 'good and evil, blessings and punishment, are from Allah, but no distress afflicts a man unless he earns it by his own mistakes or blunders'. In other words, all of the bad or unpleasant things or disasters caused by sin are from the doer of bad acts and God never does harm or wants bad things to happen to human beings. With this meaning, the process of sinning can result in disaster.

Most crises and human losses are due to failure to use available moral principles and bad governance. These verses read as follows:

So We took each one in his sin; of them was he on whom We sent a strong storm, and of them was he who was overtaken by the Cry, and of them was he whom We caused the earth to swallow, and of them was he whom We drowned. It was not for Allah to wrong them, but they wronged themselves" 29:40).... If some good befalls them, they say, "This is from Allah"; but if evil occurs, they say,

This is from yourself" ... (al-Qur'ān 4:78]. O'man: Whatever benefit comes to you, it is from Allah, and whatever misfortune or distress befalls on you, it is from yourself, and We have sent the Prophet to mankind as a messenger; and Allah is sufficient as a witness (al-Qur'ān 4:79)

The statements and lectures (Hadith) of the Prophet Mohammad (PBUH) and his companion are a valuable source of information on Islamic teaching and are complementary to the al-Qur'ān. Some of these statements of Holy Prophet Muhammad (PBUH) reported by Ashtiany (2009) can be related to the need to do good deeds to avoid issues and crises:

- "God loves those who do a deed or job correctly, perfectly and completely".
- "People should have a strong desire to do good deeds".
- "People's deeds or actions that have good intentions and produce good results are a means of worshipping God".
- "A person is not a believer when neighbours are not safe from his misconduct and when he thus behaves in a manner that will increase vulnerability". Environment around us at workplace and neighbourhood should not be of a kind in a way that creates problems for co-workers and neighbours or cause damage to them.

Recovery and Review

Four factors that greatly contributed to the company's rapid recovery and review of crises to avoid same happenings in future are as follows:

1. People and leadership.
2. Strong cash position.
3. Stakeholder support.
4. Supply chain risk mitigation.

O you who have believed, fear Allah. And let every soul look to what it has put forth for tomorrow - and fear Allah. Indeed, Allah is Acquainted with what you do (al-Qur'ān 59:18)

The concept of sin as violation of accepted norms and values, though subjective, existed in all religions and societies during all times of human history. Historically disasters and crises have usually been associated with such violations as sins committed by the members of society. There are numerous instances where Islamic traditions there are numerous instances of disasters and crises associated with the abundance or indifference towards committing sins. Any act or anything that goes against the commandments of Allah (SWT) and breaches Shari'ah (the Islamic law) is considered as sin (Ashtiany, 2009). Some aspects of sin for contemporary workplaces are further delineated as follows:

- Health, wisdom and human abilities are one of most important blessings of Allah (SWT) for human beings. Improper utilisation of these blessings leading to disaster and crises is indeed a sin.
- Negative utilisation of human intellectual and physical abilities is denial of blessings from the Almighty and may lead to personal or communal loss of the society thus considered as sin.
- Islamic work ethics advocate protection of human rights and social welfare, there is no room for violating human rights and sabotaging social cohesion.
- Practices leading to corruption and inculcating confusion & mistrust in the society are not tolerated in Islamic work ethics.

In a similar manner to sin, corruption or mischief in the management process will result in unsafe conditions and will cause damage and crises.

And do not seek to make mischief or corrupt in the land, surely Allah does not love the mischief-makers (al-Qur'ān 28:77)

Therefore, when human beings despite acquired necessary expertise as engineers, architects, town planners, developers, builders, policy makers, managers and rulers avoid implementation of relevant laws & regulations and ignore tested scientific facts or violate workplace ethics and regulations without consideration that can be considered as sin in Islamic value system leading to susceptibility for devastation and crisis (Ashtiany, 2009).

Ensuring Safety in the Wake of Crisis

Following sayings of Holy Prophet (PBUH) reported by Ashtiany (2009) can help researchers, scholars and practitioners alike to understand the spirit of Islamic workplace ethics to ensure safety in the wake of crisis. There is abundance of instances where workplaces faced crises due to the abuse of regulations and the code of conduct. Ignorance is not the excuse; everyone being involved has to ensure awareness and understanding of rules, regulations, and standard operating procedures.

Following hadith provides strong evidence that only those who abide with laws and regulations at contemporary workplaces are considered true Muslims in Islamic teachings. Islamic work ethics are compatible with the requirements of creating virtuous organisations in contemporary environments.

Those who cheat and violate the law and people's rights are not true Muslim.

In Islamic work ethics it is fundamental responsibility of individuals and equal duty of organisations to keep their employees well informed about laws, rules, regulations, rights and responsibilities of all stakeholders to promote business interests because ignorance can lead to several problems and ailments at contemporary workplaces. Following hadith is also indicating the same aspect:

Ignorance is the root of all problems and faults.

Companions of the Prophet Muhammad (PBUH) are source of inspiration for all Muslims. The fourth Caliph Hazrat Ali (ra) provided following golden principle for the success of organisations and avoiding & managing crises effectively.

Do not be part of those groups that, without using their knowledge and without doing good deeds, expect or hope for good and safe results.

Noah's Ark: A Clear Example of How to be Safe in Crisis

The story of Prophet Noah (PBUH) and his experience with crisis is one of the best examples for teaching reported in any religion. In this respect, the al-Qur'ān says: "So We revealed to him, saying: 'Construct the Ark within Our sight and under Our guidance'; then when comes Our command, and the fountains of the earth gush forth …; and address Me not in favour of the wrong-doers; for they shall be drowned" (al-Qur'ān 23:27) The lessons that should be learned from the story of Noah's Ark are:

- Even the prophets had to work hard to handle disasters as Allah (SWT) instructed Prophet Noah (AS) to build an Ark to remain safe during the typhoon.
- Preparation is the fundamental principle to remain safe during dangerous disasters and crises and

- Allah (SWT) based creation of this universe on principles of wisdom, acquiring knowledge and utilising human abilities, even most privileged human beings such as prophets also had to comply with these principles to manage crisis.

One can certainly wonder that despite robust relevant directions and knowledge about dealing with crises and disasters still Islamic communities have disappointing performance in handling crises and remain exposed to disasters. It is simply because Muslims do not follow Islamic teaching in true spirit. Islamic teaching emphasises on acquiring relevant knowledge and scientific interventions to manage crises, however, practically there seems insufficient progress towards this aspect of crisis management.

Crisis management needs relevant knowledge and its implementation to secure communities from the devastating effects of the disaster. Islamic work ethics make it mandatory for all employees of the organisation to understand and implement pertinent knowledge and abide with the guidance and recommendations of experts. Crisis management expertise can facilitate contemporary workplaces for sustainable development of the organisations. However, this can only be achieved through concerted efforts and adoption of good management practices at the workplace.

CONCLUSION

This chapter has examined ethics of multinational companies (MNCs) activities and for their workforces. The Islamic ethics system helps and enhance businesses, workforce and customers to operate in honest and transparent manner. More importantly the Islamic ethics system emphasis that our personal and business dealing should be according to commandment of Allah and ethical behaviour to be part of the faith. Key concept of Islamic ethics system to follow Islam to obey value system of Qur'ān and Sunnah. The managers, developers, engineers, builders, owners, rulers or policy makers lack faith in the common laws of nature and belief in scientific facts, and when they misuse existing know-how on safety and working principles or violate workplace regulations. People presented through value system of Qur'ān and Sunnah exhibit these qualities in their personal and professional lives.

Therefore, to identify factors which can intensify the experience during the times of crisis are aligned with the spirit of Islamic ethics. The organisations and workforce need to be prepared to deal with all known aspects and resources to handle the crisis is the essence of teachings on Islamic work ethics for contemporary workplace. This chapter has developed some key insights into the interactions between the Islamic ethics and multinational companies (MNCs) activities and their workforces. Islamic religion based on the teaching of the Prophet Mohammad (PBUH) and his companion are a valuable source of information on Islamic teaching and are complementary to the al-Qur'ān. The real problem is unfortunately most Muslims do not completely follow Islam and Islamic teaching. Crisis cannot be managed without knowledge and scientific interventions.

Discussion Questions

1. Consider and discuss the ethics of multinational companies (MNCs) activities and for their workforces.
2. Highlight and investigate the Islamic business activities which should be conducted as part of the worship and obedience to Allah?
3. Discuss and evaluate Islamic ethics system according to commandment of Allah and ethical behaviour of individual as a part of the faith?
4. Explore Islamic ethics principles of crisis management and the objective of sustainable development of business dealing within multinational companies (MNCs)?

REFERENCES

Alhabshi, S. O., & Ghazali, A. H. (1994). *Islamic Values and Management, Institute of Islamic Understanding Malaysia*. IKMI.

Alsop, R. J. (2004). *The 18 Immutable Laws of Corporate Reputation*. Kogan Page.

Asad, M. (2007). *The principles of state and government in Islam*. Islamic Book Trust Kuala Lumpur.

Ashtiany, M. G. (2009). View of Islam on earthquakes, human vitality and disaster. *Disaster Prevention and Management: An International Journal, 18*(3), 218–232. doi:10.1108/09653560910965600

Brown, J. K. (1979). *The Business of Issues: Coping with the Company's Environments*. Conference Board.

Clark, J. (1995/1996). Hope for the best, but plan for the worst – the need for disaster planning. *Employment Relations Today*, *22*(4), 41–53. doi:10.1002/ert.3910220406

Darling, J., Hannu, O., & Raimo, N. (1996). Crisis management in international business: a case situation in decision making concerning trade with Russia. *The Finnish Journal of Business Economic*, *4*.

Declining. (2012). *Declining Employee Loyalty: A Casualty of the New Workplace*. Retrieved on September 20, 2019 from:https://knowledge.wharton.upenn.edu/article/declining-employee-loyalty-a-casualty-of-the-new-workplace/

Hadisi, M. (2014). The effect of Islamic work ethics on the performance of Muslim employees of marketing sector in multinational companies. *International Journal of Organisational Leadership*, *3*(1), 31–40. doi:10.33844/ijol.2014.60402

Jackson, J. K. (2013). Codes of Conduct for Multinational Corporations: An Overview. *Congressional Research Service*. https://fas.org/sgp/crs/misc/RS20803.pdf

Kash, T. J., & Darling, J. R. (1998). Crisis management: Prevention, diagnosis and intervention. *Leadership and Organization Development Journal*, *4*(19), 179–186. doi:10.1108/01437739810217151

Loyalty. (2019). *Employee Engagement & Loyalty Statistics: The Ultimate Collection*. Retrieved on September 20, 2019 from: https://blog.accessperks.com/employee-engagement-loyalty-statistics-the-ultimate-collection#satisfaction

Mitrof, I., Harrington, L., & Eric, K. (1996, Sept.). Thinking about the unthinkable. *Across the Board*, 44–48.

Modudi, A. A. (2003). *Islami Riasat*. Islamic Publications Pvt. Ltd.

Chapter 4
Corporate Governance in Islamic Ethics

ABSTRACT

Corporate governance plays an important role in economic performance because it provides mechanisms that affect returns on investment. Organisations need a set of institutional and market mechanisms that allow managers and board members to maximise the value of the residual cash flows to the shareholders. If domestic markets including labour, goods, and capital markets of the economy are working efficiently, maximum possible growth rate can be achieved as efficient functioning also implies efficient utilisation of resources. Besides maximising the growth, it is also important to maintain the growth for sustainable performance through sound legal system, effective regulations, and transparency. These factors coupled with effective disclosure facilitate smooth and efficient functioning of markets. The purpose of this chapter is to develop an understanding of the corporate governance codes and practices according to the Islamic teaching of the Prophet Muhammad (PBUH).

INTRODUCTION

The role of corporate governance is to help the key stakeholders to deliver the long-lasting achievement for the companies. Over the last decade integration of principles of corporate governance codes has become very important since the development of the Islamic finance. In 2017 Saudi Capital Market Authority (CMA) released new wide-ranging set of Corporate Governance

DOI: 10.4018/978-1-7998-5295-7.ch004

Regulations to accommodate the Islamic principles with western corporate governance codes.

Since the Islamic finance emerged over the last 20 years as a business model for Muslim customers. It became essential for businesses to understand the how the Islamic Finance system is operated according to Quran and Sunna of Prophet Muhammad (PBUH) and meet the Shari'ah compliant financial system. The Shari'ah economic system does not allow forbidden products or services that are involved in charging interest on loans given to individual customers or businesses. Therefore, it is important that products and services which are considered for businesses need to be compatible with Islamic teaching of Prophet Muhammad (PBUH). Quran prohibits the interest rate (riba) in strongest sense, because riba represents both the return of money on money via a prearranged interest rate on a loan as a social discrimination. The riba creates social discrimination for society in general and weakens profitability of the borrowers in the completion. The Quran says that:

Allah has permitted trade and has prohibited riba (al-Qur'ān 2:275)

O you who believe, Fear Allah and give up what remains of your demand for Interest, if you are indeed a believer. If you do not, then you are warned of the declaration of war from Allah and His Messenger; but if you turn back you shall have your principal: Deal not unjustly and you shall not be dealt with unjustly (al-Qur'ān 2:278 -279)

The interest which you give to increase the wealth of people, will have no increase with Allah: But that which you lay out for charity, seeking favour of Allah (He will increase): it is these who will get a recompense multiplied (al-Qur'ān 30:39)

According to Tapanjeh, (2009) "the term 'corporate governance' had its origin from a Greek word 'kyberman' which means to steer, guide or govern. This passed on from Greek to Latin word as gubernare and the old French 'governor', but this word has been defined in different ways by different organisations or committees, according to their own ideological concerns".

This chapter will examine the discuss principles of corporate governance codes and explain how to create approachable system to support individual businesses. Also, provide examination for customers and businesses to understand and provide clear-cut accounting terms for principles of Shari'ah developed Islamic Finance.

Corporate Governance Principles

Corporate governance has diverse interpretations from accountability, transparency and fairness to balancing economics & social and individual & communal goals. Corporate governance also addresses relationships among corporate management, board of directors, shareholders and other stakeholders. It also concerns internal system of organisational policies and processes. According to Ahmed (2011) "the narrow interpretation of corporate governance has objectives which cater to the interests of shareholders whilst disciplining managers. The broad interpretation consists of ensuring a healthy business or healthy contribution to society and protecting stakeholder interests. Corporate governance is linked to the behaviour of corporations and acts as a disciplinary mechanism for managers". There are two "governance" chain models which exist throughout the world:

The "Market Model" Governance Chain

The "Market Model" governance chain is more common in US, UK, Canada and Australia. In this model there are efficient, well-developed equity markets and dispersed ownership. This model explains conditions and governance practices that are better understood, appreciated and valued by sophisticated global investors.

The "Control Model" Governance Chain

The "Control Model" governance chain exists in underdeveloped equity markets e.g. in Asia, Latin America and some eastern European countries. This model contains concentrated (family ownership), less shareholder transparency and inadequate protection of minority and foreign shareholders. Despite significant progress and wisdom to develop corporate governance, still there are three basic assumptions in corporate governance:

1. Primacy of the shareholders
2. Diversity of the shareholder group
3. Maximisation of shareholder wealth

OECD (2015) state that the corporate governance are important principles which brings the board of directors and key stakeholders to develop clear relationship.

Corporate governance involves a set of relationships between a company's management, its board, its shareholders and other stakeholders. Corporate governance also provides the structure through which the objectives of the company are set, and the means of attaining those objectives and monitoring performance are determined. (OECD, 2015 p. 9)

World Bank has gone a step further by explaining that corporate governance needs to be "fairness, transparency and accountability" (Tapanjeh, 2009). According to Parkinson, (1994), Solomon and Solomon (2004) and Abbasi (2008) "corporate governance tends to focus on accountability of corporate management to shareholders and the ability of country's legal system to protect minority shareholder rights. Corporate governance is the process of supervision and control intended to ensure that the company's management acts in accordance with the interests of shareholders".

In the practical sense, corporate governance involves the nuts and bolts of how corporations should fulfil their responsibilities to their shareholders and other stakeholders. Corporate governance is the mechanism by which agency problems of corporation stakeholders, including the shareholders, creditors, management, employees, consumers and the public at large are framed and sought to be resolved. Transparency, accountability and adequate disclosure are three essential ingredients in corporate governance Hakim (2002).

According to Tapanjeh (2009) corporate governance is a set of mechanism that facilitates fair and just dealing with all stakeholders to strengthen transparency and accountability.

Good corporate governance has long been considered a crucial role for stakeholders in the business environment. Though the goal of corporate governance differs from one firm to another or from one country to another, the main important concern is to impetus a good code of mechanisms to uplift and govern the organisation. But with the current business pressure, corporate governance structure changes very fast.

In concurrence with Tricker (1984) and Cannon (1994), Abbasi (2008) argued that "corporate governance is giving overall direction to the enterprise, with overseeing and controlling executive actions of management and satisfying legitimate expectations of accountability and regulation by interests beyond the corporate boundaries. Corporate governance is the sum of those activities that makeup the internal regulations of the business in compliance with the obligations placed on the firm by legislation, ownership and control. It incorporates the trusteeship of assets, their management and their deployment".

Peterson (2002) discussed that "corporate management have got a moral cancer or governance cancer and it's going to metastasise, if corporate leaders don't cut out this thing in a hurry or as soon as they can, into an economic cancer". Alsop (2004) considered "executive greed as one of the important factors of reputation crisis and ethical dilemma in corporate management around the globe". George (2002) said "Our system has a lot of greed, greed on investment side, greed on accounting side and greed on corporate side". Sarbanes-Oxley was an effort to strengthen law enforcement to make people accountable.

Abbasi (2008) asserted that "to control the economic cancer, to manage the greed on all sides corporate management needs a pattern where even the smallest good deed is valued, and every bad deed is counted. Islamic ethical system has the answer, where there is a just system of valuing good deeds and controlling bad deeds" as mentioned in the following verse of the Qur'ān:

Then shall anyone who has done an atom's weight of good, see it! And anyone who has done an atom's weight of evil, shall see it. (al - Qur'ān 99:7-8)

Modudi (2005b) mentioned that "this verse informs human beings about an important fact (p. 426) that every single good deed, no matter how small it is, has value and the same is for bad deed that it will be counted, it will not be ignored. Therefore, one should not leave even a small righteous deed because many little righteous deeds can become a big righteous deed in front of Allah Almighty. Also, one should not commit even a little evil because many little sins can become a big collection of sins".

In Islamic ethical system everyone is responsible for the consequences of only his/her deeds.

Nor can a bearer of burdens bear another's burden. If one heavily laden should call another to (bear) his load, not the least portion of it can be carried (by the other), even though he be nearly related (al-Qur'ān 35:18)

Modudi (2005a, p.228) stated that "burden means burden of deeds. It means in front of Allah Almighty everyone himself is responsible for his deeds, and everyone is responsible for his deeds only. There is no chance that Allah Almighty transfers the burden of responsibility of one to other. This is also not possible that anybody takes the responsibility of other and presents himself instead of other for the punishment".

This is clear in Islamic ethical system that everyone will face the consequences of his deeds. In case of leadership, IES endows even more responsibility, because it is the responsibility of leadership to ensure comfort, prosperity and happiness of people under their authority or management. If anybody is deprived of his rights, leader will be held accountable.

It is We Who have placed you with authority on earth and provided you therein with means for the fulfilment of your life: small are the thanks that ye give! (al-Qur'ān 7:10)

Daryabadi (1998) explained that "this is the address to all mankind (p. 136). Here is the mention of bodily and material blessings, which include living, eating and wearing. Two favours are mentioned here, authority and wealth. It means that these things are not bad in themselves, but arbitrary use of these two things is bad. Islamic leadership has to utilise all resources justly and it should be thankful to Almighty Allah for the resources".

Islamic Leadership is accountable to fellow beings. First Caliph Hazrat Abu Bakr Siddique said If I do the right, help me, if I do the wrong, correct me. As long as I obey Allah (SWT) and Prophet (PBUH) do obey me; and if I disobey Allah (SWT) and Prophet (PBUH) you have no obligation to obey me. (Modudi, 2003).

In Islam, everyone is guardian and supervisor in his/her own domain: husband is supervisor of home, wife and children, wife is guardian of house of her husband, and teacher is guardian of students.

Corporate governance practices have become critical to worldwide efforts to stabilise and strengthen good capital markets and protect investors (Darman, 2005). Many studies exist linking good corporate governance with better performance. There is empirical evidence to suggest that countries that have implemented good corporate governance measures have generally experienced robust growth of corporate sectors and higher ability to attract capital than those that have not (SECP, 2005). According to Tapanjeh (2009) "good corporate governance helps to bridge the gap between investor confidence and cost of capital. It also helps in ensuring company honours, its legal commitments and forms value-creating relations with stakeholders. Companies with better corporate governance enjoy higher valuation. However, there is a growing argument that corporate governance still needs to be renovated and revised. Hence, it can be concluded that issue of good corporate governance is still open for discussion".

Effective and efficient corporate governance practices can lead to increased economic efficiency and growth; corporate governance improves the use of capital and encourages foreign direct investment. These processes and mechanisms lower the risk of crisis and in the case of an external shock thus improve the robustness of the economy.

According to Maune (2017) rigorous corporate governance practices do enhances economic growth and development through two mechanisms which are its association with financing & investment and economic system efficiency. Reliable corporate governance remains significantly positively and negatively related to economic growth. Political stability and absence of violence, rule of law and voice and accountability culture have positive impact on GDP growth. Lack of control of corruption, ineffectiveness of government policies and regulatory mechanism do lead to negative impact on GDP of the country. AL Bassam (2013) also found significant relationships between economic growth as measured by GDP per capita and each indicator of the governance both before and after the onset of the 2008 economic crisis.

The OCED Principles of Corporate Governance

The Organisation of Economic Cooperation and Development in 1999 released it first set of corporate governance codes framework to improve the transparency and efficiency within financial markets. The main purpose was to create a framework for businesses to follow and be consistent with legal responsibilities set by government authorities. The following are set of principles of corporate governance developed by OCED, 2015 pp. 13-45).

Principle 1: "Ensuring the basis for an effective corporate governance framework".

Annotation: "*The corporate governance framework should promote transparent and efficient markets, be consistent with the rule of law and clearly articulate the division of responsibilities among different supervisory, regulatory and enforcement authorities*".

Principle 2: "The right and equitable treatment of shareholders and key ownership functions".
Annotation: "*The corporate governance framework should protect and facilitate the exercise of shareholders' rights and ensure the equitable treatment of all shareholders, including minority and foreign shareholders. All shareholders should have the opportunity to obtain effective redress for violation of their rights*".

Principle 3: "Institutional investors, stock markets, and other intermediaries".
Annotation: "*The corporate governance framework should provide sound incentives throughout the investment chain and provide for stock markets to function in a way that contributes to good corporate governance*".

Principle 4: "The role of stakeholders in corporate governance".
Annotation: "*The corporate governance framework should recognise the rights of stakeholders established by law or through mutual agreements and encourage active co-operation between corporations and stakeholders in creating wealth, jobs, and the sustainability of financially sound enterprises*".

Principle 5: "Disclosure and transparency".
Annotation: "*The corporate governance framework should ensure that timely and accurate disclosure is made on all material matters regarding the corporation, including the financial situation, performance, ownership, and governance of the company*".

Principle 6: "The responsibilities of the board".
Annotation: "*The corporate governance framework should ensure the strategic guidance of the company, the effective monitoring of management by the board, and board's accountability to the company and the shareholders*".

Five basic ethics emerge from OECD's above principles for effective and efficient corporate governance:

Justice

"And We place the scales of justice for the Day of Resurrection, so no soul will be treated unjustly at all. And if there is [even] the weight of a mustard

seed, We will bring it forth. And sufficient are we as accountant" (al-Qur'ān, 21:47)

It has been narrated on the authority of 'Abdullah b. 'Umar that the Messenger of Allah (PBUH) said: "Behold! the Dispensers of justice will be seated on the pulpits of light beside God, on the right side of the Merciful, Exalted and Glorious. Either side of the Being is the right side both being equally meritorious. (The Dispensers of justice are) those who do justice in their rules, in matters relating to their families and in all that they undertake to do". (Sahih Muslim 1827)

Narrated Abu Huraira: *Allah's Messenger (PBUH) said, "There is a Sadaqa to be given for every joint of the human body; and for every day on which the sun rises there is a reward of a Sadaqa (i.e. charitable gift) for the one who establishes justice among people". (Sahih al-Bukhari 2707)*

Accountability

According to Ibn 'Abbas (ra) the Prophet (PBUH) said: "We are the last of the nations, and the first to be brought to account. It will be said: 'Where is the unlettered nation and its Prophet?' So, we are the last and the first". (Sunan Ibn Majah 4431)

Narrated `Abdullah bin Abi `Aufa: Allah's Messenger (PBUH) said "on the Day of (the battle of) the Clans, "O Allah! The Revealer of the Holy Book, The Quick Taker of Accounts! Defeat the clans and shake them". (Sahih al-Bukhari 7489)

Narrated Imran ibn Husayn: The Prophet said: "If anyone swears a false oath in confinement, he should make his seat in Hell on account of his (act)". (Sunan Abi Dawud 3242)

Tapanjeh (2009) argues that "the strong belief of accountability in this world and thereafter had strong implication in every Muslim's life and governs a wider scope and extended obligations of corporate governance with that compared to conventional principles. Hence success and welfare are measured with moral and ethical obligations with a strong trust in accountability with Allah, the ultimate authority". Figure 1 below demonstrated the accountability framework within Islamic ethics.

Figure 1. Accountability Framework in Islamic Ethics
Source: Abbasi A. S. (2008). Role of Islamic Leadership in Value Based Corporate Management, PhD Thesis, NUML Islamabad, Pakistan.

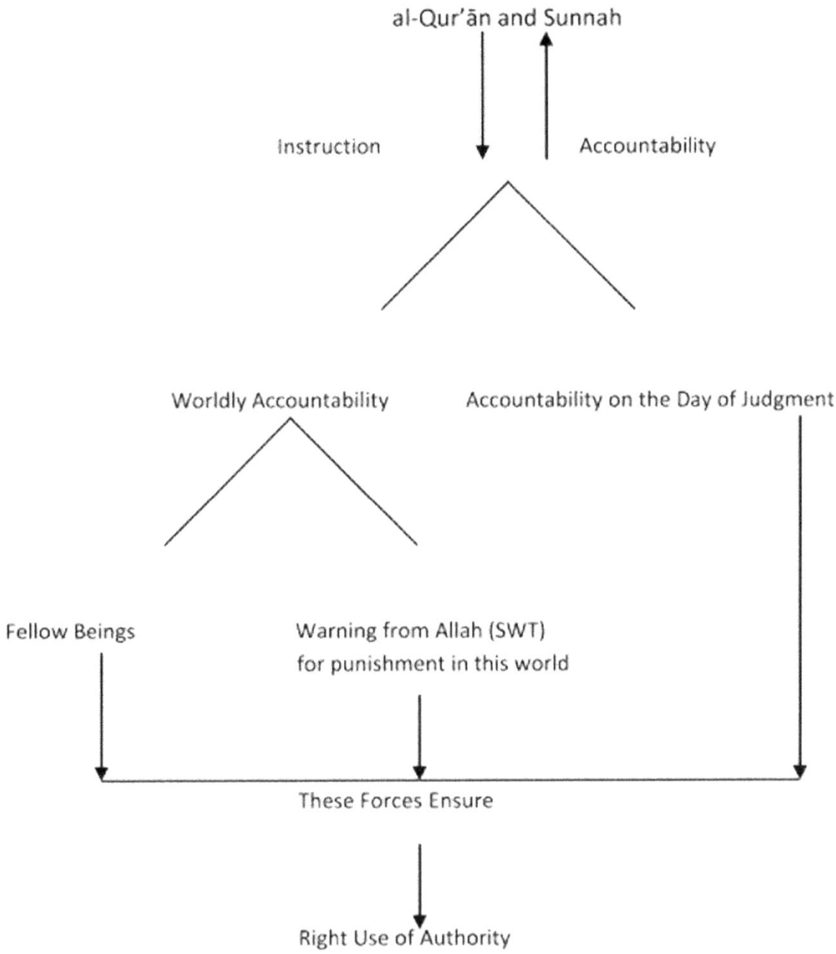

Honesty

Narrated by Abu Huraira (ra): Allah's Messenger (PBUH) said, "When honesty is lost, then wait for the Hour". It was asked, "How will honesty be lost, O Allah's Messenger (PBUH)?" He said, "When authority is given to those who do not deserve it, then wait for the Hour". (Sahih al-Bukhari 6496)

Reported by Hudhaifa (ra): Allah's Messenger (PBUH) said to us, "Honesty descended from the Heavens and settled in the roots of the hearts of men (faithful believers), and then the Qur'an was revealed and the people read the Qur'an, (and learnt it from it) and also learnt it from the Sunnah". Both Qur'an and Sunna strengthened their (the faithful believers') honesty. (Sahih al-Bukhari 7276)

...... His (the Holy Prophet's (PBUH) gatherings were the gatherings of knowledge, modesty, patience and honesty... (Shama'il Muhammadiyah Book 46, Hadith 319)

Transparency

O you who have believed, when you contract a debt for a specified term, write it down. And let a scribe write [it] between you in justice. Let no scribe refuse to write as Allah has taught him. So, let him write and let the one who has the obligation dictate. And let him fear Allah, his Lord, and not leave anything out of it. (al-Qur'ān, 2:282)

And if you are on a journey and cannot find a scribe, then a security deposit [should be] taken. And if one of you entrusts another, then let him who is entrusted discharge his trust [faithfully] and let him fear Allah, his Lord. And do not conceal testimony, for whoever conceals it - his heart is indeed sinful, and Allah is Knowing of what you do (al-Qur'ān, 2:283).

It was narrated that Wathilah bin Asqa' (ra) said:

I heard the Messenger of Allah (PBUH) say: 'Whoever sells defective goods without pointing it out, he will remain subject to the wrath of Allah, and the angels will continue to curse him (Sunan Ibn Majah 2332)

Narrated by Abu Huraira (ra):

The Prophet (PBUH) forbade the meeting (of caravans) on the way and the selling of goods by an inhabitant of the town on behalf of a desert dweller (Sahih al-Bukhari 2162)

Ibn Tawus narrated from his father that Ibn 'Abbas (ra) said:

The Messenger of Allah (PBUH) forbade a city-dweller to sell for a Bedouin" (Sahih)I (Tawus) said to Ibn 'Abbas: "What is meant by the words: 'A city-

dweller selling for a Bedouin?' He said: "He should not be a broker for him" (Sunan Ibn Majah 2261)

Saying of the Holy Prophet (PBUH),

A believer is the mirror of his brother. When he sees a fault in it, he should correct it.

A scholar derived four different meanings from above mentioned hadith of the Messenger of Allah (may Allah bless him and grant him peace):

A first meaning, he said, is that "the believer sees good qualities in his brother, so he attempts to emulate them, or he sees bad qualities in his brother, so he knows that he possesses similar qualities and attempts to eradicate them".

A second meaning is that "the believer sees a fault in his brother, so he tells him to remove it. He is thus like a mirror to his brother".

A third meaning is that "the believer appears to his brother according to his brother's inward state. If his heart is pure then he sees his brothers as being pure of heart like himself, and he holds a good opinion of them. If, however, his heart is sick he sees his brothers as being like him and he holds a bad opinion of them. The believer thus projects what is in his heart onto his brothers. Thus, if someone sees the Prophet ﷺ in a beautiful form in a dream then this shows that the person is in a good state. If, however he does not see the Prophet ﷺ in a beautiful form then this shows that the person has some kind of deficiency".

A fourth meaning is that "if a believer's faith is complete, Allah manifests Himself to his heart. One of Allah's names is 'al-Mu'min', meaning 'the Faithful.' Thus, the meaning of the hadith would be: 'the believer, or more specifically the heart of the believer is the place, or the mirror, to which Allah 'the Faithful' manifests himself".

Trusteeship

Abu Musa reported The Messenger of Allah (PBUH) as saying:

The faithful trustee who gives what he is commanded completely and in full with a good will, and delivers it to the one whom he was told to give it, is one of the two who gives sadaqah (Sunan Abi Dawud 1684)

It has been narrated on the authority of Ibn ‘Umar that the Holy Prophet (May peace be upon him) said:

Beware every one of you is a shepherd and everyone is answerable with regard to his flock. The Caliph is a shepherd over the people and shall be questioned about his subjects (as to how he conducted their affairs). A man is a guardian over the members of his family and shall be questioned about them (as to how he looked after their physical and moral well-being). A woman is a guardian over the household of her husband and his children and shall be questioned about them (as to how she managed the household and brought up the children). A slave is a guardian over the property of his master and shall be questioned about it (as to how he safeguarded his trust). Beware, every one of you is a guardian and every one of you shall be questioned with regard to his trust. (Sunan Abi Dawud 2928)

According to Tapanjeh (2009)

the Islamic religion relates directly to all spheres of life, including how to conduct the trade and commerce. Shariah covers not only religious ritual, but also many aspects of day-to-day life, politics, economics, banking, business or contract law, and social issues. Muslims are directed to conduct their business in accordance with the Shariah rules, i.e., to be fair, honest and just toward others. in Islam larger and vast guidelines with encompassing duties and practices as on how to deal with economic transactions up to the moral conduct of a Muslim without even defining the modern world corporate governance Islamic laws impetus corporate governance in every individual actions of Muslim up to the social environment.

Tapanjeh (2009) argues that:

Muslims are entitled to conduct their business activity as guided by the Shariah code of conduct, which encourage being just, fair and honest to all the people involved in the business. Therefore, a Muslim business people are hence taught to possess a high moral conduct, so not to betray, deceive or exploit his fellowships. Muslim should also not therefore overcome with their business activity with consequent results in profit making only. At the same time, Muslims require to work and produce and being not to be lazy and unproductive.

To all are degrees (or ranks) according to their deeds (al-Qur'ān 6:132)

Any system without an appropriate ethical and moral climate will not influence a proper governance mechanism. Islamic business ethics promotes transparency and rule of law. Islamic ethics extends the responsibility to fulfil obligations beyond shareholders, clients, financiers, suppliers, customers and employees.

Entire organisation is expected to contribute knowledge towards formulation and implementation of strategies for all stakeholders including employees, shareholders, customers, suppliers and the society at large (Baydoun et al., 1999). Islamic ethics are taught to maintain and strengthen good relationship with superiors, clients and the management conforming to the divine norms and rules, thus inspire the whole community with values of truthfulness, fairness, tolerance and justice.

None of you [truly] believes until he loves for his brother that which he loves for himself. (al-Bukhari) (Muslim)

Tapanjeh (2009) contends that

Islamic principle that represents a core element of corporate governance is an institution of Hisbah established under the Abbasids (750 a.d. onwards) which ensures compliance with the Shariah requirements, particularly in the business affairs. Duties like correcting weight and measures, fair trading rules, checking business, frauds, auditing illegal contracts, keeping the market free, and preventing hoarding of necessities were carried out by this office". Technically corporate governance is embedded in Islamic ethical environment; thus, it has the capacity to deal with depth and breadth of governance issues of today's organisations.

CONCLUSION

This chapter has analysed and discussed core principles of corporate governance and provided analyses of customers and businesses to understand and provide clear-cut accounting terms for principles of Shari'ah developed Islamic

Finance. Corporate governance practices play important role in alleviating and strengthen capital markets and protect investors. The empirical evidence to suggest that countries that have implemented good corporate governance measures have generally experienced robust growth of corporate sectors and higher ability to attract capital from key stakeholders. Multinational companies are adopting corporate governance to enjoy better return and higher valuation for shareholders. Corporate governance plays important role in economic performance because it provides mechanisms which affect returns on investment. Multinational companies need a set of institutional and market mechanisms that allow managers and board members to maximise the value of the residual cash flows to the shareholders.

In general public, there is a growing argument that corporate governance does not protect the rights of shareholders and further work need to be implemented to address the issue of good corporate governance within Multinational companies.

From Islamic point of view, "the strong belief of accountability in this world and thereafter plays key implication on every Muslim life and governs a wider scope and extended obligations of corporate governance with that compared to conventional principles". Islamic principle signifies key principles of corporate governance within multinational companies and individual people managing the company. Under Islamic principles companies should establish and ensures that complied with the Shariah requirements, particularly in the business affairs.

In conclusion, the use of the term principles of corporate governance in the title of this chapter does apply to multinational companies, medium sized businesses and sole trader to contribute towards formulation and implementation of strategies for all stakeholders including shareholders, suppliers, customers, workers and the local business community. Particularly, adopting the rules and principles when implementing weight and measures, fair trading rules, checking business, frauds and auditing illegal contracts.

Discussion Questions

1. Discuss and critically evaluate the Corporate Governance Code and its implementation by companies and by key shareholders?
2. Analyse the Islamic ethical environment, how to deal with depth and breadth of governance issues of today's organisations?

3. Discuss "Corporate governance is a set of mechanism that facilitates fair and just dealing with all stakeholders to strengthen transparency and accountability".
4. Explore the challenges facing Shari'ah compliance code of practice for Muslim managers and business owners the principles of Shari'ah developed Islamic Finance.

REFERENCES

Abbasi, A. S. (2008). *Role of Islamic Leadership in Value Based Corporate Management* (PhD Thesis). NUML Islamabad, Pakistan.

Ahmed, A. S. (2011). An Examination of the Principles of Corporate Governance from an Islamic Perspective: Evidence from Pakistan. *Arab Law Quarterly*, *25*(1), 27–50. doi:10.1163/157302511X540826

Baydoun, N., Mamman, A., & Mahmaud, A. (1999). The religious context of management practices: The case of the Islamic religion, accounting, commerce & finance. *The Islamic Perspective Journal*, *3*(1/2), 52–79.

Cannon, T. (1994). *Corporate Responsibility. A Textbook on Business Ethics, Governance, Environment: Roles and Responsibilities*. Pitman.

Darman, M. G. (2005). *Corporate governance worldwide*. International Chamber of Commerce.

Daryabadi, A. M. (1998). *Tafseer-e-Majidi* (Vol. 2). Majlis-e-Nashriat-e-Qur'ān.

George, W. (2002). *Online News Hour, View from the Top*. Retrieved December 22, 2006 from: https://www.pbs.org/newshour/bb/business/july-dec02/ceos_7-12.html

Hakim, S. R. (2002). *Islamic banking, challenges and corporate governance*. LARIBA.

Maune, A. (2017). The strength of sound corporate governance on economic growth in an emerging market context. *International Journal of Economics and Financial Issues*, *7*(5), 6–13.

Modudi, A. A. (2003). *Islami Riasat*. Islamic Publications Pvt. Ltd.

Modudi, A. A. (2005). Tafheem-ul-Qur'ān, vol. 4, Idara-e-Tarjaman ul Qur'ān Lahore.

Modudi, A. A. (2005). Tafheem-ul-Qur'ān, vol. 6, Idara-e-Tarjaman ul Qur'ān Lahore.

OECD. (2015). *G20/OECD Principles of Corporate Governance*. OECD Publishing. doi:10.1787/9789264236882-

Parkinson, J. E. (1994). *Corporate Power and Responsibility*. Oxford University Press.

Peterson, P. (2002). *Online News Hour, View from the Top, July 12, 2002*. Retrieved December 22, 2005 from: https://www.pbs.org/newshour/bb/business/july-dec02/ceos_7-12.html

Solomon, J., & Solomon, A. (2004). *Corporate Governance and Accountability*. John Wiley & Sons Ltd.

Tapanjeh, A. M. A. (2009). Corporate governance from the Islamic perspective: A comparative analysis with OECD principles. *Critical Perspectives on Accounting*, *20*(5), 556–567. doi:10.1016/j.cpa.2007.12.004

Tiwari, A. (2010). Corporate governance and economic growth. *Economic Bulletin*, *30*(4), 2825–2841.

Tricker, R. I. (1984). *Corporate Governance: Practices, Procedures and Powers in British Companies and Their Boards of Directors*. Gower Press.

Chapter 5
Information Technology and Islamic Ethics

ABSTRACT

The whole issue of information technology is of major interest for the whole society. The new millennium has provided some of the most exciting technological advancements, which has transformed the way businesses are managed, organised, and developed. The technology is a phenomenon, and it is dramatically changing the way businesses deal with their customers. In a climate of increased competition, expansion of new technologies, possible drop in customer numbers, one way of increasing customer numbers would be by enhancing customer experiences on the internet. It is widely accepted that relationship marketing enhances with positive experience, and the internet is a key relationship building tool. The focus of the chapter is that Islamic workplace ethics believes that confidential sharing of information should only be given to limited and relevant stakeholders in the business.

INTRODUCTION

Over the last decade many different types of technologies been developed for businesses communicate with customers. It is very difficult for ordinary individual to understand and realise that how much technologies have been changed which will impact on our daily life. This will essentially bring about a great need for fully automated environments whereby management, planning and everyday administration will be the domain of the technician. Businesses

DOI: 10.4018/978-1-7998-5295-7.ch005

will find themselves with customers that require further understanding to manage and implement procedures to enable managerial functionalities to operate better and efficiently in the given environment. Van Der Vyver (2009) states that:

We live in an era characterised by rapid change and a crucible of that change is the ICT industry. Most ICT professionals find themselves under constant pressure as they strive to deliver ever more complex technologies in the presence of increasingly severe constraints and a paradigm shift in the ICT profession. (P.19)

Therefore, information technology helps the businesses to enhance the customers buying power. The new technologies have changed the daily lives of individuals and society. The whole live is performed around information technology for following reasons.

- Shopping is done through new technologies
- Daily Banking through Internet
- Communication through social media and emails
- Working through computerised system based at home.
- Medical treatment through computerised system
- Marketing through of products and services through new technologies.

Information technologies have excessively intermingled in daily human activities. Therefore, it is imperative that computing professionals dedicate themselves to utilise the technology for better experience of people and to enhance their living standards. These professionals are first line of defence against misuse of technological provisions. Collectively information and communication technologies (ICT) exposes computing professionals to sensitive information, therefore it is important that they ensure that systems integrate in a manner that are appropriate, safe and dependable. Society expects that computing professionals are committed to ethical standards as a foundation of their professional work and engagements. Although monitoring is a part and parcel of ICT systems, however, depth of ICT operations makes it almost impossible to catch every single violation of the conduct. Therefore, it is the responsibility of every individual involved in ICT operations to remain firm on ethical guidelines to avoid any dilemma in everyday operations, because, work of computing professional can affect lives and livelihoods of dozens of people with just one click in ways that may not be intended or even predictable. Therefore, this brings multitude of complex ethical considerations into play at the workplace.

Preamble of ACM Code of Ethics (2018) says "Computing professionals' actions change the world. To act responsibly, they should reflect upon the wider impacts of their work, consistently supporting the public good".

This chapter will examine how Information Technologies has rapidly grown and changed the global communication networks ways of sharing and exchanging the information. The chapter further analyse information technology has radically changed the way businesses communicate with their customers and how ethics is being undermined in the business industry.

Global Expansion of Information Technology in the New Millennium

In the new millennium human knowledge is expanding with historically high pace which results in exponential technological advances making is a real challenge for human societies to cope with the change which seems to remain a real contest in days to come. Generally human societies take relatively longer time to change their cultural norms than change of technologies which have the capability to surprise overnight. This cultural lag phenomenon is a reality of life that material advances more rapidly than non-material culture, thus leading to a conflict due to lack of swift modifications in ethical guideline for better utilisation of technological developments. Technology is indeed a part of today's non-material culture, therefore robust mechanism to develop ethical guidelines for technology utilisation as an adaptive aspect remains imperative. Cultural lag is a critical ethical issue because failure to develop broad social consensus on appropriate application of modern technologies may lead to social unrest and rise in social conflicts. Fundamental reasons for cultural lag between technologies and ethical guidelines include the social structure and market conditions under which each are developed (Marshall, 1999).

Immeasurable new technologies that have developed have been the focus of debate regarding ethical guidelines for their application. From concerns over pornography on the Internet to fertility drugs, and from worker surveillance to the security of banking transactions, technological advances have stirred public controversy. Significant new technologies often generate a period of initial excitement and euphoria, followed by a period in which sombre professionals caution restraint based on anecdotal evidence. Finally, there is a period in which rules and guidelines are proposed and debated and varying levels of consensus develop.

Our workplaces, living environments, learning and working conditions are subject to swift change due to dynamic information and communication technologies and globalisation. ICTs are providing new and unprecedented opportunities to use and share information and knowledge for educational, scientific, cultural, social and organisational transformations. Today, all countries have a vital interest in the development of a global information society and in the benefits that flow from better access to and provision of information. It is indispensible; however, that this global information society ensures that everyone can benefit from these opportunities and that it supports initiatives to provide affordable and equitable access for all to our multicultural and multilingual human heritage. We need to explore all possible options to eliminate existing disparities and inequalities among countries and communities between the "information rich" and the "information poor" and to protect dignity and privacy in cyberspace. These concerns require proactive measures at national, regional and international levels. We also have to deal with the commercial, personal, organisational as well as the societal impact of the new technologies. Organisations such as UNESCO are particularly concerned that measures recommended should include the provision of universal access to public information by promoting the availability of the information on the global networks, the balance between legal issues of intellectual property rights and exemptions to copyright, the privacy and freedom of expression of all stakeholders in expanding globalisation (INFOethics, 2000).

Public exploration of the ethical implications of new technologies is a necessary part of the processes of social change and adaptation. How successfully ethical guidelines are developed, and social consensus is generated will affect social cohesion and solidarity (Gerwith, 1978). Such reflection is even more needed when techno logical innovation involves a great cultural shift – either due to qualitative breaks from past thought and ways of living or to rapid diffusion into a broad range of human activities (Robinson, 1981). Old principles of fairness and honesty, respect for others' rights, respect for the environment, and respect for life and its quality do apply to new technologies, but experienced and honest intellectual discussions are needed to clarify the complex issues raised by technological advances (Cordeiro, 1997)

Considering technological advances that occurred in the near past, it is now required to reflect and deliberate if new technologies introduce novel ethical problems and how Islamic principles facilitate to handle this challenge.

A variety of definitions of ethics appear in the academic press. However, for the purposes of IT, the following definition by (Marshall, 1999) deems appropriate:

Ethics are guidelines to influence human social behaviour in a manner intended to protect and fulfil the rights of individuals in a society.

It will be useful if we can define following terms at this stage:

1. Guidelines
   Guidelines do not simply mean laws or even prescriptions or proscriptions for specific behaviours – as in a code of ethics. Guidelines also include basic principles of analysis, beliefs and assumptions about the nature of Allah (SWT), the physical world, life, individuals and society, and social values.
2. Social Behaviour
   The term 'social behaviour' is intended to focus the discussion of ethics on behaviours of individuals that directly or indirectly influence other individuals.
3. Technology
   Technology means any consistent application that is employed to achieve a purpose by modifying natural world. Technology is naturally purposive. It is applied to achieve a goal. Technology differs from science in that science seeks knowledge while technology applies knowledge to the manipulation of the natural world to achieve a goal.
4. Natural world
   Natural world means the perceived physical, psychological, social and economic realms to the extent that these are believed to operate according to consistent principles derived from their nature.

Universal Declaration of Human Rights (UDHR, 1948) states "all human beings are born free and equal in dignity and rights (article 1). Everyone has the right to life, liberty and security of person (article 3). No one shall be subjected to arbitrary interference with his privacy, family, home or correspondence, nor to attacks upon his honour and reputation. Everyone has the right to the protection of the law against such interferences or attacks (article 12). Everyone has the right to freedom of thought and conscience (article 18)".

Islamic Ethics and Information Technology

Emerging mass media is largely based on electronic communications. Mass media is critical to the field of Islamic ethics because information is increasingly being processed electronically, from storage and retrieval to sharing and usage. The pervasiveness of indecent content, which was once disseminated locally with limited access, has become an issue of national and international concern with the development of the Internet, smart phones and social media platforms such as Facebook and WhatsApp.

The new media, which is a catch-all term for the Internet, email, blogs, social networking sites like Myspace, Facebook and Twitter, digital TV and mobile phones, is fast becoming a popular global information platform. It is the new form of mass media uniquely mediated by technology, especially the Internet. Unlike the traditional print and electronic media, the new media is interactive, and user driven. The users themselves, rather than editors, determine the content. It poses a great threat to new users, especially children, because of the unwanted contents on the net (Masum, Cholem and Azad (2011). It equally affects mature audience as evident by several political movements, agitations and campaigns of different interest groups around the globe. There are certain justifications to delineate Islamic ethics about information technology and related disciplines:

1. Islam forbids all types of deceptions and manipulations in every sphere of human life.
2. It is important to apprise IT professionals about ethical dimensions of Islam at the workplace
3. It is imperative to ensure that IT professionals behave responsibly at their workstations.
4. Islamic ethical framework can facilitate relevant stakeholders to avoid computer abuses and catastrophes.
5. Islamic ethics can help organisations to control inappropriate and illegal use of IT resources.

An important aspect of today's understanding of Ethics concerns issues of individual and social responsibility with regard to the impact of our choices in light of the influence of science and technology. While information and communication technologies open doors to new technological and scientific possibilities, they also act as a catalyst to an unprecedented encounter with otherness, ensuring through digital mediums the en masse collision of hitherto closed ethical systems and cultural worldviews (Rafael Capurro)

The anger, annoyance and reduction in compassion that happens when we're all stick to social media screens is not good for emerging global society. People are still people even if there is internet between them. Consider the future of digital globalisation as a global citizen, we might identify an ethical challenge that an ideal 'global citizen' faces in the shape of the 'internet troll'; a challenge that can be framed in terms of the antinomies of social togetherness and compassion. The troll is the recent phenomenon in the mass media, relation to cyber-bullying and shaming practices. 'Trolling' has been described variously as an example of 'identity deception' and as the action of 'everyday sadists' (Staunton, 2015).

Objectives of IT ethics from Western perspective are (ICIE, 2019):

1. To be able to recognise and articulate ethical conflicts in the information field,
2. To activate the sense of responsibility with regard to the consequences of individual and collective interactions in the information field,
3. To improve the qualification for intercultural dialogue on the basis of the recognition of different kinds of information cultures and values,
4. To provide basic knowledge about ethical theories and concepts and about their relevance in everyday information work.

Some of terms about ethical teachings are repeated in tens (10s) of the verses of al-Qur'ān as well as in Hadith (Masum, et al, 2011). The table 1 below looks at the frequency of the terms about ethical teaching that has been described by the Qur'ān.

Association for Computing Machinery (ACM) plays an important role to guide conduct of computing professionals who have a profound impact on both public and private lives of people. ACM delineated following code of ethics for IT professional:

1. IT professional both individually and collectively should contribute to society and to human well-being, acknowledging that all people are stakeholders in computing.
2. IT professionals should use their skills for the benefit of society, its members, and the environment surrounding them to promote fundamental human rights and protecting each individual's right to autonomy.

Table 1. Ethical Teaching in Qur'an

	Teaching	Chapters
1.	Beneficence	66 & 29
2.	Sincerity	23 & 34
3.	Forgiveness	202 & 100
4.	Honesty	65 & 66
5.	Promise keeping and secrecy	31 & 50
6.	Good ethics	61 & 250
7.	Thankfulness	235 & 142
8.	Fairness	23 & 62
9.	Truth	92 & 44
10.	Honouring Humanity	96 & 24

3. An essential aim of computing professionals is to minimise negative consequences of computing, including threats to health, safety, personal security, and privacy. When the interests of multiple groups conflict the needs of those less advantaged should be given increased attention and priority.
4. Computing professionals should consider whether the results of their efforts will respect diversity, will be used in socially responsible ways, will meet social needs, and will be broadly accessible.
5. They are encouraged to actively contribute to society by engaging in pro bono or volunteer work that benefits the public good.
6. In addition to a safe social environment, human well-being requires a safe natural environment. Therefore, computing professionals should promote environmental sustainability both locally and globally.

Information Technology Ethics From Islamic Perspective

Avoid Harm

Harm means negative consequences, especially when those consequences are significant and unjust. Intentional unjustified physical or mental injury, unjustified destruction or disclosure of information, attempt of sabotage and unjustified damage to property, reputation and the environment are some expels of harm at the workplace. Sometimes planned activities, including those that are required to accomplish designated duties, may lead to harm. In such situations those who are the cause of any harm are expected to eliminate or alleviate the harm as much as possible. Careful consideration of potential impacts on all possible affected by any decision can help avoiding situations that can lead to any harm. In case of intentional harm by the system, it becomes mandatory for all those who are responsible to justify that harm was unavoidable and at the same time remains ethically justified. In either case, visible efforts to minimise all harms are desirable (ACM, 2018).

Islamic ethics ensure that professionals avoid harming others at workplace; they must remain watchful that their actions don't lead to damage any of the stakeholders.

And those who harm believing men and believing women for [something] other than what they have earned have certainly born upon themselves a slander and manifest sin (al-Qur'ān 33:58)

Creativity

According to Al-Karasneh and Saleh (2010), Creativity is a phenomenon that comprehends and elaborates evident Divine principles and ideals and applies them according to specific needs and circumstances of contemporary environment to provide solutions for current challenges in every aspect of life. Creativity is a unique condition, attitude or state that reflects passion and commitment for work, independence, achievement, originality, flexibility, freedom, awareness, imaginations and motivation to approach matters for optimal results. Al-Mazeidy (1993) defined creativity as:

the ability of designing new forms that are beneficial for humanity and are in accordance with the Islamic shari'ah and principles.

There has come to you enlightenment from your Lord. So, whoever will see does so for [the benefit of] his soul, and whoever is blind [does harm] against it. And [say], "I am not a guardian over you" (al-Qur'ān, 6:104)

Association for Computing Machinery lays down principles for IT professional to protect intellectual property rights and copyrights, their code suggests "developing new ideas, inventions, creative works, and computing artefacts create value for society, and those who expend this effort should expect to gain value from their work. Computing professionals should therefore credit the creators of ideas, inventions, work, and artefacts, and respect copyrights, patents, trade secrets, license agreements, and other methods of protecting authors' works (ACM, 2018)". These guidelines naturally correspond with the spirit of Islamic work ethics for contemporary workplace.

Creativity in Islam has been fostered in different ways. Several methodologies to nurture creativity can be derived by studying the verses of al-Qur'ān (Al-Karasneh and Saleh, 2010):

Firstly, Allah (SWT) has guided people to travel and deeply observe what they see.

Say: Travel through the earth and see how Allah did originate creation; so will Allah produce a later creation, for Allah has power over all things (al-Qur'ān, 29: 20)

Secondly, Allah (SWT) advised us to use, effectively and efficiently, the faculty of seeing that Allah gave to human beings.

Do they not look into the realm of the heavens and the earth and everything that Allah has created and [think] that perhaps their appointed time has come near? So in what statement hereafter will they believe? (al-Qur'ān, 29: 20)

Do you not see that Allah sends down rain from the sky and makes it flow as springs [and rivers] in the earth; then He produces thereby crops of varying colours; then they dry and you see them turned yellow; then He makes them [scattered] debris. Indeed, in that is a reminder for those of understanding (al-Qur'ān, 39: 21)

Thirdly, people were advised to use the faculty of hearing in order to be able to obtain the necessary knowledge and experience.

Who listen to speech and follow the best of it. Those are the ones Allah has guided, and those are people of understanding (al-Qur'ān, 39: 18)

Fourthly, the methodology of thinking was emphasised in the Qur'an in order to use the intellectual aspect in the human beings themselves, in the universe and in the unseen world

He causes to grow for you thereby the crops, olives, palm trees, grapevines, and from all the fruits. Indeed, in that is a sign for a people who give thought. (al-Qur'ān, 16: 11)

Privacy

Islam gives great importance to the fundamental human right to privacy. This is evident from the some of the verses of al-Qur'ān:

Do not spy on one another (al-Qur'ān 49:12)

Do not enter any houses except your own homes unless you are sure of their occupants' consent (al-Qur'ān 24:27)

And if you do not find anyone therein, do not enter them until permission has been given you. And if it is said to you, "Go back," then go back; it is purer for you. And Allah is Knowing of what you do (al-Qur'ān 24:28)

.... But when you enter houses, give greetings of peace upon each other - a greeting from Allah, blessed and good... (al-Qur'ān 24:61)

A man peeped through a hole in the door of Allah's Messenger (صلى الله عليه وسلم)'s house, and at that time, Allah's Messenger (PBUH) had a Midri (an iron comb or bar) with which he was rubbing his head. So, when Allah's Messenger (PBUH) saw him, he said (to him), "If I had been sure that you were looking at me (through the door), I would have poked your eye with this (sharp iron bar)". Allah's Messenger (PBUH) added, "The asking for permission to enter has been enjoined so that one may not look unlawfully (at what there is in the house without the permission of its people) (Sahih al-Bukhari, 6901)

The responsibility of respecting privacy applies in every field. IT requires even more vigilance to ensure privacy of all stakeholders. Technology enables them to collect, monitor, and exchange personal information quickly, inexpensively, and often without the knowledge of the people affected. Therefore, an IT professional should be familiar of different aspects, forms and definitions of privacy and should understand the rights and responsibilities associated with the collection, monitoring and use of personal information. IT professionals must ensure genuine use of personal information for legitimate ends and without violating the rights of organisations, individuals and groups. This requires taking precautions to prevent re-identification of anonymised data or unauthorised data collection, ensuring the accuracy of data for quarter concerned, understanding the provenance of the data, and protecting it from unauthorised access and accidental disclosure (ACM, 2018).

Hadrat Umar Bin Khattab, the second caliph, was roaming in the city one night when he heard shouting and cursing coming from a residence; he then peeked over the perimeter and started admonishing the man:

You, the sinner, do you think that God will ignore your sins, as you're sinning against him?' The man replied: 'Woe, commander of the faithful, do not rush to judgment; if I sinned once, you sinned three times. God has forbidden you to look into someone's fault (al-Qur'ān 49:12), and you have done otherwise. God has commanded you to enter peoples' homes through the front door (al-Qur'ān 2:189) and you have intruded over the fence. And you have approached me without salutation, and God has commanded you not to enter into other peoples' homes without their permission, and without saying 'greetings' (Salam) when you enter their premises (al-Qur'ān 24:27)

This incident in early Islamic history is indicative of people's freedom at the time and clearly portrays the sanctity of the right of privacy when the Western world was not overly familiar with the concept of privacy (Hayat, 2007).

These Islamic teachings suggest that privacy is everyone's right. There are numerous possibilities to intrude anyone's privacy through IT developments and infrastructure. Therefore, it is inappropriate to access anyone's personal data or information without explicit consent. Selling personal information and preferences without permission can also be considered inadvisable. Organisations should clearly inform their employees if their emails and are subject to access. Announced monitoring may have some space in Islamic workplace ethics but still subject to certain critical limitations, however, there is absolutely no room for secret surveillance in Islamic ethics.

Confidentiality

Confidentiality is derived from the term confidence and is defined as keeping one's secret. Confidentiality in Islamic ethics is defined as not disclosing a secret. Confidentiality also known as keeping a secret, an important concept in Islam and is a highly emphasised obligation. The one who does not obey and disclose someone's secret has done a major sin and will be subjected to severe punishment. A secret can sometimes be a flaw and sometimes not. However, revealing a secret, whether a flaw or not, whether it is out of animosity, financial issues or just vice, it is an unacceptable act. In many religious resources, breach of confidentiality is defined as invading safekeeping.

Disclosing someone's secret is forbidden in Islam because it hurts people and creates distrust.

And who are shepherds of their pledge and their covenant (al-Qur'ān 23:8)

And those who keep their pledges and their covenant (al-Qur'ān 70:32)

If anyone removes his brother's anxiety of this world, Allah will remove for him one of the anxieties of the Day of resurrection; if anyone makes easy for an impoverished man, Allah will make easy for him in this world and on the day of resurrection; if anyone conceals a Muslim's secrets, Allah will conceal his secrets in this world and on the Day of resurrection; Allah will remain in the aid of a servant so long as the servant remains in the aid of his brother (Sunan Abi Dawud 4946).

IT experts are often entrusted with confidential information such as trade secrets, client data, non-public business strategies, financial information, research data, pre-publication scholarly articles, and patent applications. Ideally IT professionals should protect confidentiality in all circumstance, however, they are equally responsible to disclose or transmit evidence of the violation of law, of organisational regulations, or of the code of conduct to relevant authorities. In such situations, the nature or contents of that information should not be disclosed except to those who are either authorised or eligible to take corrective measure. An IT professional should consider thoughtfully whether such disclosures or transmissions are consistent with the Code (ACM, 2018).

Nowadays IT professionals and machines carry every important bit of information about people and organisations. Islamic workplace ethics emphasise confidentiality and allow sharing of information only with relevant stakeholders. Custodians of information are subject to reprimand if they breach given framework of confidentiality.

Avoid Deception

And give full measure and weight in justice (al-Qur'ān 6:152)

Overwhelming role of IT in our today's workplace exposes us to encounter new or enhance existing inequities. Computing professionals should try to ensure that use of technology should promote inclusion. IT facilities should be accessible to as many people as possible and they should try to avoid systems &/or technologies that disenfranchise or oppress people. Failure to design for inclusiveness and accessibility may constitute unfair discrimination (ACM, 2018).

Keep the Trust

And if one of you entrusts another, then let him who is entrusted discharge his trust [faithfully] and let him fear Allah, his Lord (al-Qur'ān 2:283)

And they who are to their trusts and their promises attentive (al-Qur'ān 23:8)

The Prophet (PBUH) said,

The signs of a hypocrite are three:

1. Whenever he speaks, he tells a lie.
2. Whenever he promises, he always breaks it (his promise).
3. If you trust him, he proves to be dishonest. (If you keep something as a trust with him, he will not return it.) (Sahih al-Bukhari 33)

A computing professional should be transparent and provide full disclosure of all pertinent system capabilities, limitations, and potential problems to the appropriate parties. Making deliberately false or misleading claims, fabricating or falsifying data, offering or accepting bribes and other dishonest conduct are violations of the Code. Computing professionals should be honest about their qualifications, and about any limitations in their competence to complete a task. Computing professionals should be forthright about any circumstances that might lead to either real or perceived conflicts of interest (ACM, 2018).

Avoid Manipulation

And do not mix the truth with falsehood or conceal the truth while you know [it]" (al-Qur'ān 2:42)

In Islamic ethics the essential rule at workplace is honesty and fair dealing; as a result, all stakeholders including employees, customers and shareholders try to maintain high ethical principles. The workplaces should be free and not subject to manipulation facilitating individuals engaging in professional activities to act fairly. Islam has several characteristics such as Sincerity (*al-Ikhlas*), Proficiency (*al-Ihsan*), Justice (*al-'Adl*), Truthfulness (*as-Sidq*), Patience (*as-Sabr*), Moderation (*'I^ctidāl*) and Promise Keeping (*Ifā'u-l-^chd*) which naturally influence and keep IT interventions at the workplace free from any kind of manipulation (AL-Aidaros *et. al.*, 2013).

Avoid Gossips

When you received it with your tongues and said with your mouths that of which you had no knowledge and thought it was insignificant while it was, in the sight of Allah, tremendous (al-Qur'ān 24:15)

Gossips cause more than 77% conflicts at the workplace (Helmy, *et. al.*, 2014). IT ethics in Islam nurture professionals with good manners facilitating people to avoid falling into difficulties and complexities of operations. Islamic ethics encourage good conduct, fulfilling promises, accuracy in business transactions and verify news before spreading to others to avoid any misunderstanding and conflict. Therefore, irrelevant conversations, gossiping, and hatred etc. are discouraged in Islamic workplace ethics especially for IT professionals. IT professionals are subject to gossips from around the globe. It indeed needs strong moral character of IT professionals to resist to gossips and transmit only verified and trusted information.

CONCLUSION

This chapter has provided argument that Information Technologies has rapidly grown and changed the global communication networks for businesses to communicate with their customers and ethics is being undermined in the business industry. The new technology has completely changed businesses communication format with customers. It is very difficult for ordinary individual to understand and realise that how much technologies have been changed which will impact on daily life of individual customers. Immense development of new technologies has been the focus of debate regarding ethical guidelines for their application. The technology seen by certain individuals in the community in general as a surveillance to the security of banking transactions, technological advances have stirred public controversy.

Emerging mass media is largely based on electronic communications. Mass media is critical to the Islamic ethics because information is increasingly being processed electronically, from storage and retrieval to sharing and usage. The Islamic ethics and Universal Declaration of Human Rights (UDHR) organisation argues that everyone has the right to life, liberty and security of person is important to safeguard from IT surveillance and interference with their personal privacy, family, home or correspondence, nor to attacks upon his honour and reputation. Islamic ethics ensure that professionals avoid harming others at workplace and they need to remain watchful that their actions that does not damage any of the stakeholders, other employees, customers and public in general. Islamic ethics clearly state that IT experts should have limited powers with confidential information such as trade secrets, client data, non-public business strategies, financial information, research data, pre-publication scholarly articles, and patent applications.

Chapter further argues that IT professionals and machines carry every important information about people and businesses. Islamic workplace ethics believe that confidentiality sharing of information should only be given to limited and relevant stakeholders in the business. Custodians of information are subject to reprimand if they breach given framework of confidentiality.

Discussion Questions

1. Critically discuss contributions of Islamic Ethics on Business World?
2. Analyse and evaluate how information technology has radically changed the way businesses communicate with their customers?
3. Evaluate and discuss Information Technology Ethics from Islamic Perspective?
4. Discuss how ethics is being undermined in the business industry?

REFERENCES

ACM. (2018). *ACM Code of Ethics and Professional Conduct*. The Association for Computing Machinery, Inc. DOI doi:10.1145/3274591

Al-Aidaros, A. H., Shamsudin, F. M., & Idris, K. M. (2013). Ethics and Ethical Theories from an Islamic Perspective. *International Journal of Islamic Thought*, *4*, 1–13. doi:10.24035/ijit.04.2013.001

Al-Karasneh, S. M., & Saleh, A. M. J. (2010). Islamic perspective of creativity: A model for teachers of social studies as leaders. *Procedia: Social and Behavioral Sciences*, *2*(2), 412–426. doi:10.1016/j.sbspro.2010.03.036

Al-Mazeidy, Z. M. (1993). Moqaddimah fi Manhaj Al-Ibda': Ro'yah Islamiyyah [An Introduction to the Methodology of Creativity: An Islamic Point of View]. Dar Al-Wafa' Littiba'a wa Al-Nashr.

Cordeiro, W. P. (1997). Suggested Management Responses to Ethical Issues Raised by Technological Change. *Journal of Business Ethics*, *16*(12-13), 1393–1400. doi:10.1023/A:1004934924242

Gerwith, A. (1978). *Reason and Morality*. University of Chicago Press.

Hayat, M. A. (2007). Privacy and Islam: From the Quran to data protection in Pakistan. *Information & Communications Technology Law*, *16*(2), 137–148. doi:10.1080/13600830701532043

Helmy, S., Labib, A., & Abou Kahf, A. (2014). The Impact of Islamic values on interpersonal relationship conflict management in Egyptian business organisations "an applied study". *Procedia: Social and Behavioral Sciences*, *143*, 1090–1110.

ICIE (International Center for Information Ethics). (n.d.). Retrieved on May 05, 2019 from https://www.i-c-i-e.org/the-field

INFOethics. (2000). *Ethical, Legal and Societal Challenges of Cyberspace: third international congress*. UNESCO. Retrieved on May 05, 2019 from https://unesdoc.unesco.org/ark:/48223/pf0000123352

Marshall, K. P. (1999). Has Technology Introduced New Ethical Problems? *Journal of Business Ethics, 19*(1), 81-90.

Masum, A. K. M., Cholem, M. U., & Azad, M. A. K. (2011). Information Technology (IT) Ethics in the Light of Islam. *IIUC Studies*, *9*, 243–260. doi:10.3329/iiucs.v9i0.24030

Rafael Capurro. (n.d.). Retrieved on May 05, 2019 from https://www.i-c-i-e.org/

Robinson, J. P. (1981). Will the New Electronic Media Revolutionise our Daily Lives. In R. W. Haigh, G. Gerbner, & R. B. Byrne (Eds.), *Communications in the Twenty-First Century*. John Wiley and Sons.

Staunton, B. (2015). Trolling the Global Citizen: The Deconstructive Ethics of the Digital Subject. *International Journal of Information Ethics*, *23*, 62–70.

UDHR. (1948). Retrieved on May 04, 2019 from https://www.ohchr.org/EN/UDHR/Documents/UDHR_Translations/eng.pdf

Chapter 6
Welfare in Islamic Ethics

ABSTRACT

Islamic ethics provides alternatives to "shareholder primacy"—the view that managers should maximise shareholder returns subject to the law. Concern for societal welfare has remained under discussion throughout the history of mankind. Theories, philosophies, policies, legislations, and what not formulates time and again to make this world a happier place to live. Still, there is a search for even better models to organise market forces to deliver in terms of welfare of society. In the corporate world, a good deal of scholarship has been devoted to articulating and justifying the responsibilities and the role of business enterprises and their managers in relation to society. This chapter aims to discuss a framework for the welfare of society being extended by key stakeholders at contemporary workplaces ensuring happiness and prosperity for all.

INTRODUCTION

The third Caliph Hazrat Usman (RA), a renowned businessman of early times of Islam, purchased a well of water and donated to entire people of that time just for the welfare of society. During the conquest of Jerusalem arrival of the second Caliph Hazrat Umar (RA) in the battlefield as a pedestrian while his slave was riding according to his turn, denotes optimum equilibrium among rights of employees and the management (according to contemporary understanding of organisational structures). This chapter aims to provide insights into Islamic ethics a fine balance between shareholders' interest and value for other stakeholders of the society.

DOI: 10.4018/978-1-7998-5295-7.ch006

Welfare in Islamic Ethics

Welfare is one of the important themes in Islamic ethics which has its roots in the concept of *Infaq* which has been used in al-Qur'ān at several places. *Infaq* is pious spending in the way of Allah (SWT) (Aziz *et al*, 2008); al-Qur'ān says:

These people ask you, how much, we will be spending in the way of Allah? Said everything beyond your requirements (2:219)

Islamic teachings limit mankind's material wants (unlike Western economic thought) if it adversely affects the society's wellbeing: no one should be denied their basic needs or sustenance and live in poverty and deprivation. Injustice is believed to ultimately impede the realisation of human welfare, exacerbate social unrest and malaise and retard development. Justice demands that all, regardless of race, colour, sex, nationality and even religion share the benefits of development equitably; and distributive justice is recognised as central to the Islamic vision of an economic system (Askari and Arfaa, 2007).

... Be ever steadfast in upholding equity, bearing witness to the truth for the sake of God, ... Whether the person concerned be rich or poor, God's claim takes precedence over [the claims of] either of them. Do not, then, follow your own desires, lest you swerve for justice.. (al-Qur'ān 4:135)

. .. Bearing witness to the truth in all equity; and never let hatred of anyone lead you into sin of deviating from justice. Be just: This is closest to being God-conscious .. (al-Qur'ān 5:8)

Behold, God enjoins justice, and the doing of good, and generosity towards [one's] fellow-men; and He forbids all that is shameful and all that runs counter to reason, as well as envy (al-Qur'ān 16:90)

Qur'ān states that poverty and denial of assistance to the needy is forbidden. The Qur'ān goes on to explain that material inequalities are not a manifestation of spiritual inequalities. Rather such inequalities should be overcome through human effort and are thus meant to foster brotherhood, again stressing the importance of zakah (Askari and Arfaa, 2007).

... We who distribute their means of livelihood among them in the life of this world, and raise some of them by degrees above other, to the end that they might avail themselves of one another's help .. (al-Qur'ān 43:32)

The role of the state includes the administration of a social security system in which the religiously decreed zakah assumes a central position. As one of the five pillars of Islam, the system levies a zakah or compulsory tax on all Muslims who meet a minimum level of wealth to help finance eight categories of welfare that are mentioned in the Quran, including poverty alleviation, the emancipation of slaves, pilgrimage, and assistance to those serving Islam (Askari and Arfaa, 2007).

Zakah expenditures are only for the poor and for the needy and for those employed to collect [zakah] and for bringing hearts together [for Islam] and for freeing captives [or slaves] and for those in debt and for the cause of Allah and for the [stranded] traveller - an obligation [imposed] by Allah. And Allah is Knowing and Wise (al-Qur'ān, 9:60)

Perhaps the most prominent alternative is stakeholder theory, according to which business enterprises are to be managed in the interests of all who are and who can be affected by managerial decisions. Other alternatives include corporate citisenship and the creation of shared value. There are also alternatives that draw explicitly on traditions in moral and political philosophy, such as Kantian theory, virtue ethics, social contract theory, Confucianism, deliberative democracy and theories of corporate social responsibility (Hsieh, 2017). In Islamic ethics roles and responsibilities of following key stakeholders of the organisation must keep collective societal welfare as one of their top priorities at the contemporary workplace. Figure. 3.1 outlines the Welfare Model of Islamic Ethics.

1. Shareholders
2. Management
3. Employees
4. Consumers

Responsibilities of Shareholders

Shareholders form the core of any business activity, they take initiatives, they face risks, and they direct major business decisions. Therefore, much

Figure 1. Welfare Model of Islamic Ethics

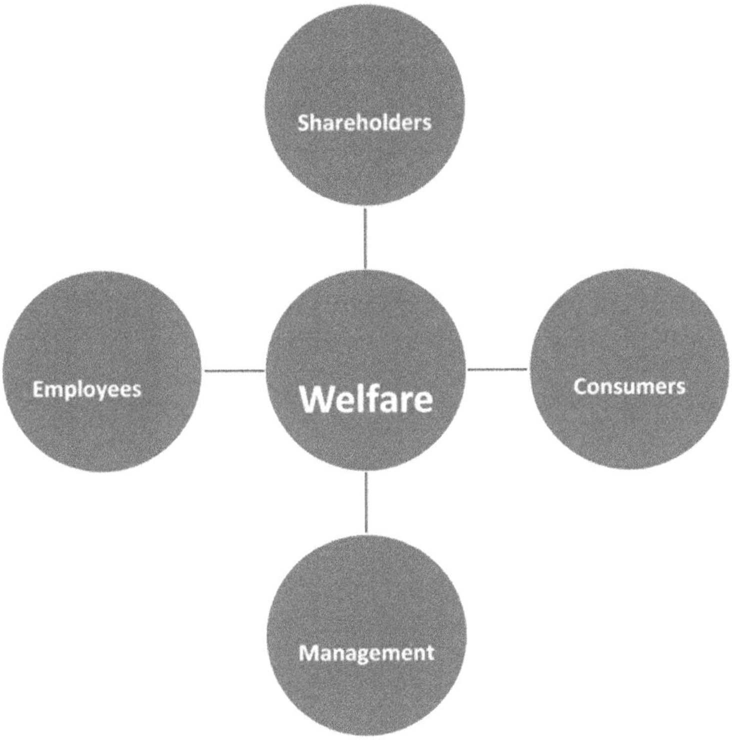

of responsibility lies on shareholders to pave the way to achieve welfare objectives for all stakeholders of the organisation. They must keep all the time following commandment in their minds:

O ye who believe! eat not up your property among yourselves in vanities: but let there be amongst you traffic and trade by mutual good-will: nor kill (or destroy) yourselves: for verily Allah hath been to you Most Merciful! (al - Qur'ān, 4:29)

Modudi (2005a) hold that all those means are illicit which are unjust and unfair from both religious and moral point of view (p. 345-6). Traffic (it may include customers and suppliers both) and trade means profit earning, which is allowed as in case of business where one person works to fulfil the needs of others and gets remuneration. He further ascertained that purpose of saying 'nor kill (or destroy) yourself is that usurping property of others through unfair means is in fact to destroy yourself because this results in spoiling the civilisation, which ultimately affects the person himself.

In above verse believers are told not to eat their properties among themselves illegally, thereby closing the door of all types of corruption. Today organisations are facing accounting abuse, illegitimate use of authority, bribes, fraud, workplace thefts etc. Islamic ethics prohibit all such immoral practice for leaders and employees both. In Islamic ethics exploiting organisational resources illegally means eating organisational properties resulting in common loss of all stakeholders.

Shareholders are expected to uphold following values during business activities for the welfare of relevant stakeholders:

(i) Consultation
(ii) Justice
(iii) Honesty
(iv) Standardisation
(v) Employee Relations

(i) Consultation

Shareholders need to ensure that culture of consultation is carried out among employees, management and key stakeholders as and when required.

and consult them in affairs (of moment) (al - Qur'ān 3:159)

Daryabadi (1998) explained that consultation has abundant value in Islam (p. 655). It is evident that if it is ordered to Hazrat Muhammad (SAW), then how much important it is for others. Jabnoun (1994) explained that participative management is the continuous involvement of people in decision making. Participatory management means that every member has input and influence over the decisions that affect the organisation. Participatory management improves the effectiveness and capacity of an organisation (Bartle, 2008). It is culture rather than a program. It is an Islamic duty for a leader to consult his/her subordinates. This consultation is called in Islam *Shura*. It is stated in the al-Qur'ān that the believers who will be rewarded in the hereafter are those who conduct their affairs with *Shura* or consultation.

Those who hearken to their Lord, and establish regular prayer; who (conduct) their affairs by mutual Consultation; who spend out of what We bestow on them for Sustenance; (al - Qur'ān 42:38)

Modudi (2005b) explained that this has been declared the best quality of believers (p. 508). On this basis consultation is the basic pillar of Islamic way of life. There are three reasons of giving so much importance to consultation (*Shura*) in Islam.

First, in a matter which is related to more than one person, it is unjust that one person takes the decision and ignores others. No one has the right to enforce his own opinion. It is necessary that all those people should be consulted to whom matter is related. If they are too many, then their representatives should participate in the process of consultation.

Second, in common affairs person tries to enforce his own will due to two reasons; either he wants to snatch the rights of others or he thinks he himself is superior and others are inferior. From moral point of view both characteristics are bad for believers. Believer is neither selfish nor arrogant.

Third, it is an important task to decide about the matters which are related to the rights and interest of others. A person who fear Allah (SWT) and knows that he will be accountable in front of Allah (SWT) for his decision, will never take the responsibility on his shoulders alone.

Jabnoun (1994) stated that *Shura* is aimed at building a consensus that will benefit the community or the business that must make the decision. In case no consensus is reached, voting is resorted too. Prophet Muhammad (PBUH) said:

My nation cannot agree upon an error and if a conflict persists be with the majority. (Ibn-e-Majah)

(ii) Justice

Justice is absolute. There is no such thing as relatively just or unjust. It is either just or unjust. Justice is a value and virtue in all religions and is upheld by all societies. As such, it is universal value which is acceptable to everyone (Alhabshi, et al, 1994). Justice is the cornerstone of Islamic ethics.

Allah commands justice, the doing of good, (al-Qur'ān, 16:90)

Islam is explicit about eradicating all forms of injustices, inequity, exploitation, oppression and wrongdoings from all management process.

(iii) Honesty

In distributing dividends, projecting profits and losses, presenting features, manufacturing information, constituents of products and services shareholders and their management must ensure honesty at every single step from raw materials to the consumption.

Once a Bedouin asked the Prophet Muhammad (PBUH) "When would the Hour (Doomsday) take place?" Prophet Muhammad (PBUH) replied, "When honesty is lost, then wait for the Hour (Doomsday)". Bedouin said, "How will that be lost". Prophet Muhammad (PBUH) said, "When the power or authority comes in the hands of unfit persons, then wait for the Hour (Doomsday)" (Beekun, 1997).

In Islamic business ethics no businessman can do dishonesty. In al-Qur'ān it is mentioned that

Give just measures and cause no loss (to others by fraud). And weigh with scales true and upright. And withhold not things justly due to men (26:181-183)

(iv) Standardisation

Before Islam has emerged as a religion in the Arabian Peninsula; it has since become a global phenomenon spanning different regions and cultures across the world. From this perspective the history and development of Islam can be read as a struggle between consistency and diversity. On one side, it has been a remarkable achievement to maintain the relative coherence of the practice and belief systems of Islam over such vast distances (Nasaruddin *et al*, 2011).

Islamisation Has Two-Fold Jobs

First: expanding, upgrading and modernising Islamic disciplines,

Second: connecting all other disciplines to Islamic faith and values. In an effort to ennoble and enrich the quality of civilisation, one should make reference to what has been mentioned in the Qur'an.

There are clear standards in Islamic teachings to follow inculcating standardisation in business processes.

Allah SWT says in surah Al-Ma 'idah verse 3: ——Forbidden to you (for food) are: dead meat, blood, the flesh of swine, and that on which hath been invoked the name of other than Allah. that which hath been killed by strangling, or by a violent blow, or by a headlong fall, or by being gored to death; that which hath been (partly) eaten by a wild animal; unless ye are able to slaughter it (in due form); that which is sacrificed on stone (altars); (forbidden) also is the division (of meat) by raffling with arrows: that is impiety... (Nasaruddin *et al,* 2011).

Sayyiduna Abd Allah ibn Umar (may Allah be pleased with him) narrates that the Messenger of Allah (peace and blessings be upon him) said:

Two types of dead meat and two types of blood have been made lawful for our consumption: The two dead meats are: fish and locust, and the two types of blood are: liver and spleen (Nasaruddin et al, 2011).

(v) Employment Relations

In terms of employment relations, Muslim scholars are divided into two camps: the idealists view relations between workers and management as harmonious, while the pragmatists consider the relationship as adversarial. Al-Faruqi represents the idealists thus emphasis normative Islamic teaching pertaining to equality and justice without analysing the reality in the marketplace. This is especially true as Al-Faruqi fails to take note of the fact that a world of unequal power and widespread inequality, the less powerful players, the workers, are not able to get fair and just share of their contributions. Indeed, his statement that all employees, be they rulers or ditch diggers, are "equally obligated to fulfil what their employers and society have hired them to do" may weaken workers' position relative to employers (Syed and Ali, 2010).

The second camp of pragmatists is represented by Al-Banna. Based on the principles enshrined in the Qur'ān, Al-Banna argues, the role of trade unions be pertaining to two essential needs: "food against hunger" and "security against fear". That is, trade union is an instrument for the protection of the weak actor in a world that is fraught with greed and exploitation. In Islamic ethics the custodianship of the poor is one of the most important responsibilities of an Islamic state. Islam takes a clear position to address the great social problem, i.e. the poor vs. the rich, the haves vs. the have-nots and stands by the poor and the have-nots. The Qur'ān also permits that those who have been oppressed may organise themselves against injustice (if any). Every individual or group can peacefully protest against unjust acts of an organisation or the state itself (Syed and Ali, 2010).

But indeed, if any do help and defend themselves after a wrong (done) to them, against such there is no cause of blame (42: 41).

The Qur'ān also suggests its followers to abide by all types of contracts and agreements. This rule is equally applicable to collective or/ individual agreements between employers and employees.

O you who have attained to faith! Be true to your covenants! (5: 1).

The objective of both idealists and pragmatists seems appropriate. It probably depends on social structures and business environments where businesses must operate. However, it is evident from above discussion that business owners must ensure security, prosperity and equality as much as possible in given dynamics of marketplace.

Role of Employees

Islam situates workers at the centre of economic activities and without them there will be no value or wealth creation. Hazrat Ali (RA), the fourth Caliph, stated that merchants and artisans are the "providers of benefits and goods". He underscored the importance of merchants and workers in improving the societal welfare and strengthening the state when he stated that they are "the people who will assure durable peace and respected allegiance". Ibn Khaldun argued that "labour belongs to the things that constitute capital" and that "profit is the value realised from labour".

Hazrat Omar (RA), the second Caliph, said "Never should anyone of you think that supplication for sustenance without work will avail him, for heaven never rains gold nor silver" (Syed and Ali, 2010). The Prophet (PBUH) said, "The worker, if employed, and takes what is right and gives what is right, is like a mujahid (struggler in the cause of God) till he returns home".

The Prophet (PBUH) also said, "When any man does any work, God wishes him to give it perfection and grace" Islam urges workers to fulfil all legitimate obligations with respect to their employment. According to the al-Qur'ān: "O you who have attained to faith, Be true to your covenants" (al-Qur'ān, 5:1).

Hazrat Ali (RA), the fourth Caliph, said, "Persist in your action with a noble end in mind [. . .] Failure to perfect your work while you are sure of the reward is injustice to yourself". He further states "One who does not perfect one's work, will bring confusion to self"

Employees have greater responsibility to nurture the concept of welfare in contemporary workplace. Islamic ethics emphasise:

Help ye one another in righteousness and piety, but help ye not one another in sin and rancour. Fear Allah, for Allah is strict in punishment (al-Qur'ān, 5:2)

With the concept of helping one another in righteous deeds and avoiding malice can solve dozens of issues of contemporary workplaces. Employees who follow Islamic ethics can contribute welfare and benevolence in the organisation.

Employment Ethics From Islamic Perspective

In contemporary thoughts the concept of employment revolves around material gains to increase wealth and to obtain luxuries for life provided basic needs are fulfilled. Islamic ethics capture a broader view and consider employment beyond physical exertion as a natural component of life to develop a model behavior and a sound personality to contribute towards the sustainable development of human society. Islamic ethics for employment are based on following aspects:

1. Employment as 'Ibadah

The concept of seeking bounties of Allah (SWT) is closely connected with one of the most important ritual of Islam i.e. Jumm'ah (weekly congregational prayer).

O you who have believed, when [the adhan] is called for the prayer on the day of Jumu'ah [Friday], then proceed to the remembrance of Allah and leave trade. That is better for you, if you only knew (al-Qur'ān 62:9)

Importance of Jumm'ah is evident from following sayings of the Prophet (PBUH):

The Prophet (PBUH) said: He who leaves the Friday prayer (continuously) for three Friday on account of slackness, Allah will print a stamp on his heart. (Sunan Abi Dawud 1052)

In the very next verse Allah (SWT) ordained that:

And when the prayer has been concluded, disperse within the land and seek from the bounty of Allah, and remember Allah often that you may succeed (al-Qur'ān 62:10)

This close linkage suggests that seeking from the 'bounty of Allah' is part of the 'ibadah. Offering Jumm'ah is important for religious and spiritual gains and after the Jumm'ah prayer believers are encouraged to disperse and start working for the prosperity of their own self, their organizations and their communities to build a happy and affluent society.

Islamic work ethics suggest that employees have to work with religious commitment and dedication to make contemporary workplaces more productive, reliable, and comfortable for all stakeholders of the society.

2. Employment as Responsibility

Islamic work ethics consider employment as a responsibility which employees must fulfil according to their contractual obligations, as mentioned in al-Qur'ān:

O you who have believed, fulfill [all] contracts (al-Qur'ān 5:1)

Employments are based on mutual agreements between employees and employers. Islamic work ethics are about the delivery of prescribed responsibilities according to the contract between both parties. Therefore, Islamic work ethics expects fulfilment of contractual responsibilities as one of the most important aspects of employment ethics for contemporary workplaces provided operations are not in contradiction with fundamental articles of faith. It is paramount in Islamic work ethics that people render back the trust to those, to whom they are due:

Indeed, Allah commands you to render trusts to whom they are due … (al-Qur'ān 5:1)

There is almost no room in Islamic work ethics for treachery in employment relations:

O you who have believed, do not betray Allah and the Messenger or betray your trusts while you know [the consequence] (al-Qur'ān 8:27)

3. Employment as Reciprocal Success

Islamic work ethics emphasize continuous struggle with clear intentions and optimum utilization of available resources and abilities. It is mentioned in the Qur'ān that the good, the achievement, the success all depend upon sincere and committed efforts of people.

And that there is not for man except that [good] for which he strives (al-Qur'ān 53:39)

Employment ethics in Islam suggest that employees should strive for the best outcomes for their organisations, without transgressions, which will lead to their own exceptional achievements both in this world and the world hereafter (In Sha Allah).

4. Employment as a Prospect for Collaborations, Innovations and Inventions

Islamic work ethics view employment as a potential prospect for collaborations. These collaborations can range from small scale local initiatives to global partnerships for innovations and inventions.

And cooperate in righteousness and piety, but do not cooperate in sin and aggression (al-Qur'ān 5:2)

Islamic ethics expect from employees to join hands with leading organisations in today's global village to disseminate their achievements and learn from the accomplishments of other leading individuals and institutions.

5. Employment as Accomplishment

Islamic work ethics consider employment as a source of accomplishment in both lives. One can utilise employment to beautify life in this world and can make the life hereafter full of joy and happiness.

But seek, through that which Allah has given you, the home of the Hereafter; and [yet], do not forget your share of the world. And do good as Allah has done good to you. And desire not corruption in the land. Indeed, Allah does not like corrupters (al-Qur'ān 28:77)

Islamic employment ethics also inspire employees to return and contribute to the society the wellbeing and happiness they secured during their professional careers. However, all that exists belongs to the Almighty Allah (SWT) and He will recompense accordingly:

And to Allah belongs whatever is in the heavens and whatever is in the earth - that He may recompense those who do evil with [the penalty of] what they have done and recompense those who do good with the best [reward] - (al-Qur'ān 53:31)

6. Employment as Dignity

Human dignity is of high importance in Islamic work ethics. Employment is the source of promoting individual dignity and self-reliance. Brief working protocols can be determined by following saying of the Prophet (PBUH):

Your employees are your brothers upon whom Allah has given you authority, so if a Muslim has another person under his control, he/she should not overburden them with what they cannot bear and if you do so, help them in their jobs (Sahih al-Bukhari)

7. Employment as Part of Tawakkal

Islamic work ethics stimulate tawakkal in employment as an institution; both employees and employers must have tawakkal on the Almighty Allah (SWT):

And whoever fears Allah - He will make for him a way out. And will provide for him from where he does not expect. And whoever relies upon Allah - then

He is sufficient for him. Indeed, Allah will accomplish His purpose. Allah has already set for everything a [decreed] extent (al-Qur'ān 65:2-3)

8. Employment as a Source of Halal Lifestyle

Islamic work ethics provide a very good opportunity to employees to adopt Halal lifestyle. If employees give their best through their heart and soul to their workplaces, they actually earn Halal livelihoods for their families. If an employee is physically present at workplace but unable to deliver his or her best, without any solid reason, s/he is going to earn luqma-e-mushtabeh (doubtful earnings) for their families, which can have grave consequences in the long run.

Therefore, to adopt Halal Lifestyle employment ethics in Islam expect from employees to bring their best abilities to contemporary workplaces.

9. Employment as a Tool of Holistic Advancement

Islamic work ethics consider employment as an instrument of holistic advancement of the society including personal, professional and communal achievements.

a. Personal

Islamic work ethics are based on the concept of personal gains in both worldly life and the life hereafter to advance individual motives and ensure high achievements for extraordinary progressions in their personal lives and professional careers.

But among them is he who says, "Our Lord, give us in this world [that which is] good and in the Hereafter [that which is] good and protect us from the punishment of the Fire (al-Qur'ān 2:201)

b. Organisational

Professional excellence remains a central point in Islamic work ethics. Hassan (2013, p. 2-3) stated that:

In the Qur'ān, the word 'amal (work) appears 360 times, and a synonymous term fi'l (also translated as work) is mentioned in another 109 places. So altogether the concept of work appears 469 times in the Qur'ān. This recurrent use of the concept of work in the Qur'ān and in innumerable ahadith emphasizes the need for the believers to be exemplary professionals to ensure advancement of their organisations towards set objectives

Had Allah willed He could have made you one community. But that He may try you by that which He hath given you (He hath made you as ye are). So vie one with another in good works. Unto Allah ye will all return, and He will then inform you of that wherein ye differ (al-Qur'ān 5:48)

c. Communal

The concept of community in Islamic ethics has several interpretations from mere a localised geographical community of adherents of Islam to national or even global community of believers (ummah) transcending geographical, cultural and national boundaries. All believers in the community are required to remain united to pursue collective objectives.

And hold firmly to the rope of Allah all together and do not become divided (al-Qur'ān 3:103)

The Prophet (PBUH) said, "None of you will have faith till he wishes for his (Muslim) brother what he likes for himself." (Sahih al-Bukhari 13)

Islamic work ethics through these strong communal bindings have great potential to make contemporary workplaces an ideal environment for shared progress.

10. Employment as an Opportunity to Promote Good

Islamic work ethics view employment as an opportunity to promote values such as proficiency, truth, justice, cooperation and so on, in and around the workplace.

And let there be [arising] from you a nation inviting to [all that is] good, enjoining what is right and forbidding what is wrong, and those will be the successful (al-Qur'ān 3:104).

Role of Management

In Islamic ethics huge responsibility lies on the shoulders of those who are management any of the organisations.

It has been narrated on the authority of Abu Malik that Ubaidullah b. Ziyad visited Ma'qil b. Yaser in the latter's illness. Ma'qil said to him: "I am narrating to you a tradition. If I were not at death's door, I would not narrate it to you. I heard the Messenger of Allah (may peace he upon him) say: A ruler who, having obtained control over the affairs of the Muslims does not strive for their betterment and does not serve them sincerely shall not enter Paradise with them" ("A ruler", 2007).

It has been reported on the authority of Abd al-Rahman b. Shumasa who said: I came to A'isha (RA) to inquire something from her. She said: "From which people are thou? I said: I am from the people of Egypt. She said: What was the behaviour of your governor towards you in this war of yours? I said: We did not experience anything bad from him. If the camel of a man from us died, he would bestow on him a camel. If any one of us lost his slave, he would give him a slave. If anybody was in need of the basic necessities of life, he would provide them with provisions. She said: Behold! the treatment that was meted out to my brother, Muhammad b. Abu Bakr, does not prevent me from telling you what I heard from the Messenger of Allah (may peace be upon him). He said in this house of mine: O God, who (happens to) acquire some kind of control over the affairs of my people and is hard upon them-be Thou hard upon him, and who (happens to) acquire some kind of control over the affairs of my people and is kind to them-be Thou kind to him. ("Behavior", 2007)

There is direct link between business growth and management excellence. Management of an organisation must work very hard in Islamic ethics to achieve set objectives through just and equitable means. Illegal ways and means are considered to spoil the whole system of corporate organisation. People who are managing must strengthen integrity of organisation by promoting and establishing just and honest culture. Illicit practices are dangerous not only for the organisation but also for those who are involved in these practices, because they will have to face the consequences in case of failure of the organisation. Islamic ethics suggest that management must respect.

(i) Equal Opportunity
(ii) Diversity

(iii) Social Welfare

(i) Equal Opportunity

Islam ensures that all individuals have an equal opportunity for employment, regardless of characteristics, such as sex, race, colour or religion.

O mankind, indeed We have created you from male and female and made you peoples and tribes that you may know one another. Indeed, the most noble of you in the sight of Allah is the most righteous of you. Indeed, Allah is Knowing and Acquainted (al-Qur'ān, 49:13).

Prophet Muhammad (PBUH) said: "O mankind, your Lord is One and your father is one. You all descended from Adam, and Adam was created from earth. He is most honoured among you in the sight of God who is most upright. No Arab is superior to a non-Arab, no coloured person to a white person, or a white person to a coloured person except by *taqwa* (piety)" (Ahmad and At-Tirmithi), (Equality, 2018).

In another narration, the Prophet (PBUH) was asked: "Who among men is most favoured by Allah?' He (PBUH) replied: "A man who does the most good to people" (At-Tabaraani), (Equality, 2018).

(ii) Respect Diversity

Islam and the Quran are clearly appreciative of diversity and dissimilarity -in creation, culture, and beliefs- within human world. Discarding the pre-Islamic tribal culture inculcating tight groupings based on family and lineage the Quran describes all human beings as part of one super unit which is humanity. It addresses the totality of humanity as 'Bani Adam' (children of Adam) in several places. For example, the following verses from the Quran endorse the principle of diversity as an essential element of the scheme of creation (Zaidi, na).

O ye who believe! Let not some men among you laugh at others: it may be that the latter are better than the former. Nor let some women laugh at others: it may be that latter are better than the former. Nor defame nor be sarcastic to each other, nor call each other names......(al-Qur'ān, 49:11)

O mankind! We created you from male and female and made you into nations and tribes, that ye may know each other (not that ye may despise each other). Verily, the most honoured of you in the sight of Allah is he who is the most righteous of you. And Allah has full knowledge and is fully informed... ... (al-Qur'ān, 49:13)

If thy Lord had so willed, He could have made mankind One People: but they will not cease to be diverse... ...(al-Qur'ān, 11:118)

In the first verse the Quran upholds unity by exhorting its adherents to respect the dignity of all human beings. The next two verses affirm the diversity among human beings through nations and tribes. The Quran recognises and respects the facets of identity determined by these divisions forming smaller and larger collectives of humankind. While the Quran conveys respect for everyone, it does not confer nobility or higher worth upon any group or ethnicity. Instead the single evaluative standard for the Quran remains moral consciousness of God (taqwa) (Zaidi, na).

(iii) Societal Welfare

Societal welfare is an obligation beyond statutory requirements where organisations voluntarily take steps for prosperous society. Societal welfare has many dimensions in Islam. Society is made up of human beings and Islam ensures welfare of every segment of society. Therefore, businesses must endeavour to contribute towards relatively less privileged segments of the society. There are different modes of contribution for the welfare of society, some are obligatory, and some are voluntary. Islam prioritises the welfare of different segments of society, as explained in following verses.

Alms are for the poor and the needy, and those employed to administer the (funds); for those whose hearts have been (recently) reconciled (to the truth); for those in bondage and in debt; in the cause of Allah; and for the wayfarer: (thus is it) ordained by Allah, and Allah is full of knowledge and wisdom (al - Qur'ān 9:60)

They ask thee what they should spend (in charity). Say: Whatever ye spend that is good, is for parents and kindred and orphans and those in want and for wayfarers. And whatever ye do that is good, Allah Knoweth it well (al-Qur'ān, 2:215)

Responsibilities of Consumers

A consumer is a person or organisation that spends wealth for the satisfaction of wants such as food, clothing, housing, articles of daily use, health, education, and other organisational, personal or family needs. There is no limit to human wants which are insatiable. It is required that one should be very careful in the consumption of wealth. Islam, therefore, enjoins moderation, self-control and prudence in spending of wealth (Chaudhry, 2003).

Islam educates consumers to manage their choices of consumption and control spontaneous temptations. Consumers with high buying powers are not allowed to be wasteful because Islamic work ethics discourage wastage of resources. It is the responsibility of consumers to maintain moderation in consumption:

And do not make your hand [as] chained to your neck or extend it completely and [thereby] become blamed and insolvent (al-Qur'ān 17:29)

Islamic ethics emphasise conservation of resources and discourage wastefulness because wastefulness depicts ungratefulness on the part of consumers for rich ecosystem of resources which Allah (SWT) created around human lives from cultivation to the environment.

Indeed, the wasteful are brothers of the devils, and ever has Satan been to his Lord ungrateful (al-Qur'ān 17:27)

Principles of Consumption in Islam

The basic principles of consumption laid down by Islam are three: Consumption of lawful (Halal) things, consumption of pure and clean things and moderation in consumption.

(i) Principle of Halal

It is mandatory for a Muslim to consume only 'Halal' (lawful and permitted) food and not to take that which is 'Haram' (unlawful and forbidden). The Qur'ān says:

And eat of what Allah has provided for you [which is] lawful and good. And fear Allah, in whom you are believers (al-Qur'ān, 5:88).

In another verse, the al-Qur'ān has mentioned prohibited or Haram items of food and has said:

Prohibited to you are dead animals, blood, the flesh of swine, and that which has been dedicated to other than Allah, and [those animals] killed by strangling or by a violent blow or by a head-long fall or by the goring of horns, and those from which a wild animal has eaten, except what you [are able to] slaughter [before its death], and those which are sacrificed on stone altars, and [prohibited is] that you seek decision through divining arrows. That is grave disobedience. ...... (al-Qur'ān 5:3)

The principle of Halal and Haram also applies to items of expenditure besides food. The followers of Islam are required to spend their earnings on Halal or permitted expenses and refrain from spending on Haram or prohibited things such as wine, narcotics, prostitutes, gambling, luxuries, etc. Following are the principles of consumption in Islamic ethics (Chaudhry, 2003).

(ii) Principle of Cleanliness and Wholesomeness

The Qur'ān commands upon mankind:

O mankind eat from whatever is on earth [that is] lawful and good and do not follow the footsteps of Satan. Indeed, he is to you a clear enemy (al-Qur'ān, 2:168).

The Qur'an addresses its followers and says:

O you who have believed, eat from the good things which We have provided for you and be grateful to Allah if it is [indeed] Him that you worship (al-Qur'ān, 2:172).

The Qur'an also says:

Then eat of what Allah has provided for you [which is] lawful and good. And be grateful for the favour of Allah, if it is [indeed] Him that you worship (al-Qur'ān, 16:114).

Thus, the Holy Qur'an impresses upon the people to eat good things which Allah has bestowed upon them. Another word used by the Qur'ān besides Halal is 'Tayyab' which means anything one finds pleasing, sweet, agreeable, wholesome, pure and conducive to health. The word 'Khabaith' is opposite of Tayyab which means things one finds impure, displeasing, bad, and disagreeable in sight, smell or eating. The believers have been exhorted to take for food those things which are Halal and Tayyab and avoid those which are Khabaith. Prophet Muhammad (PBUH) in his following A hadith has stressed cleanliness in food:

- Salman reported that the Messenger of Allah said: "The blessing of food is washing of hands before it and washing of hands after it". (Tirmizi)
- Abu Qatadah reported that the Messenger of Allah said: "When one of you drinks, he should not blow into the vessel". (Bukhari)
- Jaber reported that the Messenger of Allah said: "When you go to sleep, put out the lamp and shut the doors and cover the food and drink". (Bukhari)

(iii) Principle of Moderation

The principle of moderation in consumption means that one should take the food and drinks with moderation and avoid excess because excess of intake is harmful to health.

The Qur'ān says:

O children of Adam, take your adornment at every masjid, and eat and drink, but be not excessive. Indeed, He likes not those who commit excess (al-Qur'ān, 7:31).

O you who have believed, do not prohibit the good things which Allah has made lawful to you and do not transgress. Indeed, Allah does not like transgressors (al-Qur'ān, 5:87).

Islamic ethics prohibit overloading of stomach. It is also forbidden that one should adopt self-denying practices followed by ascetics and monks and deprive himself of some foods which Allah (SWT) has made lawful. The principle of moderation is also applicable to spending. One must not be miser in spending nor extravagant.

And [they are] those who, when they spend, do so not excessively or sparingly but are ever, between that, [justly] moderate (al-Qur'ān, 25:67)

CONCLUSION

In conclusion, this chapter defines the welfare concept in Islamic ethics a fine balance between shareholders and stakeholders. Islamic ethics guide businesses not to denied ordinary shareholders of their basic needs or sustenance and live in poverty and deprivation. Injustice in Islam seen as an obstruction to the human welfare, deepen social unrest and dissatisfaction among society in general. In Islam, the role of the state includes the administration of a social security system in which the religiously decreed zakat assumes a central position.

The welfare system is clearly been a responsibility of Islamic state as Prophet Muhammad (PBUH) stated. The companions of Prophet followed the Islamic ruling on developing welfare system. The second Caliph Hazrat Umar (RA) in the conquest of Jerusalem, his slave was riding according to his turn, signifies optimum equilibrium among rights of employees and the management (according to contemporary understanding of organisational structures).

The Prophet (PBUH) said, "When any man does any work, God wishes him to give it perfection and grace" Islam urges workers to fulfil all legitimate obligations with respect to their employment.

The Second Caliph Hazrat Umar (RA) during his term as leader of the Islamic state, wrote to his governors instructing them to welfare of the people and their hardships in the basic responsibility of the government create welfare state. Islam states that workers rights need to be at the centre of economic activities and without them there will be no value or wealth creation. Hazrat Ali (RA), the fourth Caliph, stated that merchants and artisans are the "providers of benefits and goods". He emphasised the importance of merchants and workers in improving the societal welfare and strengthening the state.

Chapter also argued that management of an organisation must work toward achieving Islamic ethics through just and equitable means. Illegal ways and means are considered to spoil the whole system of corporate organisation. The management and consumer should always follow the principle of Halal and Haram when conducting dealing with each other.

Discussion Questions

1. Discuss and explore the principles of consumption laid down by Islam?
2. Describe and discuss the concept of helping one another in righteous deeds and avoiding malice issues at contemporary workplaces?
3. Evaluate the relationship between Islamic ethics a fine balance between shareholders' interest and value for other stakeholders in business environment?
4. Critically evaluates accounting abuse, illegitimate use of authority, bribes, fraud, workplace thefts in relations to Islamic ethics?

REFERENCES

A ruler who having obtained control over the affairs. (2007). Retrieved August 13, 2007 from: www.iiu.edu.my/deed/hadith/muslim/020_smt.html#009_b20

Al-Faruqi, I., & Al-Banna, G. (1985). *Towards Islamic Labour and Unionism*. The International Islamic Confederation of Labour.

Al-Faruqi, I. R. (1992). *Al Tawhid: Its Implications for Thought and Life*. International Institute of Islamic Thought.

Askari, H., & Arfaa, N. (2007). Social Safety Net in Islam: The Case of Persian Gulf Oil Exporters. *British Journal of Middle Eastern Studies*, *34*(2), 177–202.

Aziz, F., Mahmud, M., & Karim, E. (2008). The Nature of Infaq and Its Effects on Distribution of Wealth. *KASBIT Business Journal*, *1*(1), 44–48.

Bartle, P. (2008). *Participatory Management: Methods to increase staff input in organisation*. Retrieved May 06, 2008 from: http://www.scn.org/cmp/modules/pm-pm.htm

Beekun, R. I. (1997). *Islamic Business Ethics*. The International Institute of Islamic Thought. doi:10.2307/j.ctvk8w1zv

Chaudhry, M. S. (2003). *Consumption*. Retrieved on May 06, 2019 from http://www.muslimtents.com/shaufi/b16/b16_6.htm#III-Moderation in Consumption

Daryabadi, A. M. (1998). *Tafseer-e-Majidi* (Vol. 1). Majlis-e-Nashriat-e-Qur'ān.

Hassan, M. M. (2013). *Islam and Professionalism: In Search of Excellence.* Retrieved on March 28, 2020 from: https://www.researchgate.net/publication/273909683_Islam_and_Professionalism_In_Search_of_Excellence

Hsieh, N.-h. (2017). The Responsibilities and Role of Business in Relation to Society: Back to Basics? *Business Ethics Quarterly*, *27*(2), 293–314.

Jabnoun, N. (1994). *Islam and Management.* Institute Kajian Dasar (IKD).

Le Caire, Gene`ve Alhabshi, S. O., & Ghazali, A. H. (1994). *Islamic Values and Management.* Institute of Islamic Understanding Malaysia (IKMI).

Modudi, A. A. (2005). Tafheem-ul-Qur'ān, vol. 1. Idara-e-Tarjaman ul Qur'ān Lahore.

Modudi, A. A. (2005). Tafheem-ul-Qur'ān, vol. 4. Idara-e-Tarjaman ul Qur'ān Lahore.

Nasaruddin, R. R., Fuad, F., Jaswir, I., & Hamid, H. A. (2011). The Importance of a Standardised Islamic Manufacturing (IMP) for Food and Pharmaceutical Productions. *2nd International Conference on Professional Ethics and Education in Engineering 2011 (ICEPEE'11).*

Syed, J., & Ali, A. J. (2010). Principles of employment relations in Islam: A normative view. *Employee Relations*, *32*(5), 454–469.

Zaidi, A. (n.d.). *Islam and Diversity.* Retrieved on May 16, 2019 from: https://www.masrif.net/index.php?option=com_content&view=article&id=92:islam-and-diversity-by-az&catid=39:blog&Itemid=58

Chapter 7
Islamic Work Ethics in Marketing

ABSTRACT

Islam ethics are being overlooked by multinational companies (MNCs) with growing Muslim markets. Islam sees business as an essential pillar of society, and before the noble Prophet Mohammad (PBUH) commencement his mission, he was a very successful businessman with his honesty, reliability, and trustworthiness towards his customers. This clearly advocates that Islamic ethical principles need to be adopted by multinational companies (MNCs) to meet the welfare of Muslim customers. Although profit maximisation is not the ultimate goal of trade in Islam, Islam accepts profits and trade and does not aim to remove all differences in income and wealth that may result in various social and economic classes. The chapter discusses the conceptual implications of companies planning to engage the Muslim customers, employees, and other stakeholders.

INTRODUCTION

This chapter will examine the organisations operating in Muslim communities need to know fundamental beliefs that drive the behaviour of Muslim customers. Today organisations are embracing multiculturalism as business pragmatism. Awareness about permissibilities can facilitate consumptions on macro level. Religion is getting much importance to attract customers. Internationally both public and private organisations are adapting their procedures, rules and

DOI: 10.4018/978-1-7998-5295-7.ch007

regulations to provide sufficient space to Muslim customers, employees and other stakeholders to contribute towards growth and expansion of economies and societies.

In Arabic the word Souq (sometimes spelt Souk; the plural is Aswaq or Aswak) means the place where selling and sales take place. The name is an exact linguistic description of how goods are brought into the market; sellers would Souq (herd, shepherd, lead or bring) their goods in. However, the word Souq as a concept has been defined during the life of Prophet Mohammad as 'any place where a sale occurs'; it is tied to the transaction itself not to the place. Thus, in Islam, a market is held wherever and whenever an exchange takes place between buyers and sellers under mutually agreed-on terms and conditions (Alserhan, 2011).

An organisation cannot create an Islamic brand or position itself as Islamic if it promotes its business through un-Islamic means. The use of the word 'Islamic' to describe a company's operations has huge implications, starting from how the product is developed and handled till consumption by the end-user. Islamic is not just a name, it is an entire business philosophy that incorporates every single aspect of the business (Alserhan, 2011).

Islam prohibits fraud and cheating and warns marketers against exaggerating or lying about their products or services. It is forbidden to gain wealth by fraud, deceit, theft or other falsehoods. Marketers involved in fraud are committing a sin. Chapter 83 in the Quran (The Dealers in Fraud) contains the following verses:

1. 'Woe to those who deal in fraud.'
2. 'Those who, when they have to receive by measure from men, exact full measure.'
3. 'But when they have to give by measure or weight to men, give less than due.'

Other clear Islamic teachings in this regard include:

1. 'God permits selling but forbids usurious gain' (Quran 2:275).
2. 'O my people! Give full measure and full weight in justice, and wrong not people in respect of their goods' (Quran 11:85).
3. 'Oh ye who believe! Eat not up each other's property by unfair and dishonest means' (Quran 4:29).

4. 'On the day of judgment, the honest Muslim merchant will stand side by side with the martyrs' (Prophet Mohammad (PBUH)).
5. 'Sell the good and bad separately. He who deceives is not of us' (Prophet Mohammad (PBUH)).
6. 'Swearing produces ready sale but blots out blessing' (Prophet Mohammad (PBUH)).

According to Alserhan (2011), in general, all Muslim practices and acts are classified under the following categories.

1. Halal, or permissible. It has three levels:
    a. "Wajib, or duty; obligatory acts. Failure to perform them is a sin. Duty can be described as the Core Halal, without which a firm can't be Shariah-compliant. Implications: firms must perform Wajib. Examples include being honest and transparent".
    b. "Mandoob, or likeable; preferable but not obligatory. Not performing Mandoob is not a sin. Likeable can be described as the Supplementary Halal. Implications: do if possible. Examples include being helpful and going the extra mile".
    c. "Makrooh, or despised; not preferable, discouraged by religion and usually seen as a last resort. Engaging in Makrooh doesn't result in a sin unless it leads to one. The most obvious example of Makrooh in Islam is divorce! Although it is Shariah compliant, it represents the border between compliance and non-compliance. It is loathed by society. Implications: avoid if possible".
2. "Businesses should refrain as much as they can from engaging in doubted activities for the fear of being perceived to be unscrupulous by Muslim consumers. Firms engaging in these activities risk a Fatwa being issued against them".
3. "Haram, or not permissible; all acts condemned explicitly or implicitly by the Islamic religion. Engaging in them or in activities leading to them is a sin".

These categories have obvious implications on what companies planning to engage the Muslim marketplace should and shouldn't do. It is of no relevance whether these companies are Muslim or not, what is of relevance is what they should do, i.e., value maximisation, and how they do it – by fair play and just dealing. To illustrate, the duty Wajib of a company in Islam is to maximise the good of the society, not only profit maximisation. Therefore, a company (its personnel) will be committing a sin if it doesn't actively seek societal value maximisation. A company however is at ease in choosing the means to do that, as long as those means are not Haram (as long as they are permissible or not a sin). In fact, Islam acknowledges that people will differ and that this difference is for a purpose:

'It is We Who portion out between them their livelihood in this world, and We raised some of them above others in ranks, so that some may employ others in their work. But the Mercy of your Lord is better than the (wealth of this world) which they amass.' (Quran 43:32).

The implications of these categories on the marketing aspect of business are very thorough and encompass the entire marketing mix for both services and goods. The first component of the conventional marketing mix, e.g., is the product.

Reputation of Marketing in Islam

Islam gives a special attention to the market and urges people to go into markets to trade and make gains. Trade as a profession has been encouraged to earn livelihood and blessing of Allah (SWT).

'O ye who believe! Squander not your wealth among yourselves in vanity, except it be a trade by mutual consent' (Quran 4:29).

'And when the Prayer is finished, then may ye disperse through the land, and seek of the Bounty of Allah' (Quran 62:10).

In another verse, traders were even compared to those who fight in the cause of Allah (SWT):

'He knows that there must be among you sick, and others who travel in the land seeking of the bounty of Allah, and others who fight in Allah's way' (Quran 73:20).

Prophet Mohammad (PBUH) said: 'The one who brings merchandise to our market is like the one who fights in Allah's cause.'

In Islam, believers are not only dwellers in Mosques or monks in monasteries. They are people of profession and trade, although their worldly activities don't take toll on their religious duties.

'Men whom neither merchandise nor sale beguileth from remembrance of Allah and constancy in prayer and paying to the poor their due' (Quran 24:37).

The centrality of the market in Islam is expressed in the fact that God counts the market as one of His major blessings on the people of Macca.

'Have We not established for them a sure sanctuary, whereunto the produce of all things is brought (in trade), a provision from Our presence? But most of them know not' (Quran 29:57).

Prophet Mohammad (PBUH), who was a merchant before he became a Prophet, when asked about the best ways to gain, said: 'A sale that is accepted by God and a man working with his hands.' The Prophet used to go to the market to make a living until the non-believers of his time, trying to criticise him, counted that as non-prophet-like behaviour.

'What sort of a messenger is this, who eats food, and walks through the streets? Why has not an angel been sent down to him to give admonition with him?' (Quran 25:7).

According to Alserhan (2011), "markets in Islam were under the Hisbah authority chaired by the market governor or the Muhtasib. The Muhtasib would have a dedicated place – later it became an office – in the market and would have employees assisting him. His duties included continuous inspection and supervision of transactions in the market including terms, conditions, and quality. He would have to be of good character, knowledgeable of both trade and Shariah, and fair. He would ensure that the market operations didn't violate the teachings of Islam".

Job Specification and Description of Muhtasib

In recent time role of muhtasib has deviated, however, historically regulating and controlling the marketplace remained central responsibility of muhtasib. Men and women both can perform duties as muhtasib. Women muhtasib will be appointed for women markets. The second Muslim caliph appointed

Ashshifa, daughter of Abdullah, as a Muhtasib in one of the markets of the Prophet Mohammad's city (Medina) (Alserhan, 2011). In Islamic work ethics muhtasib has to be Muslim for Muslim markets to ensure Shariah compliance. However, every religion and faith have the right to appoint muhtasib according to their specific religious requirements.

Nomenclature

In contemporary marketplace societies can opt for any alternative nomenclature for muhtasib according to their norms and requirements. But for this publication authors preferred to continue with the same title of the office.

Position

Muhtasib has to be a fulltime public employee to

- Resolve disputes and complaints of the marketplace
- Maintain the discipline in the market
- Continuously monitor the markets for violations and providing remedies
- Muhtasib will have the provision of required staff and other facilitates, such as offices, vehicles and amenities, according to the size of the market
- Ensure compliance
  With Shariah guidelines in trading, manufacturing, slaughtering and distribution

A Muhtasib is accountable to the appointing authority and the public both. Muhtasib has to maintain the secrecy as long as violations are evident to public. However, if offender violates rules openly then s/he has to be reprimanded publically maintain the discipline. Muhtasib has to have polite nature, courteous behaviour and well-mannered attitude to facilitate communication and interaction with all stakeholders of the marketplace. The Prophet says, 'Allah, the Blessed and Exalted is kind and loves kindness. He is pleased with it and helps you with it as long as it is not misplaced' (Hadith).

Duties of Muhtasib

According to Alserhan (2011) following are the duties of muhtasib in Islamic work ethics:

1. Market accessibility. To monitor roads and paths in the market and ensure that they remain uncongested and their roofs high enough to allow easy access to shops. Shopkeepers are not allowed to exhibit their goods on these paths because such an act is seen as a transgression on pedestrians.
2. Division of market. To divide markets according to the type of the product or service being provided. Those whose professions require the use of fire, such as blacksmiths, cooks and bakers, must have shops located far away from garments and scents shops. The Muhtasib appoints to each of these divisions supervisors who know the ways of traders in them and their possible violations. The local supervisor would also report to the Muhtasib on prices and on availability of goods in their respective divisions.
3. Monitoring scales, weights and measures. These must be inspected without the knowledge of sellers in many cases and must weigh or measure at least as much as they should. It is OK to give buyers more but not less, 'Give just measure, and cause no loss (to others by fraud). And weigh with scales true and upright. And withhold not things justly due to men, nor do evil in the land, working mischief' (Quran 26:181–3). A companion of the Prophet also reports the following story, 'I and Makhrafah al-Abdi imported some garments from Hajar and brought them to Mecca. The Apostle of Allah (peace be upon him) came to us walking, and after he had bargained with us for some trousers, we sold them to him. There was a man who was weighing for payment. The Apostle of Allah (peace be upon him) said to him: Weigh out and give overweight' (Hadith).
4. Money market. To inspect the money market and to make sure that coins are produced to exact measures and specifications and to ensure that a balance is achieved between the amount of money available in the market and the economic situation in the country to ensure stability of prices.
5. Deals and transaction. To thwart unlawful deals and transactions and to prevent the sale of products declared impermissible in Islam. Examples of unlawful transactions include, as instructed by the Prophet (peace be

upon him): 'The price paid for a dog, the price given to a soothsayer, and the hire paid to a prostitute are not lawful' (Hadith).

6. Prevention of monopoly. To prevent monopolies and to force traders to sell at equal value if there is a need to do so.
7. Brokers and middlemen. To oversee the operations of brokers and middlemen and to prevent them from selling until they know who the seller is and to document that information in their books in order to ensure that what is being sold is not stolen, disputed, taken by force or acquired through any other illegal means.
8. The production of meat. To supervise the slaughter of animals, making sure that these are free from disease, to prevent butchers from blowing between the skin and the body of the animal when it is being skinned to avoid human breath from changing the flavour of the meet, to ensure the place where the meat is prepared and sold is clean, and that adequate procedures are used to preserve meat.

Shariah Compliant Islamic Business

In modern times we can safely suggest that irrespective of location and ownership, Islamic company is an organisation that specialises in the production or distribution of products that comply with the teachings of Islam, i.e., Halal, are classified as Islamic companies. These companies might be located anywhere and owned by anyone. The key differentiating criterion in this category of companies is that their products are manufactured as Shariah-compliant. Clearly, their main target market is consumers in one or more of the three types of Islamic market: primary (predominantly Muslim majority societies), secondary (societies with Muslim minority) and emerging (non-Muslim societies exposed to Shariah compliant products).

Conventional Marketing

The American Marketing Association (AMA) reviews definition of marketing every three-year by a panel of five scholars who are active researchers in the area of marketing. According to the most recently approved definition of marketing by AMA, "marketing is the activity, set of institutions, and processes for creating, communicating, delivering, and exchanging offerings that have value for customers, clients, partners, and society at large" (AMA, 2017).

The Chartered Institute of Marketing (CIM) defines marketing as, "the management process responsible for identifying, anticipating and satisfying customer requirements profitably" (CIM, 2019).

Islamic Marketing

According to Alom and Hoq (2011) Islamic marketing can be defined as "the process and strategy (Hikmah) of fulfilling need through Halal (Tayyibat) products and services with the mutual consent and welfare (Falah) of both parties i.e. buyers and sellers for the purpose of achieving material and spiritual wellbeing in the world here and the hereafter".

According to Abuznaid (2012) Islamic marketing is "the wisdom of satisfying the needs of customers through the good conduct of delivering Halal, wholesome, pure and lawful products and services with the mutual consent of both seller and buyer for the purpose of achieving material and spiritual wellbeing in the world here and hereafter and making consumers aware of it through the good conduct of marketers and Islamic ethical advertising".

In above mentioned two definitions of Islamic Marketing we can find following key concepts:

1. Hikmah (Strategy)
2. Needs vs. Wants
3. Halal (Tayyibat)
4. Mutual Consent
5. Good Conduct
6. Islamic Ethical Advertising

Hikmah (Strategy)

In Islamic ethics, as Alom and Hoq (2011) argued, "the word Hikmah is very close to the strategy which indicates 'Wisdom'. It signifies sound perception and sound judgment, which is time befitting approach, adaptable to the situation. Marketing allows us to consider the subject as being flexible and dynamic, just like the world we live in. Islamic Marketing can achieve long term goals in this world and the hereafter through interacting with changing environment, situation and even it can purify the beliefs, outlook, morals, habits, customs, and social, cultural, economic and political life of man in its totality". The holy Qur'ān tells of Hikmah in different verses such as:

Our Lord, and send among them a messenger from themselves who will recite to them Your verses and teach them the Book and wisdom and purify them. Indeed, You are the Exalted in Might, the Wise (al-Qur'ān 2:129)

Just as We have sent among you a messenger from yourselves reciting to you Our verses and purifying you and teaching you the Book and wisdom and teaching you that which you did not know (al-Qur'ān 2:151)

He gives wisdom to whom He wills, and whoever has been given wisdom has certainly been given much good. And none will remember except those of understanding (al-Qur'ān 2:269)

Needs vs. Wants

Islamic marketing is based on 'needs' instead of 'wants' as in conventional marketing concepts. The scope of wants is much wider than needs, thus ultimately leads to frustration, dissatisfaction, hostility and crimes. Although needs vary from person to person, society to society and culture to culture, however, needs seem manageable and can be addressed according to real capacity of people. The holy Qur'ān recognises human needs as:

Indeed, it is [promised] for you not to be hungry therein or be unclothed (al-Qur'ān 20:118)

And indeed, you will not be thirsty therein or be hot from the sun (al-Qur'ān 20:119)

The Tayyibat

In Islam, 'products' are associated with values and ethics. The word Taiyyibat, which is mentioned in the Quran 18 times, has been explained by Islamic scholars to carry the meanings of beauty, purity, physical and spiritual cleanliness, and attractiveness, and it is usually used along with the word Rizq (sustenance). Because in Islam Allah is the sole sustainer (Razzaq) and because He is Taiyyib then Rizq –which is provided by Him – can be nothing else but Taiyyib. Therefore, Muslims are obliged by the teachings of their religion to make Taiyyib everything that they do, including each and every single action leading to or involved in the making of the product.

From the Islamic religious perspective, Taiyyibat can be defined as the goods and services that are Shariah-compliant. It is the plural of Taiyyib, which is the opposite of Khabeeth: 'Say (O Muhammad): Not equal are Al-Khabîth (all that is evil and bad as regards things, deeds, beliefs, persons and foods) and At-Taiyyib (all that is good as regards things, deeds, beliefs, persons, foods), even though the abundance of Al-Khabîth may please you. So, fear Allah, O men of understanding in order that you may be successful' (al-Qur'ān 5:100)

Taiyyibat means 'the useful and beneficial material granted by Allah to his servants. The consumption of these leads to material, ethical, and spiritual benefits to the consumer.' Turkumani (1990) defined Taiyyibat in a similar manner but emphasised in the last part of the definition that the consumption of these leads to material, ethical, and spiritual meanings. These definitions make it clear that Taiyyibat is what a Muslim can benefit from in accordance with the Shariah guidance and that Khaba'ith (plural of Khabeeth) is all that which cannot benefit a Muslim in a Shariah-compliant manner under normal circumstances. Under other circumstances, however, Khaba'ith can be made use of or consumed but within the limits of 'absolute necessity'. For example, a Muslim is allowed to consume 'just enough' of a non-Shariah compliant product, i.e., Haram, pork, e.g., to allow him to survive if he could not find any other source of food and his survival was clearly at risk. Once this necessity is lifted the licence to consume is cancelled and consumption of that product becomes a sin. It must be made clear that Khaba'ith cannot be considered products from an Islamic perspective. In Islam only that which is Shariah-compliant can be referred to as product (Alserhan, 2011).

Mutual Consent

Mutual consent in Islamic ethics, according to Alom and Hoq (2011), means that the exchange goods and services should happen under the free will of buyers and sellers without any pressure, fraud and deception. Mutual consent leads to cooperation among all stakeholders without elements of compulsion or cheating. According to a hadith the seller and buyer have the right to keep or return the goods so long as they have not parted or till, they part. The holy Qur'ān also educates mutual consent in trading activities:

O you who have believed, do not consume one another's wealth unjustly but only [in lawful] business by mutual consent. And do not kill yourselves [or one another]. Indeed, Allah is to you ever Merciful (al-Qur'ān 4:29)

And those who have responded to their lord and established prayer and whose affair is [determined by] consultation among themselves, and from what We have provided them, they spend (al-Qur'ān 42:38)

The Messenger of (PBUH) said: "The contract of sale becomes lawful with the consent of both parties"

Good Conduct

Good conduct is important in Islamic ethics. In every business activity all stakeholders have to abide with good conduct. There are several dimensions of good conduct in Islamic work ethics. Following verses from al-Qur'ān and saying of holy Prophet Muhammad (PBUH) suggest some of relevant aspects of good conduct for marketers.

And the servants of the Most Merciful are those who walk upon the earth easily, and when the ignorant address them [harshly], they say [words of] peace (al-Qur'ān 25:63)

And when you are greeted with a greeting, greet [in return] with one better than it or [at least] return it [in a like manner]. Indeed, Allah is ever, over all things, an Accountant (al-Qur'ān 4:86)

And be moderate in your pace and lower your voice; indeed, the most disagreeable of sounds is the voice of donkeys (al-Qur'ān 31:19)

And speak to him with gentle speech that perhaps he may be reminded or fear [Allah] (al-Qur'ān 20:44)

Invite to the way of your Lord with wisdom and good instruction and argue with them in a way that is best. Indeed, your Lord is most knowing of who has strayed from His way, and He is most knowing of who is [rightly] guided (al-Qur'ān 16:125)

An-Nawwas bin Sam'an (RA) narrated, 'I asked the Messenger of Allah (PBUH) about virtue and sin and he replied, "The essence of virtue is (manifested in) good morals (Akhlaq) whereas sinful conduct is that which turns in your heart (making you feel uncomfortable) and you dislike that it would be disclosed to other people". (Muslim, Book 16, Hadith 1483)

Abu Hurairah (May Allah be pleased with him) reported: Messenger of Allah (PBUH) was asked about the deed which will be foremost to lead a man to Jannah. He replied, "Fear of Allah and the good conduct". Then he was asked about indulgence which will admit a man to Hell (Fire), and he answered, "The tongue and the genitals". (At- Tirmidhi, Book 1, Hadith 627)

Islamic vs. Ethical Advertising Approach

According to Nebenzahl and Jaffe (1998) ethical advertising is concerned with the extent of harm advertising deception and content cause to the consumer. Deception is generally defined as false and misleading claims in advertising while ethical issues related to advertising contents include the use of informative versus emotional persuasive advertising. In ethical of advertising harm may be defined as:

1. Violation of autonomy by control or manipulation
2. Invasion of Privacy
3. The violation of the right to know

Islamic advertising approach includes avoidance of following three dimensions in addition to the aspects covered under conventional ethical advertising.

1. Advertising of Haram products
   The basic principle is the permissibility of the product/service. To make (anything) lawful and to prohibit (anything) is the right of Allah (SWT) alone and interfering with these is tantamount to committing shirk (Shafiq *et. al.*, 2016).

2. Exaggeration
   In Islamic ethics exaggeration is considered inappropriate:

"O People of the Scripture, do not commit excess in your religion or say about Allah except the truth" (al-Qur'ān 4:171)

3. Sexual Appeal
   According to Ismail and Melewar (2014) "the attitude of Muslims toward high sex appeal female model ads was significantly lower than non-Muslims attitudes toward the same ad. Similar results were

obtained when subjects were exposed to high sex appeal male models. The Muslims' attitudes toward the ad were significantly lower than non-Muslim attitudes toward the same ad. Muslim subjects' attitudes toward the low sex appeal female model ad were also significantly lower than non-Muslims' attitudes toward the same ad. However, no significant differences were detected between Muslims and non-Muslims in relation to their attitudes toward the low sex appeal male model ad. These findings indicate that for Muslim consumers, the old marketing cliché, "sex sells," may not hold true. The Islamic religion in is still an important factor that determines people's values. From the Islamic perspective, Muslim behaviour has to be in line with Shari'ah and to be considered an act of worship ('ibadah). The use of sex appeal in advertisements whereby advertisers expose, exploit, and objectify the woman and her body is rejected in Islam".

(O' Prophet!) Say to the believing men to lower their gaze and protect their private parts. This is purer for them. Verily, Allah is All-Aware of what they do. And say to the believing women that they should lower their gaze and guard their private parts, that they should not display their beauty and ornaments except what ordinarily appear thereof. . . (al-Qur'ān 24:30-31)

Islamic vs. Conventional Marketing Concept

The basic difference between Islamic and conventional marketing concept is satisfying needs through Halal and Tayyib products and services in case of Islamic wisdom through mutual consent; while conventional concept suggests anticipating, identifying and creating requirements for customers. There is thin but significant difference between two ideologies. One takes the responsibility while other utilises circumstances. This conceptual approach takes contemporary business approach apart from Islamic business attitude. A companion once established a business which flourished unusually. One day he suddenly decided to close the business, his neighbours asked the reason for abandoning such a lucrative venture. He replied that once he heard the Prophet (PBUH) mentioning reward of taking back sold commodity as securing a house in paradise, today a customer returned a product, my objective has been achieved, and thus I am winding the business.

In Arabic, the word "selling" means "meeting something with something else "like exchanging money with money, a product for product, service for service and or money for a product, etc. thus causing ownership". In Islam, the word "selling" is considered one of the opposing names, which means "it can be used for something and its opposite" like buying and selling, buyer and seller. Originally the Arabic word bay'a (sell) is taken from "Baa" which means "the arm". Therefore, it means that both the buyer and the seller extend their arms to each other in a sign for giving and taking thus resulting in relationship (Abuznaid, 2012). This concept builds Islamic marketing on the solid footings to provide, disseminate and promote products and services which extend material, social and psychological benefits to end-users with lasting relationships between producers or providers and consumers.

The Islamic Product

These are products that are manufactured and promoted as Shariah-compliant, i.e., Halal. They are produced and consumed mainly in the primary and secondary Islamic markets and they are rarely known in non-Islamic markets. However, many non-Islamic multinationals produce Halal brands that are specifically destined to Islamic markets. Many of Nestlé's products are being produced according to Halal principles and are being heavily advertised and distributed to Muslim consumers in both secondary and primary Islamic markets. The same products can be found on the shelves of numerous stores in non-Islamic markets since making these products Islamic required minimum changes to the production process, or the use of alternative yet similar ingredients.

Classification of Products n Islam

Lawful or Taiyyibat products have been classified by Islamic scholars into four different categories:

1. Dharuriyyat (necessities)
   These are the products which are necessary to satisfy basic needs and necessary for surviving. In Islamic marketing strategies these products should be available in abundance with variety of quality perspectives and price range to fulfil basic needs of people according to their purchasing capacities. However, a minimum standard has to be maintained to ensure required benefit is available to the consumer. Manufacturers and service providers are expected to keep minimal profit margins for the benefit of masses.

2. Hajiyyat (needs)
   Products and services required to improve quality of human life. Consumers and providers have to maintain reasonable balance of demand and supply to ensure excess of people to required products and service to enhance their quality of life. Manufacturers and service providers have to keep profit margins reasonable and state has the role to intervene if there is any exploitation at any stage in the process.

3. Kamaliyyat (improvements)
   Kamaliyyat are goods and services that lead towards perfect experience of human life. Those who have the capability and capacity to consume kamaliyyat should consume and with gratitude to the Almighty for His bounty, however, such consumers have greater responsibility about their surroundings to facilitate less fortunate people to fulfil their basic needs. Manufacturers and providers of kamaliyyat can keep their profit margins high and create aspiring brands for people to affiliate with.

4. Tarafiyyat (extravagances)
   Tarafiyyat are Halal products by nature but may be considers as extravagant and wasteful. Although this is subjective, however, consumers of tarafiyyat being wealthy people have to remain cautious to be extravagant and wasteful. They should consume justifiable quantities of tarafiyyat with valid reasons. Manufacturers and providers of tarafiyyat can have exceptional profits because market size is usually remaining small for such products.

Pricing Strategies in Islamic Work Ethics

There are several dimensions of pricing strategies in Islam work ethics. Manufacturers and providers of goods and services are expected to keep prices of necessities and needs in affordable range of masses. However, if there are special circumstances such as famine or drought then following saying of holey Prophet Muhammad (PBUH) will be the guideline for all stakeholders:

The people said: Messenger of Allah, prices have shot up, so fix prices for us. Thereupon the Messenger of Allah (PBUH) said: Allah is the one Who fixes prices, Who withholds, gives lavishly and provides, and I hope that when I meet Allah, none of you will have any claim on me for an injustice regarding blood or property. (Sunan Abi Dawud 3451)

If traders' resort to hording, then following analysis by Ibn Taimiyah will be helpful, as cited by Bashar (1997), for price control strategies of dharuriyyat and hajiyyat:

Imam Muslim reports in his Sahih from Muammar bin Abdullah that the Prophet said that hoarding is practiced only by a sinner (wrong-doer). A hoarder is a person who buys the grains that are most needed by people with a view to putting them out of their reach so the price will rise. Such a man commits injustice against people. So, the authorities have the right to force such trader to sell the grains at the market price when people need it... That is why the jurists are of the opinion that if a person needs another person's grains (for his survival) then he can buy it from him at the market price even against the wish of the owner, and even if he insists on charging a higher price. The owner deserves only the market rate.

Consumers can also set prices of commodities in Islamic ethics as a following incident has been cited by Alserhan (2011):

The companion of the Prophet, Jareer Ibn Abdullah (died circa 671 AD), said 'We made a covenant to the Prophet, may peace be upon him, that we listen and obey and give advice to all Muslims'. Jareer, may Allah be pleased with him, sent his servant to buy a horse. The servant found a horse for 300 dirhams and brought it back along with the seller so that his master could complete the purchase and give the seller the money. When Jareer saw the horse, he estimated that it was worth much more than the agreed price; he told the seller that the horse was worth more and offered the seller 400 dirhams. The seller agreed. Then Jareer offered 500 and the seller agreed again. Jareer kept on raising the price until it reached 800 dirhams and gave that amount to the seller. The servant was bewildered by the act of his master and asked him why did he do that? Jareer explained that he made a covenant to the Prophet to give advice to all Muslims and therefore that was the only right thing to be done: to inform the seller, his Muslim brother, the accurate price of the horse.

Market dynamics also have complete liberty to develop price setting mechanism because all traders and consumers in Islamic work ethics are allowed to engage in free exchange of commodities and agreed prices with mutual consent.

Promotional Activities

Perhaps there is no other religion in the history of mankind that has relied so heavily on promotions to support its causes as much as Islam. The religion, which was inaugurated with the words read, teach and write in an era when only the privileged were literate, is no stranger to the professional use of promotional means in the propagation. Islam is a religion that is based on dissemination of information and awareness creation (Alserhan, 2011).

According to Islamic work ethics there should not be wrong promises, false hopes and deception is any of the promotional activity.

Halal Supply Chain

Halal supply chains include everything from the procurement and preparation of genuine Halal ingredients to the manufacturing and delivery of the final product all the way to customer shelves. This includes the separation of Halal ingredients or finished products from non-Halal products, such as alcoholic or pork-related products, throughout the entire chain. This long chain of activities preceding the final step and the activities following consumption is usually overlooked and thus a product might end up being classified as Halal despite being moved through a Haram channel. This short-sightedness in defining Halal is being corrected now as accreditation authorities, governments and businesses come to realise that such an extension of the activities considered does actually represent an advantage to be had, not a burden to be avoided (Alserhan, 2011).

CONCLUSION

In this chapter Islamic marketing principles and ethics were discussed. The chapter analysed that the Islamic values, beliefs and principles has been overlooked by the multinational companies within developing and distribution of products to Muslim customers. Islamic marketing perspective, the product that a company sells must be entirely Halal. This means that all inputs, processes and outputs must be Shariah-compliant, i.e., the product and all that has been involved in its creation, delivery, and consumption must be environmentally friendly and totally harmless, as Islam clearly prohibits causing harm to anything that God created (all-embracing harmony in the universe). An un-Halal or Haram product will be very difficult to sell to the Muslim consumer because the Muslim consumer's behaviour is mostly dictated by the common understanding of what is permissible and what is prohibited under the Shariah law. Being Shariah-compliant is the quickest way to promote the company and its products.

The Shariah-compliant products are being very important for Muslim customers. The halal products and services are satisfying needs of customer through Islamic wisdom and mutual consent. While conventional products and services are anticipating, identifying and creating requirements for customers. There is thin but significant difference between two ideologies. One takes the responsibility while other utilises circumstances of needs of the individual customer. Islamic marketing considers taking in account the values and beliefs of the Muslim customers within Islamic principles and ethics. The Islamic ethics make it very clear to manufacturers and traders not to make false promises, false hopes and deception is any of the promotional activity. Perhaps there is no other religion in the history of mankind that has relied so heavily on Islamic ethics in promoting the products and services to support its causes. The prophet Mohammad (PBUH) set the standards for business dealing even before he declared the prophethood that traders should follow honesty, reliability and trustworthiness towards his customers.

Discussion Questions

1. Discuss and analyse the importance Shariah-compliant products are being very important for Muslim customers?
2. What are the Islamic principles that traders should follow to attract Muslim customers?
3. How do Islamic values, beliefs and principles have been overlooked by the multinational companies within developing and distribution of products to Muslim customers?
4. Discuss, how traders and consumers in Islamic work ethics can engage in free exchange of commodities and agreed prices with mutual consent?

REFERENCES

Abuznaid, S. (2012). Islamic Marketing: Addressing the Muslim Market, An-Najah Univ. *J. Res. (Humanities)*, *26*(6), 1473–1503.

Alom, M. M., & Haque, M. S. (2011). Marketing and Islamic Perspective, *World. Journal of Social Sciences*, *1*(3), 71–81.

Alserhan, B. A. (2011). *The Principles of Islamic Marketing*. Gower-UK.

AMA. (2017). *Definitions of marketing*. Retrieved on November 21, 2019 from: https://www.ama.org/the-definition-of-marketing-what-is-marketing/

Bashar, M. L. A. (1997). Price Control in an Islamic Economy. *JKAU: Islamic Econ.*, *9*, 29–52.

Beekun, R. I. (1997). *Islamic Business Ethics*. The International Institute of Islamic Thought. doi:10.2307/j.ctvk8w1zv

CIM. (2019). *What is marketing*. Retrieved on November 21, 2019 from: https://www.cim.co.uk/qualifications/get-into-marketing/

Ismail, A. R., & Melewar, T. C. (2014). Attitude of Muslim Consumers toward Sex Appeal in Advertising: A Comparative Study between Subcultures in Malaysia. *Journal of Promotion Management*, *20*(5), 553–570. doi:10.1080/10496491.2014.946204

Nebenzahl, I. D., & Jaffe, E. D. (1998). Ethical Dimensions of Advertising Executions. *Journal of Business Ethics*, *17*(7), 805–815. doi:10.1023/A:1005850812845

Shafiq, A., Haque, A., & Abdullah, K. B. (2016). *A Collection of Islamic Advertising Principles*. Retrieved on June 29, 2019 from: https://www.researchgate.net/publication/309490921

Turkumani, A. K. (1990). Islamic Economic System. Jeddah, Saudi Arabia: Sawadi Library.

Chapter 8
Islamic Ethics in Finance

ABSTRACT

Islamic banking and finance have been very attractive features for Muslim as well as non-Muslim customers. Where a Muslim customer would investigate Shariah compliance when choosing an Islamic financial institution for its services, a non-Muslim customer prefers ethical banking as a main feature of any financial institution. This awareness of ethical banking has been a decisive factor for many customers when choosing a financial institution. Before delving into Islamic ethics in finance, the authors explore factors of production in Islamic ethics and how they differ from conventional concepts. Secondly, most important in Islamic financial ethics is that the al-Qur'an strictly forbids charging interest or riba to businesses or individual customers. This chapter focuses on reviewing the development of Islamic banking vs. conventional banking.

INTRODUCTION

This chapter will discuss the Islamic ethics in finance as a moral principle which control or influence an individual's personal and professional behaviour. It is system of moral principles or rules of behaviour. It relates to beliefs and principles about what is right and wrong. Islamic finance over the last few decades is one of the fastest growing area in the world. Leading Muslim countries started to adopt the Islamic finance as a key and important financial transaction tool for trading.

DOI: 10.4018/978-1-7998-5295-7.ch008

In order to understand the Islamic point of view, it would be better to have a look at the systems of the distribution of wealth in capitalist and socialist economies. Capitalistic theory can be briefly stated as:

Wealth should be distributed only over those who have taken a part in producing it, and who are described in the terminology of economics as the factors of production.

According to the conventional concept, these are following four factors:

1. Capital: which has been defined as "the produced means of production" – a commodity which has already undergone one process of human production and is again being used as a means of another process of production.
2. Labour: any exertion on the part of man.
3. Land: has been defined as ''natural resources'' (those things which are being used as means of production without having previously undergone any process of human production).
4. Entrepreneur or Organisation: The fourth factor that brings together the other three factors utilise them and bear the risk of profit and loss in production.

Under the capitalist economy, the wealth produced by the cooperation of these four factors is distributed over these very four factors as follows:

a) One share is given to capital in the shape of interest
b) The second share to labour in terms of wages
c) The third share to land as rent
d) The fourth share is reserved for the entrepreneur as profit

On the other hand, in a socialist economy, capital and land instead of being private property are national or collective property. The question of interest or rent does not arise at all under this philosophy. In the socialist system, the entrepreneur too is not an individual but the state itself. So profit as well is out of the question here - at least in theory. Now there remains only one factor, namely labour. And labour alone is considered to have a right to wealth under the socialist system, which it gets in the shape of wages (Usmani, 2015).

Islamic vs. Conventional Factors of Production

Islamic System of Distribution of Wealth

The Islamic system of the distribution of wealth is different from both the Capitalist and Socialist economic system. From the Islamic point of view, there are two kinds of people who have a right to the wealth:

1. Primary Right to Wealth

The primary right denotes the right to wealth which is directly in consequence of participation in the process of production. In other words, primary right is for those factors of production that have contributed in the process of producing wealth.

2. Secondary Right to Wealth

The secondary right holders are those who have not directly contributed in the process of production, but it has been made obligation upon the producers to make them partners in their wealth e.g. beneficiaries of zakah, sadaqah al-fitr, etc.

Islamic Concept of Factors of Production

In Islam there are three factors of production in contrast to the conventional concept. This is the point of departure from ideology of exploitation to the principles of prosperity. In Islamic concept of factors of production money is not considered as standalone factor, it is treated almost in the same manner as raw material required for producing a commodity. Second, human efforts are not considered only as labour; rather all faculties of human efforts are recognised and rewarded as a factor of production according to the role under different arrangements.

1. Modifiable Components: Those factors of production which cannot be used in the process of production until and unless during the process of production they are either wholly consumed or completely altered e.g. liquid money or raw materials etc.
2. Fixed Elements: Those factors of production which maintain their original and external characteristics during the process of production and hence can be used again e.g. land, building, machinery etc.

3. Human Effort: Physical or intellectual human efforts in managing organisations, developing plans, bringing together all factors of production, marketing, customer service, manufacturing activities all come under this factor of production in Islamic concepts.

In Islamic economy wealth produced by the combination of all above mentioned three factors of productions would be distributed in following manner:

a. A share would go to modifiable components in the form of profit only (not interest) according to agreed terms
b. Second share would go to fixed elements in the form of rent
c. Third share would be given to human efforts in the form of wages

Purpose of Wealth Circulation in Islam

According to the injunctions of al-Qur'ān, there are following three purposes of circulation of wealth in Islam:

1. Establishing Free, Fair and Halal Economy
2. Channelising Wealth to Entitled
3. Eradicating Concentration of Wealth

Establishing Free, Fair and Halal Economy

The first purpose of wealth circulation is establishing free, fair and Halal economy in the world. Predictable, natural practicable economy which, without using any compulsion or force, allows every individual to function in a normal way according to his ability, his aptitude, his own choice and liking, so that his activities may be more fruitful, healthy and useful. This cannot be achieved without a healthy relationship between the employer and the employee, without proper utilisation of the natural force of supply and demand. That is why Islam recognises all these factors. A comprehensive indication of this principle is to be found in the following verse.

We have distributed their livelihood among them in worldly life and have raised some above others in the matter of social degrees, so that some of them may utilise the services of others in their work (al-Qur'ān 43:32)

The condition of proper utilisation has been assumed because it is possible to make an improper use of these forces as it has been in the case of capitalism. Islam has struck at the very root of such an improper use and has thus eradicated the unbridled exploitation of private property (Usmani, 2015).

Channelising Wealth to Entitled

The second purpose of wealth circulation is Islam is to enable everyone to get what is rightfully due to every person. But in Islam the concept and criteria of this right is somewhat different from what it is in other systems of economy. Under materialistic economic systems, there is only one way of acquiring the right to wealth and that is a direct participation in the process of production.

Those factors that have taken a direct part in producing wealth are supposed to be entitled to a share in wealth and none other. On the contrary, the basic principle of Islam in this respect is that wealth in principle is the property of Allah Himself and He alone can lay down the rules as to how it is to be used. So according to the Islamic point of view, not only those who have directly participated in the production of wealth but also those to whom Allah has made it obligatory upon others to help, are the legitimate sharers in wealth. Hence, the poor, the helpless, the needy, the paupers and the destitute - they too have a right to wealth. For Allah has made it obligatory on all those producers of wealth among whom wealth is in the first place distributed that they should pass on to them some part of their wealth. And the al-Qur'ān makes it quite explicit that in doing so they would not be obliging the poor and the needy in any way, but only discharging their obligation, for the poor and the needy are entitled to a share in wealth as a matter of right. Says the al-Qur'ān:

In their wealth there is a known right for those who ask for it and those who have need for it (al-Qur'ān 70:24-25)

In certain verses, this right has been defined as the right of Allah. For example:

And pay what is rightfully due to Him on the day of harvesting (al-Qur'ān 6:142)

The word "right" in these two verses makes it clear that participation in the process of production is not the only source of the right to wealth and that the needy and the poor have as good a right to wealth as its primary owners. Thus, Islam proposes to distribute wealth in such a manner that all those who have taken a part in production should receive the reward for their contribution to the production of wealth, and then all those too should receive their share that Allah has given a right to wealth (Usmani, 2015).

Eradicating Concentration of Wealth

The third purpose of wealth circulation, which Islam considers to be very important, is that wealth, instead of being concentrated in a few hands, should be allowed to circulate in the society as widely as possible, so that the distinction between the rich and the poor should be narrowed down as far as is natural and practicable. The attitude of Islam in this respect is that it has not permitted any individual or group to have a monopoly over the primary sources of wealth but has given every member of society an equal right to derive benefit from them. Mines, forests, unowned barren lands, hunting and fishing, wild grass, rivers, seas, spoils of war etc., all these are primary sources of wealth. With respect to them, every individual is entitled to make use of them according to his abilities and his labour, without anyone being allowed to have any kind of monopoly over them.

So that this wealth should not become confined only to the rich amongst you (al-Qur'ān 59:7)

Beyond this, wherever human intervention is needed to produce wealth and a man produces wealth by deploying his resources and labour, Islam gives due consideration to the resources and labour thus deployed and recognises right of property in the wealth produced. Everyone shall get his share according to the labour and resources invested by him.

We have distributed their livelihood among them in worldly life and have raised some above others in the matter of social degrees, so that some of them may utilise the services of others in their work (al-Qur'ān 43:32)

Despite this difference among social degrees or ranks certain injunctions have been laid down in order to keep this distinction within such limits as are necessary for the establishment of a practicable system of economy, so that wealth should not become concentrated in a few hands. Of these three purposes of wealth circulation, the first distinguishes Islamic economy from socialism, the third from capitalism, and the second from both at the same time (Usmani, 2015).

Islamic vs. Ethical Banking and Finance

Ethical Banking and Finance

Ethical banking and finance encompass any financial system that embraces environmentally and socially conscious practices, while the financial institutions still try to earn profits. The key to ethical banking and finance is deciding on the common set of principles and abiding accordingly. An ethical banking and finance are also known as a social, alternative, civic, or sustainable financial intermediation concerned with the social and environmental impacts of its financial interventions.

As the result, lower-income individuals have fewer opportunities to save and borrow money. This, in turn, limits their ability to improve their lives and their communities. Proponents of ethical banking argue that this traps low-income communities and developing countries in a cycle of poverty, since they do not have the means or the funding to improve their situation. The development of poor communities benefits the country and the world as a whole; since it increases national tax revenues and lowers the number of people who are dependent on government aid. But to achieve this, profit-based policies alone would not suffice.

Ethical banking and finance ensure:

- Community involvement: The financial institution takes an active interest in community welfare and takes steps to improve it. Among other things, this can include funding affordable housing projects, providing scholarships for students in local high schools, sponsoring community events and holding seminars to educate members of the community about their services.
- Sustainable practices: The bank tries to apply environmentally friendly practices whenever possible, as well as to support clients who practice those policies.
- Client screenings: The bank screens its clients in order to avoid doing business with individuals, organisations and corporate entities with a history of unethical and immoral practices. For example, it may avoid doing business with a company that has a history of using child labour.

- Consistent internal and external ethics: the bank practices what it preaches. Bank applies the same ethical standards to its internal processes as it does to its external operations. For example, if a bank is not going to do business with a company having unsafe and unhygienic working environment, it has to offer safe and hygienic work environment to its own employees.

It is important to remember that while financial institutions that practice ethical banking try to serve the disadvantaged; those are not the only services they provide. It is also important to remember that just because a bank is ethical does not mean it should not keep an eye on its bottom line. Good intentions and humanitarian efforts don't protect banks from financial weaknesses and economic downturns. Ethical banks need to make sure they remain profitable for sustainability of operations ("What is Ethical Banking", 2019).

Ethical banking is a quest to make "a market in money and not to make money in the market". Ethical banking as a system that works based on equity, responsibility, accountability and promotion of sustainable development. Integrity, responsibility and affinity are the three integral aspects of ethical banking. The growth of ethical banking is believed to have given a boost to Islamic banking. Many scholars are of the view that Islamic banking is riding on the idea of ethical banking. Ethical prerogatives and socio-economic development become salient determinants of the Islamic financing modes. Islamic financial institutions have a mandate that extends beyond simply serving their clientele by securing funds in the abovementioned kinds of portfolios. They become development institutions, and thereby play an important role in the economic and moral uplift of the Islamic society or community aligning it within the Shariah framework (Gilani, 2015).

Islamic Banking and Finance

Islamic banking and finance have a much wider canvas than ethical banking and finance. Islamic financial intermediations share fundamental values with socially responsible investing (SRI), environmental, social and governance (ESG) models and Ethical Finance. Besides, Islamic banking and finance offers even more vigilance to human and societal prosperity and avoiding investments in some fatal areas, details will be available in following discussion.

Islamic banking and finance are based on following four fundamental principles:

1. Rabbaniyyah
2. Akhlaqiyah
3. Insaniyyah
4. Wasatiyyah

The main goal of Islamic banking and finance is to provide opportunities of happiness and prosperity through appropriate economic activities to all people irrespective of religion including both Muslim and non-Muslim. These values reflect the uniqueness of the Islamic economic and financial system being different from conventional systems.

1. Rabbaniyyah

Rabbaniyyah means the economy is not based purely on material interests, but it is associated with divinity or *Ilahiyah*. Man-made economies consider property as private, a matter for its owner alone. On the other hand, Islam teaches us that the property is the property of Allah (SWT), which is created and provided for human use ("Morals", 2014).

2. Akhlaqiyah

Akhlaqiyah means there is no separation between economic activities and moral character. A Muslim is bound by faith and morals in every economic activity that he is in. Islam prohibits the elements of fraud, corruption, misconduct and breach of trust in economic activities because it conflicts with Islamic morals ("Morals", 2014).

3. Insaniyyah

Insaniyyah means economic activities are aimed for the betterment of human lives. Islamic economics is laid in line with human nature; it recognises the instinct for ownership, propensity to pursue wealth and love of material possession for the purpose of empowering the human being ("Morals", 2014).

4. Wasatiyyah

Wasatiyyah means balanced. In the Islamic ethics, it refers to the 'middle way' or 'moderation', a justly balanced way of life, avoiding extremes and experiencing things in moderation ("Morals", 2014).

And thus, we have made you a just community that you will be witnesses over the people and the Messenger will be a witness over you. And We did not make the qiblah which you used to face except that We might make evident who would follow the Messenger from who would turn back on his heels. And indeed, it is difficult except for those whom Allah has guided. And never would Allah have caused you to lose your faith. Indeed, Allah is, to the people, Kind and Merciful (al-Qur'ān 2:143)

The Prophet Muhammad (PBUH) said, "The religion (of Islam) is easy, and whoever makes the religion a rigour, it will overpower him. So, follow a middle course (in worship); if you can't do this, do something near to it and give glad tidings and seek help (of Allah) at morn and at dusk and some part of night". (Sahih al-Bukhari, 145)

Allah's Messenger (PBUH) said, "Do good deeds properly, sincerely and moderately and know that your deeds will not make you enter Paradise, and that the most beloved deed to Allah is the most regular and constant even if it were little" (Sahih al-Bukhari 6464).

Allah's Messenger (PBUH) said, "O `Abdullah! Have I not been formed that you fast all day and stand in prayer all night?" I said, "Yes, O Allah's Messenger ((PBUH))!" He said, "Do not do that! Observe the fast sometimes and also leave them (the fast) at other times; stand up for the prayer at night and also sleep at night. Your body has a right over you, your eyes have a right over you and your wife has a right over you" (Sahih al-Bukhari 5199)

Investment Ethics

Islamic banking system does not commit just blind investments in projects, but they also make sure that the investment they make positively contributes to the society, as providing funding to projects that would affect humanity is considered as Haram:

They ask you about intoxicants and gambling: say, 'In them there is a gross sin and some benefits for the people'. But their sinfulness far outweighs their benefit (al-Qur'ān 2:219)

Conventional banks do not have this principle, they go onto invest on pretty much any project that has a high return, so that they could earn their fair share of profit and satisfy their stake holders. Customers who prefer ethical baking do not wish their money to be invested in instruments that could harm anyone (Gilani, 2015).

Operational Ethics

The operations of Islamic banking and indicate the ethical factors behind it, we will use one method of operations, i.e. Mudarabah. Mudarabah is one of the alternatives for Riba as a form of return for the investment made by clients. The remuneration for the amount invested is Mudarabah profit and loss sharing. This is whereby the bank acts as the manager or also known as the Mudarib manages the funds invested by the investor also known as Rab-al-mal. The profit is then shared in accordance with the percentage agreed. Losses are absorbed by the financier of Tan-al-mal. all Islamic transactions are based on the Shariah, the Sunnah and the Quran, which restrict Islamic banks to invest their money in unlawful and Haram activities. Unlike equity-based financing, Mudharabah financing does not increase the firm's risk through increased financial leverage. This again shows us that excessive risk which is also considered as "mysir" is avoided in Mudharabah-based transactions (Gilani, 2015).

Watch List for Islamic Financial Institutions

Employees and Islamic financial institutions (IFIs) need to be vigilant all the time to remain away from indulging in any of the following aspect during any of the transaction or contract.

Riba

The word Riba means excess, increase or addition. According to Shariah it implies any excess compensation without due consideration except time value of money (Usmani, 2015). This definition of Riba is derived from al-Qur'ān.

There are two types of Riba

1. Riba an-Nasiyah
2. Riba al-Fadl

Riba an-Nasiyah

Riba an-Nasiyah is defined as excess which results from predetermined interest which lender receives over and above the principal amount (ras ul mall) in any loan transaction. Riba an-Nasiyah is the primary form of Riba. Due to its origin in dark ages before Islam, therefore Riba an-Nasiyah is also known as Riba al-Jahiliyyah. There is direct prohibition of Riba an-Nasiyah in al-Qur'ān, therefore it also called Riba al-Qur'ān.

O you who have believed, fear Allah and give up what remains [due to you] of interest, if you should be believers (al-Qur'ān, 2:278)

And if you do not, then be informed of a war [against you] from Allah and His Messenger. But if you repent, you may have your principal - [thus] you do no wrong, nor are you wronged (al-Qur'ān, 2:279)

And if someone is in hardship, then [let there be] postponement until [a time of] ease. But if you give [from your right as] charity, then it is better for you, if you only knew (al-Qur'ān, 2:280)

And fear a Day when you will be returned to Allah. Then every soul will be compensated for what it earned, and they will not be treated unjustly (al-Qur'ān, 2:281)

Islam has categorically made a clear distinction between the excess in capital resulting from sale and excess resulting from interest. Growth in capital due to business is permissible, while excess resulting from interest is prohibited, as ordained in following verse of al-Qur'ān:

Those who consume interest cannot stand [on the Day of Resurrection] except as one stands who is being beaten by Satan into insanity. That is because they say, "Trade is [just] like interest" But Allah has permitted trade and has forbidden interest. So, whoever has received an admonition from his Lord and desists may have what is past, and his affair rests with Allah. But whoever returns to [dealing in interest or usury] - those are the companions of the Fire; they will abide eternally therein (al-Qur'ān 2:275)

Riba al-Fadl

Riba al-Fadl means excess in exchange of specific homogeneous commodities encountered in their hand-to-hand purchase and sale.

That the Prophet (PBUH) said: "Gold for gold, kind for kind; silver for silver, kind for kind; dried-dates for dried-dates, kind for kind; wheat for wheat, kind for kind; salt for salt, kind for kind; and barley for barley, kind for kind. Whoever increases or seeks an increase, then he dealt with Riba. Sell gold for silver as you wish, hand to hand; and sell wheat for dried-dates as you wish, hand to hand; and sell barley for dried-dates as you wish, hand to hand". (Jami` at-Tirmidhi 1240)

Interest as a component has always been opposed on the basis that it is something that creates a gap in the society. The fact that borrowers borrow money in times of hardship is taken advantage of by charging a high interest. Interest acts as component which systematically transfers money from people who have less money to people who have more. It is seen as tool for exploiting the needy and benefiting the rich. This is a major hurdle for social inequity which is not present in Islamic banking (Gilani, 2015). This view is further supported by al-Qur'ān and goes on to say:

O you who believe! Devour not usury, doubling and quadrupling (the sum lent). Observe your duty to God, that ye may be successful (al-Qur'ān 3: 130)

The word Riba has been extracted from Raba, which literally means to increase, to grow, to rise, to add, to swell. Riba in the Shari'ah, technically refers to the "premium" that must be paid by the borrower to the lender along with the principal amount as a condition for the loan or for an extension in its maturity. In fiqh terminology, Riba means an increase in one of two homogeneous equivalents being exchanged without this increase being accompanied by a return. The rate of interest is what decides the wealth of an individual, thus creating an inequality in the society. The fact that people with high risk are charged high interest, and the returns are given to the lenders, this is complete injustice on the borrowers as the sole purpose of borrowing money is because they are in need, lenders take this as an advantage for themselves and earn more money out of it at the exchange of the borrowers. Also, the fact that they earn more money as a result of this makes them richer and make the borrower poorer which then goes on to create a wealth gap (Gilani, 2015).

Gharar

Uncertainty (Gharar) means "making predictability difficult", in other words, a high level of uncertainty is what results in hedging. The recently reported Netflix hedging deal resulted in a $200 million loss (Forbes.com, 2011, www.forbes.com). These types of massive losses are what Islamic institutions try to avoid by avoiding uncertainty. It is completely banned in contractual terms and that conditions are not allowed, unless that all parties involved are previously kept informed of the risks that will be associated, and also importantly, they must be understood by the parties. There is no systematic risk in Islamic banking and finance, because in conventional finance, the interest rate is what creates a large equity premium, and this is not present in Islamic banking as interest is considered as Haram in Islamic finance (Gilani, 2015).

The Prophet (PBUH) "forbade the type of sale which involves risk (or uncertainty) and a transaction determined by throwing stones" (Sunan Abi Dawud 3376)

Abu Huraira (Allah be pleased with him) reported that "Allah's Messenger (PBUH) forbade a transaction determined by throwing stones, and the type which involves some uncertainty" (Sahih Muslim 1513)

Maisir and Qimar

Maisir refer to games of chance, but Qimar is a kind or subset of Maisir. Maisir is defined as

wishing something valuable with ease and without paying an equivalent compensation for it or without working for it, or without undertaking any liability against it by way of a game of chance (Ayub, 2007).

Qimar means "receipt of money, benefit or usufruct at the cost of others, having entitlement to that money or benefit by resorting to chance" (Ayub, 2007).

They ask you about wine and gambling. Say, "In them is great sin and [yet, some] benefit for people. But their sin is greater than their benefit". And they ask you what they should spend. Say, "The excess [beyond needs]". Thus, Allah makes clear to you the verses [of revelation] that you might give thought (al-Qur'ān 2:219)

O you who have believed, indeed, intoxicants, gambling, [sacrificing on] stone alters [to other than Allah], and divining arrows are but defilement from the work of Satan, so avoid it that you may be successful (al-Qur'ān 5:90)

Satan only wants to cause between you animosity and hatred through intoxicants and gambling and to avert you from the remembrance of Allah and from prayer. So, will you not desist? (al-Qur'ān 5:91)

Khiyar

Khiyar refers to an option or right of the buyer and seller to rescind a contract of sale. There are five types of khiyar in a sales contract.

1. Khiyar-e-Shart (Optional Condition)
2. Khiyar-e-Roiyyat (Option of Inspecting Goods)
3. Khiyar-e-Aib (Option of Defect)
4. Khiyar-e-Wasf (Option of Quality)
5. Khiyar-e-Ghaban (Option of Price)

Dharar

Dharar refers to all sources of damage, detriment, harm, or loss inflicted by an individual on others or even on one's self. In the context of transactions/contracts, it is any such inflictions that arise from a transaction/contract between two parties or more. More specifically, dharar constitutes all factors that negatively affect another party's rights associated with the transaction/contract. Dharar is more intense and widespread than *izaa* (minor damage). Based on this principle, contracting parties can terminate a contract in which they have been inflicted with serious prejudices as a result of execution (Dharar, 2019).

And spend in the way of Allah and do not throw [yourselves] with your [own] hands into destruction [by refraining]. And do good; indeed, Allah loves the doers of good (al-Qur'ān 2:195) and do not keep them, intending harm, to transgress [against them]. And whoever does that has certainly wronged himself (al-Qur'ān 2:231)

It was narrated from Ibn 'Abbas that the Messenger of Allah (PBUH) said: "There should be neither harming nor reciprocating harm" (Sunan Ibn Majah 2341)

Code of Ethical Business Conduct

There are two notable global bodies to provide guidelines for code of ethical business conduct in Islamic finance:

1. Accounting and Auditing Organisation for Islamic Financial Institutions (AAOIFI)
2. Islamic Financial Services Board (IFSB)

Accounting and Auditing Organisation for Islamic Financial Institutions (AAOIFI, 2015) outlines following structure of code of ethics for Islamic finance professionals:

1. Integrity

Islam is a religion that highly values integrity and makes it govern all acts. Islam also values the capability to perform duties, which requires that the accountant and others who are in charge be competent and adequately qualified. This is confirmed in the Holy Qur'ān:

Verily, the best of men for you to hire is the strong, the trustworthy. (al-Qur'ān 28:26)

2. Sincerity

This means the IFI professional should seek to obey Allah in performing his work, and not to seek hypocrisy, fame flattery, boasting or ostentation. Being sincere entails that the professional does not subject himself to external influences and pressures but applies himself to his work as a religious commitment as well as a performance of his professional duty. Thus, his ordinary occupational and professional duty turns into a form of worship, because one of the established Shari'a fundamentals is that good intention turns a habit into worship. Hence, the professional becomes worthy of reward from Almighty Allah, apart from the material gain, and the usual praise he receives for his efforts, without making such gains and praise his sole objective.

3. Righteousness and Perfection

IFI professionals should strive to attain the degree of righteousness and perfection in their work by performing their duties assigned to them in the best manner possible. This cannot be realised except through academic qualifications, practical experience and acquisition of religious knowledge, which is a religious duty in the scope of their work. Allah, the Almighty, says:

{"Verily, Allah enjoins A-Adl (i.e. justice and worshiping none but Allah Alone – Islamic Monotheism) and Al-Ihsan [i.e. to be patient in performing your duties to Allah, totally for Allah's sake and in accordance with the Sunnah (legal ways) of the Prophet in a perfect manner]..."}, (al-Qur'ān 16:90) and:{"... and do good Truly, Allah loves Al-Muhsinun (the good-doers)"} (al-Qur'ān2:195). The Prophet (peace and blessing be upon him) says: "Allah likes when someone performs his work to do it perfectly, (al-Bayhaqi) and Allah has prescribed righteousness in everything" (Sahih Muslim, 6:72).

4. Legitimacy

The IFI professional should be fair, impartial and unbiased, free from conflicts of interest and independent in fact as well as in appearance. Objectivity also entails that IFI professional should not subordinate his professional judgment and duties to suggestions of others.

5. Competence and Diligence

The IFI professional should be competent and well equipped for carrying out tasks required in the course of performing professional duties or services so that they can perform such tasks diligently and properly, saving no effort in order to discharge their responsibilities towards Almighty Allah and towards their society, profession, superiors, clients, and himself.

6. Professional Conduct and Technical Standards

While performing their duties, the IFI professionals should observe the rules of professional conduct and comply with the accounting and auditing standards for Islamic financial institutions.

According to Islamic Financial Services Board (IFSB) Guiding Principles on Conduct of Business for Institutions offering Islamic Financial Services (IFSB, 2009), "The sound functioning of a financial system depends, *inter alia*, on the users of the system having confidence in the quality of the conduct of business by the participants offering financial products and services, and that there are adequate systems of control over the conduct of business. A framework of the principles and rules that govern effectively the conduct of business of Islamic financial services industry (IFSI) participants, whether mandatory or voluntary, can play a significant role in supporting the growth of the IFSI. Such a framework would not only promote a climate of confidence and a supportive environment that upholds transparency and fair dealing comparable to the conventional frameworks, but would also strengthen the relevant moral, social and religious dimensions in conducting business".

The code of ethical business conduct of Islamic financial institutions is derived from following principles of the Shariah as set out in al-Qur'ān and the Sunnah of the Prophet.

Successful indeed are the believers ... those who are faithfully true to their Amanât (all the duties which Allah has ordained, honesty, moral responsibility and trusts) and to their covenants (al-Qur'ān 23:8)

Woe to those that deal in fraud, – those who, when they have to receive by measure from men, exact full measure, but when they have to give by measure or weight to men, give less than due. Do they not think that they will be called to account – on Mighty Day when (all) mankind will stand before the Lord of the Worlds (al-Qur'ān 83:1–6)

Prophet Muhammad's (PBUH) teachings on business and economic issues in general are many and they cover almost every aspect of business and economics. The Prophet emphasised that honesty and truthfulness will raise the level of rewards that will be given to the merchant in the hereafter. He said:

God shows mercy to a person who is kindly when he sells, when he buys and when he makes a claim" (Shahih Bukhari, 1934)

Fairness in Islam means placing something in its rightful place. Three very important aspects of fairness in this context are: (1) placing someone in a post or function appropriate to his capabilities; (2) meting out sentence or making a decision appropriate to a situation or the person about to receive it; and (3) placing wealth or property with those who rightly deserve them.

Eat not up each other's property by unfair and dishonest means (al-Qur'ān 4:29)

According to IFSB (2009), Principle 1(12), "The fundamental requirement with regard to truthfulness, honesty and fairness is that an IIFS should not, either deliberately or through negligence, issue information that is potentially misleading to stakeholders or the market, nor should it manipulate prices by using any of the means whereby this may be done. Such means include making a false market, issuing misleading price-sensitive information and price-fixing in conjunction with other market players. In addition, an IIFS should not, either deliberately or through negligence, issue information that is misleading to stakeholders or the market regarding the Shariah compliance of its products or services, or of Sukuk issuances with which it is involved. Nor should an IIFS mislead clients or the market through the withholding of material information".

IFSB (2009) in its Principle 1(13) states, "A further key requirement implied by this principle is the existence of appropriate procedures whereby whistle-blowers are treated honestly and fairly, with no coverups or victimisation. With regard to fairness, IIFS should follow best practice in establishing procedures for handling complaints from clients".

According to the Shariah Governance Framework (SGF, 2018) issued by the State Bank of Pakistan (SBP) it is imperative for Islamic financial institutions (IFIs) to "comply with the principles of Shari'ah as enshrined in the Holy Quran and the Sunnah of the Prophet (peace be upon him) is the essence and raison d'être of Islamic banking industry.

A sound and effective Shari'ah compliance framework is thus critically important to give confidence to the general public about Shari'ah conformity of Islamic banking institutions' (IBIs') products and services. State Bank of Pakistan (SBP) endeavours to ensure that the operations of IBIs remain in conformity with the rules and principles of Shari'ah". SGF 2018 is attached as an annexure for the reference and convenience of relevant stakeholders.

Ethical Spirit of Islamic Finance

Despite significant theoretical and applied developments in the field of Islamic finance still there is a considerable debate among Muslim scholars about permissibility of contemporary operations of Islamic financial institutions. This confusion has roots in a strong financial infrastructure for social wellbeing of the society that exist in Islamic teachings. Scholars usually failed to draw a line between measures taken by Islamic teachings for social wellbeing through mandatory and voluntary financial interventions and business operations of financial institutions.

In Islamic ethics both mandatory and voluntary financial instruments for social wellbeing have altogether different aspirations based on compassion and responsibility. Islamic ethics consider people with financial resources as responsible citizens to remain connected with ground realities of the society and continuously remain engaged to contribute to resolve difficulties of those who are relatively less privileged. Focus of Islamic ethics remained on encouraging people to spend (infāq). We can hardly find motivation for wealth accumulation in Islamic teachings because of human instinct to find ways to multiply the wealth. However, expansion in wealth through business activities are significantly encouraged in Islamic ethics to ensure prosperity of businessmen and the society, because business activities bring opportunities for several segments of society to earn their livelihoods.

It is, in fact, the prosperity that enables an individual to extend both mandatory contributions such as zakat and voluntary sadaqat. A school of thought overwhelmed with strong Islamic social finance instruments usually undermines business potential of Islamic financial institutions which is a disservice to both the Islam and the humanity. Business model of Islamic financial institutions is built on fundamental Islamic financial ethics which will be discussed later in this section. However, pressurising Islamic financial institutions in the business market to adapt to the social finance structure given in Islamic teachings will probably not contribute much to the existing parallel financial structure of zakat, sadaqat and waqf in Islamic society and effectively contributing to the welfare of masses for centuries now.

One of the important reasons that the social fabric in Islamic societies has maintained its strength over a millennium is the strong footing of these instruments of social finance among followers of Islam. Islamic ethics motivate people to do 'good' to almost every segment of society irrespective colour or creed.

Worship Allah and associate nothing with Him, and to parents do good, and to relatives, orphans, the needy, the near neighbor, the neighbor farther away, the companion at your side, the traveler, and those whom your right hands possess. Indeed, Allah does not like those who are self-deluding and boastful (al-Qur'ān 4:36)

Who are stingy and enjoin upon [other] people stinginess and conceal what Allah has given them of His bounty - and We have prepared for the disbelievers a humiliating punishment - (al-Qur'ān 4:36)

And establish prayer and give zakah, and whatever good you put forward for yourselves - you will find it with Allah. Indeed, Allah of what you do, is Seeing (al-Qur'ān 2:110)

These instructions are providing relief to communities for centuries in Muslim majority societies. However, at the same time, now these teachings are transcending into the business operations of Islamic financial institutions and expecting the same kind of role from these organizations to serve as institutions of social service due to their affluence, which is probably not the right expectation. Islamic financial institutions can certainly contribute in philanthropic activities, some are contributing significantly, out of their specific social responsibility allocations; but we must view business organisations as entities providing opportunities of earning through permissible (halal) ventures.

Business operations of Islamic financial institutions are based on compact ethical guidelines from scope to the structure of products and services. Islamic financial institutions cannot join hands with businesses such as manufacturing and distribution of alcohol, slaughtering and distribution of swine, activities which lack environmentally responsible behaviour, prostitution etc.

Islamic financial institutions (IFIs) take dual responsibility of the success of both their shareholders and clients. Unilateral view of diligence to protect the interest of the financial institution as pursued conventionally has limited scope for IFIs due to multi levelled monitoring of conventional audits and Shari'ah compliance. Ethics has become increasingly important in the financial services sector because of the emerging focus of the business activities in general and financial services in particular on value creation for all stakeholders of the organization including shareholders, consumers, environment and the society (Musa, 2015).

Careful analysis of products and services of Islamic financial institutions suggests an array of ethical considerations which distinguish Islamic finance from conventional institutions of financial services.

1. Avoiding Exploitation

It is generally agreed that humanity experience financial crises repeatedly due to failed morality which manifests in the form of exploitation of financial resources through ever exploiting usury embedded in the operations of conventional financial institutions. Islamic financial products remain away from usury to avoid exploitation. According to Adebayo and Hassan (2013) the wisdom of Qur'ānic prohibition of usury can be summed up in following points:

a. Usury amounts to appropriation of another person's property without giving him anything in exchange
b. Usury prevents people from working to earn money, as it reduces the value of work. The rich will have no interest in investing his money on a business or risking his money in trade or industry. This therefore paralyses commerce, trade and industry
c. Usury discourages benevolent acts which is important to promote brotherhood. It also weakens the feeling of goodwill and friendliness toward the lender by the borrower.
d. Usury allows exploitation of the poor by the rich and this makes the lender wealthier and the borrower poorer.

2. Avoiding Excessive Uncertainties

Spirit of Islamic finance is to avoid excessive uncertainties; certain level of uncertainty is always present in business transactions, however, if the existence or description of risks associated with the transaction is not available due to the lack of information or knowledge of the ultimate outcome of the transaction then it is prohibited in Islamic finance. In Islamic finance the term Gharar is used to describe uncertainties in financial transactions. Hanafi scholars have defined Gharar as "something which in its consequence is undetermined."

While Shafi'i scholars have described it as "something which in its manner and its consequence is hidden".

3. Avoiding Irrational Speculations

Islam holds a very clear position that hope and luck must be associated with tireless work before a decision is exercised.

And when you have decided, then rely upon Allah. Indeed, Allah loves those who rely [upon Him] (al-Qur'ān 3:159)

According to Salamon et al. (2015, p. 374):

This verse clearly states that God not only commands humans to be immersed in al-tawakkul but that He also loves those who surrender to Him after the work of surrender is performed tirelessly. Hope, therefore, is certainly present but it is directed towards God with Whom all luck (benefit) originates. Hence, Islam does not accord with the idea of al-tawakkul minus the onerous detail of real work as understood by some Muslims. The implication is that Islam rejects 'blind tawakkul'. Those who depend purely on hope and luck without responsibly undertaking hard work are considered by God as people without faith. This is because a man's surrender without doing work is the same as abandoning hope in God.

O my sons, go and find out about Joseph and his brother and despair not of relief from Allah. Indeed, no one despairs of relief from Allah except the disbelieving people (al-Qur'ān 12:87)

Speculation is not to be integrated with elements denounced by Islam such as blind hope, pure luck and betting, or the taking advantage of those who remain ignorant of realistic economic fundamentals. Such forbidden matters are of grave concern as their implementation undermines and, thus also, jeopardizes participation in the permitted activities of rational speculation (Salamon et al. 2015, p. 377).

4. Recognising Expertise

Products and services of Islamic financial institutions give due consideration to the expertise of the people and institutions, which facilitates people &/

institutions to utilise financial resources for business activities as partners e.g. in mudarbah contract an investor (rabb ul maal) joins a business venture may be as silent partner while a managing partner extends expertise and both share profits &/ fee for expertise according to mutual agreement.

5. Rewarding Worth

Worth of an individual or an organisation has always been recognised in the history of Islamic ethics. Hazrat Usman (RA) bought a well named "Bi'r-i-Rumah" from a Jew paying twenty thousand dirhams and donated for free use of Muslims. That was the first trust ever made in the history of Islam. The Holy Prophet (PBUH) gave him the glad words of paradise for this act of generosity (Ghani, 2017). The worth of Hazrat 'Abdur Rehman Ibn 'Awf, one of the Ten with Glad Tidings of Paradise (*al-'Asharaa al-Mubasharûn bi-l-Jannah*), was approximately more than 525 billion USD in cash other than thousands of livestock and vast area of land. These examples suggest that there is no restriction in Islamic ethics on developing worth through permissible (halal) means.

Products and services of Islamic financial institutions such as mudarbah also recognizes and rewards the worth of investment account holders depending either as silent partner or active participant in the business operations.

6. Maintaining Equity

One of the important objectives of Islamic ethics is to ensure equitable distribution of resources.

And what Allah restored to His Messenger from the people of the towns - it is for Allah and for the Messenger and for [his] near relatives and orphans and the [stranded] traveler - so that it will not be a perpetual distribution among the rich from among you. And whatever the Messenger has given you - take; and what he has forbidden you - refrain from. And fear Allah; indeed, Allah is severe in penalty (al-Qur'ān 59:7)

Product portfolio of Islamic financial institutions such as murabaha, mudarbah, musharkah and so on also suggest equitable share of investment account holders, fund managers and business enterprises.

7. Promoting Partnerships

Promoting partnerships through musharkah financing is a unique strength of Islamic financial institutions and tries to eliminate drawbacks of conventional financial system such as exploitation and speculation.

Musharkah gives strength to the borrower and lender both to join hands and put their efforts according to their expertise to ensure maximum returns through invested funds. The spirit of musharkah is collaboration and cooperation instead of seeking returns through toils of other parties.

8. Safeguarding Vulnerabilities

Products such as Salam are examples of safeguarding, supporting and facilitating those who are subject to vulnerabilities due to natural dynamics. It has always been difficult for farmers to avoid exploitations and vulnerabilities. According to Ehsan and Shahzad (2015, p. 74):

The true spirit of Salam financing is to provide maximum possible financial benefit to the farmer. Salam is an exception of sale contract and it is allowed by the Prophet (PBUH) specifically for farmers. The main objective of allowing this exception to the sale contract by Prophet (PBUH) was to provide an alternative to interest-based loans, which farmers used to take for growing their crops

9. Complementing Capacities

Islamic financial institutions try to find opportunities to complement capacities of the fancier and the customer as in the diminishing musharkah contract, where financier extends resources while customer pays rent on financier's share in the property and continues to purchase the share of financier in instalments. Progression of contract results in increased share of customer in the property with reduced payments of rent overtime according to the reference rate till the predetermined termination time of the agreement. In case if property is destroyed the customers cannot be compelled to continue paying rent. This reflects ethical spirit of Islamic finance to complement capacities of both the financier and the customer as partners.

10. Promoting Togetherness

Islamic finance promotes a sense of togetherness through takaful in communities where members of a community contribute to support each other in case of loss or calamity. According to Khan et al. (2018, p. 219):

Takaful is a scheme based on brotherhood, solidarity and mutual assistance which provides mutual financial aid and assistance to the participants in case of need whereby the participants mutually agree to contribute for the purpose

CONCLUSION

This chapter explored the Islamic ethics in finance as a moral principle which control or influence an individual's personal and professional behaviour. The Islamic ethics in finance support the economic monetary system that is designed to operate according to Quran and Sunna of Prophet Muhammad (PBUH). The Islamic Finance is comparable system to conventional banking that sets up capital markets, banks, investment and insurance companies. It is essential for Islamic banks and financial institutions to follow Shari'ah compliant financial system. Islam ethics in finance has categorically made a clear distinction between the excess in capital resulting from sale and excess resulting from interest.

Mudarabah is one of the alternatives for riba as a form of return for the investment made by clients. The remuneration for the amount invested is Mudarabah profit and loss sharing. This is whereby the bank acts as the manager or also known as the Mudarib manages the funds invested by the investor also known as Rab-al-mal. This system helps Muslim investors to access to capital that is according to their individual investors personal beliefs.

Ethical Islamic banking is a quest to make "a market in money and not to make money in the market". Ethical Islamic banking as a system that works based on equity, responsibility, accountability and promotion of sustainable development. Integrity, responsibility and affinity are the three integral aspects of ethical banking. The growth of ethical banking is believed to have given a boost to Islamic banking. The code of ethical business conduct of Islamic financial institutions is derived from the principles of the Shariah as set out in al-Qur'ān and the Sunnah of the Prophet Muhammad (PBUH).

Discussion Questions

1. Critically evaluate and conduct the comparative analysis of the impact of financial crisis on Islamic Banks?
2. Discuss a framework of the principles and rules that govern effectively the conduct of business of Islamic financial services industry (IFSI)?
3. Evaluate and discuss the Islamic ethics in finance as a moral principle which control or influence an individual's personal and professional behaviour?
4. Investigate ethical banking has been a major decisive factor for many customers when choosing a financial institution?

REFERENCES

AAOIFI. (2015). Accounting, Auditing and Governance Standards. Accounting and Auditing Organisation for Islamic Financial Institutions, Manama, Bahrain.

Adebayo, R. I., & Hassan, M. K. (2013). Ethical Principles of Islamic Financial Institutions. *Journal of Economic Cooperation and Development*, *34*(1), 63–90.

Ayub, M. (2007). *Understanding Islamic Finance*. Wiley.

Dharar. (2019). Retrieved on June 23, 2019 from: https://www.investment-and-finance.net/islamic-finance/d/dharar.html

Ehsan, A., & Shahzad, M. A. (2015). Bay Salam: A Proposed Model for Shari'ah Compliant Agriculture Financing. *Business and Economic Review*, *1*(7), 67–80. doi:10.22547/BER/7.1.4

Ghani. (2017). *Life History of Hazrat Usman Ghani (R.A)*. Retrieved on March 31, 2020 from: http://quranreading.com/blog/life-history-of-hazrat-usman-ghani-r-a/

Gilani, H. (2015). Exploring the ethical aspects of Islamic banking. *International Journal of Islamic and Middle Eastern Finance and Management*, *8*(1), 85–98. doi:10.1108/IMEFM-09-2012-0087

IFSB. (2009). *Guiding Principles on Conduct of Business for Institutions Offering Islamic Financial Services*. Islamic Financial Services Board.

Khan, M. J., Anwar, J., Zubair, M., Ammad, H., Akhter, W., & Abbasi, A. S. (2018). *A Textbook of Islamic Finance*. COMSATS Institute of Information Technology Lahore.

Morals. (2014). *Morals, Ethics in Islamic Finance*. Retrieved on June 21, 2019 from: https://www.nst.com.my/news/2015/09/morals-ethics-islamic-finance

Musa, M. A. (2015). Islamic business ethics and finance: An exploratory study of Islamic banks in Malaysia. In *Ethics, Governance and Regulation in Islamic Finance*. Bloomsbury Qatar Foundation.

Salamon, H. B., Ebrahimi, M., & Yusoff, K. (2015). Speculation: The Islamic Perspective; A Study on Al-Maisir (Gambling). *Mediterranean Journal of Social Sciences*, *6*(1), 371–378. doi:10.5901/mjss.2015.v6n1s1p371

Usmani, M. I. A. (2015). *Islamic Finance Revised & Updated Edition of Meezan Bank's Guide to Islamic Banking*. Maktab Ma'ariful Quran.

What is Ethical Banking. (2019). Retrieved on June 22, 2019 from https://www.finweb.com/banking-credit/what-is-ethical-banking.html

Chapter 9 Islamic Ethics and Corporate Social Responsibility

ABSTRACT

The core principles of Islamic corporate social responsibility (CSR) are derived from al-Qur'ān and Sunnah, while the major foundations of Islamic CSR principles are unity, viceregency and trusteeship, justice and equilibrium, and rights and responsibilities. Man is a vicegerent (khalifah) or representative of Allah on Earth and trustee of resources provided by Allah (SWT). As a khalifah or leader in organisation, they have greater responsibility to utilise all these given things and facilities by Allah to the best of their abilities to create maximum added value to the organisation itself and to the whole community. The purpose of this chapter is to explore how Islamic ethics and corporate social responsibility (CSR) are two compatible concepts.

INTRODUCTION

Corporate social responsibility (CSR) is a concept that has attracted worldwide attention and acquired a new resonance in the global economy. Heightened interest in CSR in recent years has stemmed from the advent of globalisation and international trade, which have reflected in increased business complexity and new demands for enhanced transparency and corporate citisenship. Governments have traditionally assumed sole responsibility for the improvement of the living conditions of the population, society's needs have exceeded the capabilities of governments to fulfil them. In this context,

DOI: 10.4018/978-1-7998-5295-7.ch009

the spotlight is increasingly turning to focus on the role of business in society and progressive companies are seeking to differentiate themselves through engagement in CSR (Elasrag, 2015).

This chapter further discuss that corporate social responsibility (CSR) is an idea that has been constantly evolving as business firms are continually more aware of the community around them. CSR encompasses a business firm's obligation to society beyond simply maximising its profits. The business organisations involving charitable giving and reflecting the highly competitive environment of the 1990s has been termed ''strategic charity''. It involves corporate giving which serves dual purposes: contributing funds to charitable causes while simultaneously benefiting the firm's financial bottom line and enhancing business political legitimacy.

Dimensions of Corporate Social Responsibility

Several terms and definitions are used, including, corporate responsibility, corporate accountability, corporate ethics, corporate citizenship, sustainability, stewardship, triple bottom line and responsible business. CSR could be defined as the voluntary integration of environmental, social and human rights considerations into business operations, over and above legal requirements, contractual obligations and spirit of business i.e. growth and prosperity (Elasrag, 2015).

According to Dahlsrud (2008) despite numerous efforts to bring about a clear and unbiased definition of CSR, there is still some confusion as to how CSR should be defined. He developed following five dimensions of CSR through content analysis of 37 definitions.

1. The Environmental Dimension
    a. The natural environment
        i. 'a cleaner environment'
        ii. 'environmental stewardship'
        iii. 'environmental concerns in business operations'
2. The Social Dimension
    a. The relationship between business and society
        i. 'contribute to a better society'
        ii. 'integrate social concerns in their business operations'
        iii. 'consider the full scope of their impact on communities'

3. The Economic Dimension
    a. Socio-economic or financial aspects, including describing CSR in terms of a business operation
        i. 'contribute to economic development'
        ii. 'preserving the profitability'
        iii. 'business operations'
4. The Stakeholder Dimension
    a. Stakeholders or stakeholder groups
        i. 'interaction with their stakeholders'
        ii. 'how organisations interact with their employees, suppliers, customers and communities'
        iii. 'treating the stakeholders of the firm'
5. The Voluntariness Dimension
    a. Actions not prescribed by law
        i. 'based on ethical values'
        ii. 'beyond legal obligations'
        iii. 'voluntary'

Religiosity and Corporate Social Responsibility

A specific body of CSR literature has examined the link between religiosity and CSR, suggesting that religiosity influences individual preferences, managerial attitudes and decision making. Studies also indicated that individuals with a religious orientation are likely to have different attitudes toward CSR than those without such an orientation. Moreover, religious individuals are likely to hold a broader conception of the responsibilities of corporations than nonreligious individuals (Khurshid, *et. al.*, 2014).

Religiosity is among the important informal institutional, corporate governance mechanisms that affect a firm's adoption and implementation of CSR practices. Religiosity is more likely to influence attitudes and to increase CSR practices and disclosure thus resulting in increased stakeholder satisfaction (Zaman, *et. al.*, 2018). Literature reveals that religion affects corporate behaviours in following four broader ways:

1. The firms operating in a religiously dominated region may represent a handful of religiously motivated employees at various organisational levels. Thus, influencing management behaviour, corporate culture and preferences about investments and CSR initiatives.

2. Religiously motivated employees are more likely to be whistle blowers, resulting in more cautious corporate behaviour by organisations.
3. An organisation with religiously dominated workforce can influence behaviour of managerial positions, although not being active religious participants, leading to same collective norms.
4. Highly religious workforce has greater concerns regarding the ethical value of CSR and a weaker orientation toward the economic value of CSR thus undermining economic dimension of Carroll's model.

Islamic vs. Contemporary Concepts of Corporate Social Responsibility

Contemporary notions of CSR irrespective of their approach lack genuine sincerity and stem from profit motives. Friedman's concept of 'one and only one social responsibility of business is to earn profit' carries weight that if a business is unable to sustain then what to expect of other responsibilities. Social contract, instrumental approach, legitimacy concerns and considerations of stakeholders are all good ideas to direct business activities towards collective wellbeing. However, contemporary approaches failed to connect to the core of social responsibility i.e. empathy, care and support.

Islamic concept of socially responsible activities is based on seeking pleasure and protection of Allah (SWT) in this life and in the life hereafter.

But among them is he who says, "Our Lord, give us in this world [that which is] good and in the Hereafter [that which is] good and protect us from the punishment of the Fire" (al-Qur'ān 2:201)

Seeking specific monetary, economic or strategic benefits from socially responsible activities is against the spirit of Islamic ethics. Multifold financial and spiritual payback of socially responsible activities is considered a natural outcome for both lives.

Those who spend their wealth in the way of Allah and then do not follow up what they have spent with reminders [of it] or [other] injury will have their reward with their Lord, and there will be no fear concerning them, nor will they grieve (al-Qur'ān 2:262)

Technically CSR is voluntary initiative in contemporary concepts; however, in Islam charity for the welfare of society is obligatory:

Zakah expenditures are only for the poor and for the needy and for those employed to collect [zakah] and for bringing hearts together [for Islam] and for freeing captives [or slaves] and for those in debt and for the cause of Allah and for the [stranded] traveller - an obligation [imposed] by Allah . And Allah is Knowing and Wise (al-Qur'ān 9:60)

Islamic Ethics and Corporate Social Responsibility

The goal of an Islamic social system is based on falah (human well-being) and hayat-e-tayyibah (good life), both of which stress brotherhood and socio-economic justice, as well as a balance between the material and spiritual requirements of all human being that is necessary to preserve and enrich faith, life, intellect, posterity and wealth. The concept of social responsibility and justice in Islam in the light of the holy Qur'ān and Hadith suggests that there seems to be congruence between the ideals of social responsibility & justice and business transactions in Islam that has a resonance with prevailing notions of corporate social responsibility (CSR). In Islam the relationship between commercial activity and civil society is taken as natural and the rules of practice are embedded in the Islamic precepts (Elasrag, 2015).

Western theorists have failed to provide a single ethical justification in this regard whereas; Islam provides a holistic view, derived from the divine commandments of the holy Qur'ān and sayings of Allah's Apostle (peace be upon him). The divine revelations provide strong moral and ethical principles that are more eternal, absolute and enduring. Islam encouraged Muslims to perform socially responsible activities (Mir, et. al., n.d.).

While drawing linkages of CSR with Islamic principles, it is revealed that its theoretical foundations are much similar to the Islamic and Shariah doctrines. Just like work ethics (khulq) in Islam is considered as a virtue and determines a man's interaction with other individuals and the society, similarly, CSR is an obligation that an organisation must fulfil in order to determine its relationship with the individual and the socio-economic environment (Ilyas, 2018).

Islam provides a complete code of life; it directs every phase of human life, including spirituality, business and social justice. The concept of Tazkia, or growth and purification, is the idea of active contribution in the material world. This concept entails that Muslims are required to participate in worldly activities with the provision that any material development and growth should also guarantee social justice and spiritual improvement. One of the key features of the Islamic ethical system is that it provides no separation between an individual's public and private lives (in the eyes of God). Islamic ethical system does not distinguish between public and private lives. Therefore, Islam influences the decision-making of its followers in every facet of their lives. In Islamic teaching, there is a great emphasis on trusteeship (amanah); business is considered a sacred trust with managers. Therefore, managers are expected to act in the best interests of owners and not to indulge in any activity that could harm owners. However, this expectation does not mean that owners and managers can use any means in pursuit of profit maximisation. Although the right to personal property and profit is not negated in Islam, the religion does not allow these objectives to be achieved at the expense of other stakeholders (Khurshid, *et. al.*, 2014).

Islamic Global Economy (IGE)

The Islamic world is currently experiencing a time of reinvigoration with respect to population growth with almost 1.3 billion Muslims worldwide, which comprises approximately one fifth of the collective population of the planet and socioeconomic development. Some of this progress can be attributed to the success of national and international development programs, as well as the shift to responsive administrative or governmental structures. Muslim majority countries (MMCs) such as Pakistan, Saudi Arabia, Turkey, Malaysia, and Indonesia, to name a few, have been ushered into the global economic order through their ascension to supranational multilateral organisations like the World Trade Organisation (WTO), G20, and Organisation of Petroleum Exporting Countries (OPEC), as well as regional free trade blocs like the Gulf Cooperation Council (GCC), the Association of Southeast Asian Nations (ASEAN), South Asian Association of Regional Cooperation (SAARC) and Shanghai Cooperation Organisation (SCO). As a result of these economic and social gains, world is beginning to witness an emergence of industries which cater to the needs of this large ever-growing global demographic. The IGE, based on Islamic values such as social justice, reciprocity and the spiritual, moral, intellectual, social, and material well-being of individuals and society at large, as of 2013 was valued at US$2 trillion, and is forecasted to grow to reach US$3.7 trillion by 2019. In addition, the Islamic finance and insurance industry is estimated to cross US$3 trillion by 2019. However, less known industries within the IGE, namely, Islamic fashion/modest clothing, halal food, halal pharmaceuticals, halal cosmetics, as well as Islamic values-influenced tourism, media, and recreation, also contribute substantially to improved living standards in MMCs and are poised for growth. These achievements demonstrate that some MMCs are remerging as major contributors to the global economy. Hence, it is important for scholars, practitioners, and public officials to understand the Islamic stance and underpinnings on CSR for better interaction with relevant stakeholders (Murphy and Smolarski, 2017).

Islamic Ethics and Corporate Social Responsibility Principles

Concern for others and the environment where one lives is deeply inscribed in the teachings of Islam. Human being is considered a social being in Islam who cannot ignore his role and responsibility to the society and fellow beings. Islam discourages people to isolate even for the purpose of worship. Dusuki (n.d) cited that Prophet Muhammad (peace be upon him) once said as narrated by Abu Hurayrah (RA) who said: One of the Prophet's Companions passed a ravine where a freshwater spring ran. He liked the ravine and said,

How I would like to isolate myself from other people to worship Allah! I will not do so before asking permission from the Messenger of Allah (peace be upon him)". The man told the Prophet of his wish, and the Prophet said, "Do not do it. Your striving for the path of Allah is better than Praying in your house for seventy years. (Narrated by Tirmidzi and al-Hākim).

Therefore, in Islamic ethics it is unconceivable that organisations remain oblivious of their CSR responsibilities. Following key principles can provide required impetus to CSR commitments of organisations and their employees to discharge their obligatory and voluntary responsibilities as depicted in figure 1.

Taqwa

Taqwa facilitates people in continuously monitoring their behaviour and understanding their responsibilities.

And fear a Day when you will be returned to Allah. Then every soul will be compensated for what it earned, and they will not be treated unjustly (al-Qur'ān 2:281)

O you who have believed, fear Allah. And let every soul look to what it has put forth for tomorrow - and fear Allah. Indeed, Allah is Acquainted with what you do (al-Qur'ān 59:18)

As for he who gives and fears Allah (al-Qur'ān 92:5)

And believes in the best [reward] (al-Qur'ān 92:6)

We will ease him toward ease (al-Qur'ān 92:7)

Morality

O you who have believed, fear Allah and be with those who are true (al-Qur'ān 9:119)

O you who have believed, fear Allah and speak words of appropriate justice (al-Qur'ān 33:70)

O you who have believed, be persistently standing firm for Allah, witnesses in justice, and do not let the hatred of a people prevent you from being just. Be just; that is nearer to righteousness. And fear Allah; indeed, Allah is Acquainted with what you do (al-Qur'ān 5:8)

Balancedness

And [they are] those who, when they spend, do so not excessively or sparingly but are ever, between that, [justly] moderate (al-Qur'ān 25:67)

Say, "Not equal are the evil and the good, although the abundance of evil might impress you" So fear Allah, O you of understanding, that you may be successful (al-Qur'ān 5:100)

Islamic Corporate Social Responsibility Model

Islamic CSR model contains following dimensions as:

1. Benevolence
2. Economic Dimensions
3. Legal Dimensions

Figure 1. Islamic Ethics and CSR Principles

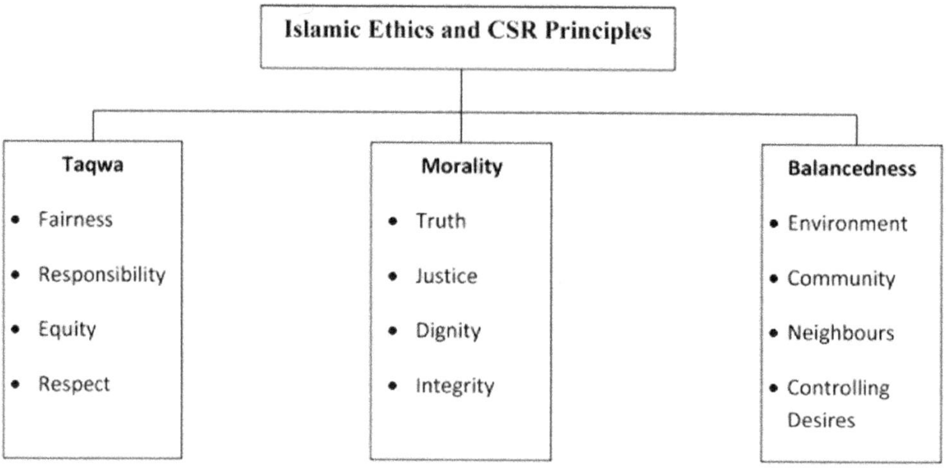

4. Ethical Dimensions
5. Philanthropic Dimensions
6. Environmental Dimensions
7. Fard al-Ayn and Fard al-Kifayah
8. Societal Dimensions

Benevolence

Benevolence is one of the core values of Islamic ethics contributing towards social responsibilities as depicted in Figure 2. Benevolence means compassion without obligation to seek pleasure of Allah (SWT) as mentioned in al-Qur'ān:

O you who have believed, do not invalidate your charities with reminders or injury as does one who spends his wealth [only] to be seen by the people and does not believe in Allah and the Last Day. His example is like that of a [large] smooth stone upon which is dust and is hit by a downpour that leaves it bare. They are unable [to keep] anything of what they have earned. And Allah does not guide the disbelieving people. (*al-Qur'ān 2:264)*

Economic Dimensions

Business organisations have played a vital role in the economic and social life of people throughout history. In Islam, business activities are not assumed to satisfy only material needs and desires; rather, these activities should be undertaken to fulfil religious responsibilities as well. Therefore, the purpose of the Islamic system of business is not primarily materialistic but is based on the concepts of human well-being and the overall achievement of a good life (Khurshid, *et. al.*, 2014). Allah (SWT) permitted buying and selling but has forbidden riba.

Muslims are directed to conduct all business activities according to Shariah rules; they ought to be transparent, fair and honest towards society and the general public. Wealth accumulation for oneself is only permitted in line with Islamic ethics and alleviation of poverty is to be considered from this aspect. The main virtue of wealth utilisation in Islam is based on the prohibition of riba (Zaman, *et. al.*, 2018).

Those who consume interest cannot stand [on the Day of Resurrection] except as one stands who is being beaten by Satan into insanity. That is because they say, "Trade is [just] like interest" But Allah has permitted trade and has forbidden interest. So, whoever has received an admonition from his Lord and desists may have what is past, and his affair rests with Allah. But whoever returns to [dealing in interest or usury] - those are the companions of the Fire; they will abide eternally therein. (al-Qur'ān 2:275)

The prohibition of riba in Islam fulfils two objectives; first, it promotes risk sharing in a business transaction which promotes business responsibility towards society and its stakeholders. Second, riba is perceived as a form of operation with unfairness and exploitation, and thus, it can cause damage to the economy which is also against the norms of CSR (Zaman, *et. al.*, 2018).

Allah (SWT) has encouraged mankind to exercise mutual cooperation in good deeds but has forbidden people from helping one another to further evil acts and enmity.

And cooperate in righteousness and piety, but do not cooperate in sin and aggression. And fear Allah; indeed, Allah is severe in penalty (al-Qur'ān 5:2)

Trade practices also draw heavily on the life of the Prophet Mohammad (PBUH) and on the lives of many of his companions and their followers, who were actively engaged in trade and who established the ethical foundations of Islamic business practices at the inception of the religion. Profit considerations are not independent of an ethical system but are part of prevailing norms that govern conduct and business exchange functions. Profit assumes a central place in Islamic ethics; however, Islamic prescriptions do not condone profit that leads to exploitation and mischief in the marketplace. Islamic view is similar but broader than stakeholder theory in advocating that value creation results in profits rather than the reverse (Khurshid, *et. al.*, 2014).

Islam introduced the concept of *halal* (lawful) and *haram* (unlawful) in its comprehensive system of life. These concepts reign supreme in the areas of production and consumption. Certain means of earning and wealth are considered unlawful, such as interest, bribery, gambling and games of chance, speculation, short weighing and short measuring and business negligence. Unlawful means of earning are strictly forbidden; followers of Islam are permitted to earn income only through lawful and fair means. Similarly, in the area of consumption, certain food items are unlawful, such as dead animals, blood, swine products (including meat and lard) and animals that are slaughtered in a name other than that of God. Even expenses for certain items, such as alcoholic drinks, narcotics, debauchery, prostitution, pornography, items that promote obscenity and vulgarity, lotteries and gambling, are strictly inadmissible (Khurshid, *et. al.*, 2014).

Legal Dimensions

Islamic market is categorised by certain norms that ensure the safety of both buyers and sellers. There are certain ethical regulations in Islamic commercial transactions even in the absence of written contracts. These rules manifest a code of good manners, decency and ethical excellence. All these rules are pursuant to the concept of lawful and unlawful practices in Islam and reflect features of social responsibility in every aspect of transactions (Khurshid, *et. al.*, 2014).

In Islamic ethics organisations and their employees must be honest, sincere and truthful in their business dealings and should ensure accuracy in terms of promised product specifications, such as weights, measures and other attributes.

Give full measure when you measure, and weigh with a balance that is true: that is the most fitting and the most advantageous in the final determination […] (al-Qur'ān 17: 35)

Islam condemns cheating, lying and hoarding products to create shortages in the market to increase prices. Islam requires businesspersons to be straightforward in all their dealings and transactions. Justice in Islam also

Figure 2. Islamic CSR Model

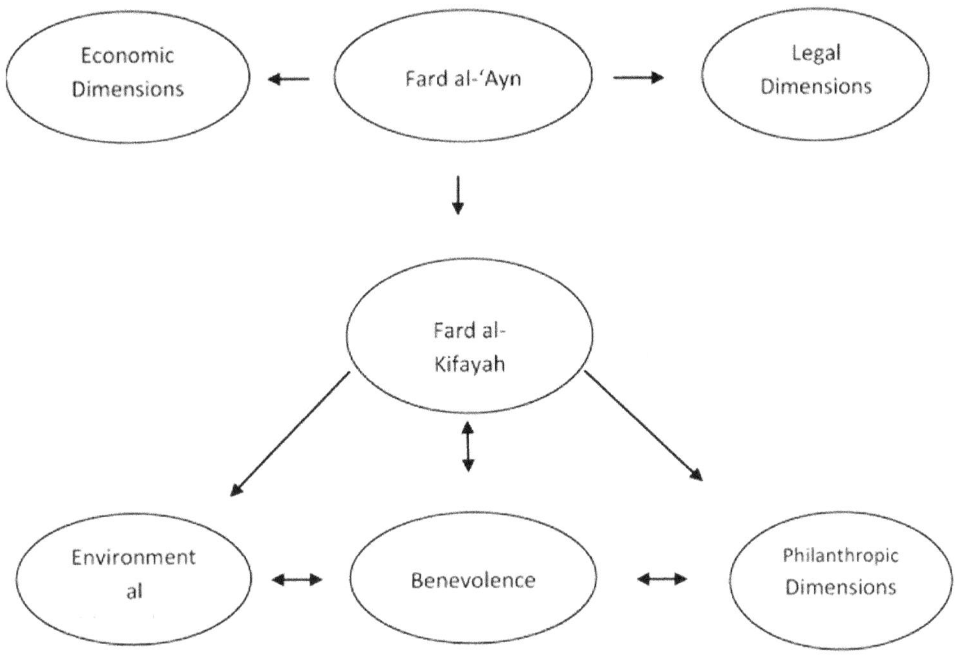

includes the equitable distribution of wealth. Although inequality in terms of wealth is justified, all members of society have the right to be provided with basic needs, regardless of their race, religion, language, colour, sex, age, health and status. Islam encourages people to take appropriate measures to redistribute resources, to avoid concentration of wealth, to minimise social gaps and to share the fortunes of the wealthy with unfortunate members of society by paying *Zakat* (alms) and *Sadaqah* (charitable donations).

Ethical Dimensions

According to Islamic ethics, the behaviour, deeds, words, feelings, thoughts and intentions of Muslims should be guided by such values as honesty, humanity and respect for the law. Islam asks its followers to consider certain norms and moral codes and to follow Islamic rules and regulations in their family affairs, business transactions, social affairs and interactions with others. Compliance with ethical behaviour is part of *Iman* (faith); as such, social responsibility and justice are considered subsidiaries of the Muslim belief system.

Islamic business system is based on the concepts of human well-being and the achievement of a good life. Islam emphasises community values, socioeconomic justice and a balance between the material and spiritual needs of its followers. Islam restricts riba (interest/usury), pornography, prostitution, gambling and speculation (Khurshid, *et. al.*, 2014).

Islam requires its followers to adhere to the same cohesive code of behaviour and that every human action is undertaken for Allah (SWT). Only Allah (SWT) is to be feared; therefore, morality follows automatically. As the al-Qur'ān states:

Say: Lo! My worship and my sacrifice and my living and my dying are all for God, Lord of the Worlds". This philosophy encourages a focus on altruism and awareness of social responsibility (al-Qur'ān 6:162)

Philanthropic Dimensions

In Islam, charity for the welfare of the society is obligatory in the shape of *Zakah*, al-Qur'ān mentions regarding those beneficiaries of *Zakah.*

Zakah expenditures are only for the poor and for the needy and for those employed to collect [zakah] and for bringing hearts together [for Islam] and for freeing captives [or slaves] and for those in debt and for the cause of Allah and for the [stranded] traveller - an obligation [imposed] by Allah. And Allah is Knowing and Wise (al-Qur'ān 9:60)

The Islamic perspective for business organisations includes accountability, covering business legitimacy (prohibition of harmful activities), the fulfilment of zakah and obligations to help deprived members of society. The stakeholder perspective of zakah argues that it is vital for the development of the country as it contributes to social security and harmony by reducing discrimination and the wealth difference between rich and poor. In addition, zakah guarantees a compulsory and permanent redistribution of wealth to those who suffer from poverty. The role of zakah in social welfare has been widely cited in the extended literature. Zakah distribution not only reduces the inequalities in society but also increases the wealth circulation. This wealth circulation in return reduces the probability of recession, increases the consumption of goods and services and ultimately increases business value (Zaman, *et. al.*, 2018).

Islam allows its followers to conduct business for profit without harming others or the environment. People are expected to ensure justice to stakeholders and welfare to mankind.

Indeed, Allah orders justice and good conduct and giving to relatives and forbids immorality and bad conduct and oppression. He admonishes you that perhaps you will be reminded (al-Qur'ān 16: 90)

Islam also encourages people to take appropriate measures to redistribute resources, to minimise social gaps and to share the fortunes of the wealthy with unfortunate people in society by paying *Zakah* (alms) and *Sadaqah* (charitable donations).

The payment of *Zakah* can help balance the economy of a country by helping the poor and needy to pursue a better life. Therefore, the payment of *Zakah* may help companies fulfil their responsibilities both to God and to society. In Islam, *Sadaqah* (charitable payments) are another social dimension to which companies can contribute through donations. These donations can be given in the form of money to help the poor, needy persons or orphans or to build public facilities, such as mosques, public halls and recreational parks. These donations can benefit society as a whole. In summary, socially responsible activities, *Zakah*, and *Sadaqah* can help people obtain *Barakah* (blessings) from God. At the same time, *"a'amalsaliha"* (good deeds) is the key to the achievement of *Falah* (success in this world and in the hereafter) (Zaman, *et. al.*, 2018).

From an Islamic perspective, all possessions, wealth, expertise, abilities, positions and power belong to God. Humans are only trustees. As trustees, human beings must manage these possessions to the best of their abilities to create maximum value in social responsibility with the intention of benefiting the community (Khurshid, *et. al.*, 2014).

Fard al- 'Ayn vs. Fard al-Kifayah

Murphy and Smolarski (2017) precisely discussed another set of important *Shariah* concepts, which link Islam to CSR, fard al- 'ayn and fard al-kifayah.

Fard al- 'ayn defines what is obligatory upon each individual Muslim in Islamic legal doctrine. For instance, the five pillars of Islam (i.e., the declaration of faith, the five daily prayers, paying alms to the poor, fasting during the month of Ramadan, and the pilgrimage to Mecca) are prime examples of fard al ‘ayn. If one fails to fulfil this individual obligation, then he or she will personally be held responsible to God.

Fard al-kifayah is the Islamic legal concept that defines what is obligatory upon the *ummah* (the Muslim community/society) as a whole. If this obligation goes unfulfilled, then the entire *ummah* will be held accountable to Allah (SWT) for negligence of duty; however, if enough people from the *ummah* fulfil this duty, then the rest of the *ummah* is discharged from having to carry it out. Some examples of fard al-kifayah are competence environmental protection initiatives and philanthropic activities.

Fard al-kifayah in CSR perspective would require some companies in the society to utilise their resources to support the development priorities of the state, while also lobbying the state on behalf of stakeholders who do not possess the political or social resources to advocate for themselves. In particular, the latter would encompass those minority groups (be they racial, tribal, gender, religious, etc.), as well as the environment, whose interests are rarely, if ever, recognised in the institutions responsible for public policy making. This phenomenon is even more acute in many contemporary Muslim majority countries, wherein democratic values of freedom, equality, dignity, transparency, and sustainability are not always held in high esteem in practice though they are clearly mandated in Islamic teachings (Murphy and Smolarski, 2017). Hence, within these societies normative Islam asserts that powerful firms have even more of a fard al-kifayah obligation to advocate for and protect the rights of the weak and those who cannot do so for themselves e.g. animals, plant, environment etc. The Qur’ān states:

And what is wrong with you that you struggle not in the Cause of God, and for those weak, ill-treated and oppressed among men, women, and children (al-Qur’ān 4:75)

The Prophet Muhammad (PBUH) further substantiates this point in the following *hadith*:

Help your brother, whether he is an oppressor, or he is an oppressed one. People asked, “O God’s Apostle! It is all right to help him if he is oppressed, but how should we help him if he is an oppressor?” The Prophet said, “By preventing him from oppressing others” (Sahih Bukhari).

Environmental Dimensions

Islamic teachings are quite explicit to protect the environment. Cleanliness is one of the important requirements to be a Muslim. Therefore, Islamic ethics ensures that every member of organisation adopts and practices cleanliness and purity.

For Allah loves those who turn to Him constantly and He loves those who keep themselves pure and clean (al - Qur'ān 2:222)

Daryabadi (1998) explained that here cleanliness means purity from both physical and spiritual dirt (p. 419).

A saying of Prophet Muhammad (PBUH) that "Cleanliness is half the Faith" further endorses the importance of cleanliness,

The prophet Muhammad (PBUH) said, "If the last hour strikes and finds you carrying a nursling tree to the grove for planting go ahead and plant it".

Islamic ethics emphasises cleanliness and purity and expects from all the followers to practice and promote cleanliness in everyday life to make the surrounding environment free from all kinds of pollutions. One can address today's popular issue of environmental pollution through practicing Islamic values in the life. It is one of the important responsibilities of organisations to protect the environment within and outside the organisation from all hazards, and to improve it even further for healthy and clean life of all stakeholders.

Emphasis on plantation is an indication of deep concern for protection of environment and keenness for the healthy living of people, because plants do contribute significantly to the world's environmental stability.

Wastefulness is one of the important contributors to the environmental instability. Islamic ethics do not allow people to be extravagant in their personal spending and educate to avoid carelessness in utilising collective and natural resources. The Qur'ān says:

Indeed, the wasteful are brothers of the devils, and ever has Satan been to his Lord ungrateful (al-Qur'ān 17:27)

Societal Dimensions

So, establish regular Prayer and give regular Charity; and obey the Messenger; that ye may receive mercy (al - Qur'ān 24:56)

deal not unjustly, and ye shall not be dealt with unjustly (al - Qur'ān 2:279).

Daryabadi (1998) explained that here absolute fact about Islamic law has been narrated (p. 509) that neither you should be unjust to others nor others should be unjust to you. The other angle of the fact is that as you sow so shall you reap.

There are two-fold motivations for people in Islamic ethics to be more active in welfare of society: first reward is in this world in the shape of loyalty, sincerity and devotion from within and outside the organisation and second reward is in the Life Hereafter:

But give glad tidings to those who believe and work righteousness, that their portion is Gardens, beneath which rivers flow (al-Qur'ān 2:25)

Allah will admit those who believe and work righteous deeds to Gardens beneath which rivers flow: they shall be adorned therein with bracelets of gold and pearls; and their garments there will be of silk (al-Qur'ān 22:23)

Mufsidah and Corporate Social Responsibility

Maslahah denotes a good, right, just or honest person or thing. Legally, al-Shatibi (d.790) defined it as: "all concerns that promote the subsistence of human life, the completion of man's livelihood and the acquisition of all his physical and intellectual qualities which are required for him". Its antonym, mufsidah indicates anything that is harmful and destructive. The use of maslahah as an independent legal source has been advocated by many contemporary jurists and reformists (Shaharuddin, 2010).

Any harmful activity that puts society at risk through the violation of Islamic rules is considered to be mufsidah. Shaharuddin (2010) considered that any social activity that contributes to promoting the public interest is considered as maslahah, in contrast to mufsidah, which consists of any harmful activities to violate the public interest. Islam does not prevent commercial business transactions, as these support wealth and prosperity. However, Islam emphasises that business transactions should avoid harmful practices known as mufsidah. These include the factors that prevent wealth from smooth circulation, lead to unfair financial dealings or thwart justice (Zaman *et. al.*, 2018).

The institution of maslahah is derived from the survey and scrutiny of all Islamic teachings and injunctions available in the al-Qur'ān and Hadith. This means that the Shariah in all its teaching aims at the attainment of good, welfare, advantage, benefits, etc., and the warding off evil, injury, loss, etc., for all creatures on this planet. Al-Ghazali explains the maslahah as the "preservation of the religion, life, mind, offspring and wealth". According to him, "everything that leads to the preservation of these five foundations is considered maslahah, and everything that leads to the disruption of these foundations is mufsidah, and its removal is maslahah,". As a principle, each matter that increases the welfare of people from the Sharia point of view is considered as maslahah or utility. Similarly, every matter that decreases the welfare of people from the Shariah point of view is considered as mufsidah or disutility (Jalil, n.d.).

The goal of an ideal organisation from the perspective of Islamic work ethics should be based upon the principles of promoting maslahah and avoiding mufsidah engagements. Theoretical evaluation of CSR concepts leads to some new aspects such as huquq (rights) and responsibilities in line with the CSR best practices. The stakeholder perspective of mufsidah depends on respecting the society by considering the social benefits and costs while not compromising on the religious instructions (Zaman *et. al.*, 2018).

Teachings about Fasad in al-Qur'ān are given below:

And when it is said to them, "Do not cause corruption on the earth," they say, "We are but reformers". Unquestionably, it is they who are the corrupters, but they perceive [it] not (al-Qur'ān 2:11-12)

Indeed, the penalty for those who wage war against Allah and His Messenger and strive upon earth [to cause] corruption is none but that they be killed or crucified or that their hands and feet be cut off from opposite sides or that they be exiled from the land. That is for them a disgrace in this world; and for them in the Hereafter is a great punishment (al-Qur'ān 5:33)

Who break the covenant of Allah after contracting it and sever that which Allah has ordered to be joined and cause corruption on earth. It is those who are the losers (al-Qur'ān 2:27)

CONCLUSION

In conclusion, this chapter has explored and discussed theoretically and empirically, the linkage between Islamic ethics and corporate social responsibility (CSR) are two compatible concepts which are very interesting to be explored especially on how core rules in Islamic ethics provide a solid ground for CSR. Islam in the light of the holy Qur'ān and Hadith suggests that there seems to be congruence between the ideals of social responsibility and justice and business transactions in Islam that has a character with prevailing notions of corporate social responsibility (CSR). Corporate social responsibility (CSR) since early 1990 has attracted worldwide attention and acquired a new reverberation in the global economy. Heightened interest in CSR in recent years has stemmed from the advent of globalisation and international trade, which have reflected in increased business complexity and new demands for enhanced transparency and corporate citizenship.

Corporate Social Responsibility (CSR) principles and practices which are been implemented in the companies are persistent with Islamic principles stated in Qur'an and Hadith. In Islamic ethics spending is the preferred activity for the welfare of society. Spending is the indicator of sympathy and care of other fellow beings. Habit of spending from personal account for the welfare of people of society may fight against common and most challenging ailments of today's world of management i.e. selfishness and executive greed, which are the root causes of corruption in many organisations. Finally, Islamic work ethics are being practiced by modern businesses in two dimensions in corporate world as individual and organisation. Islamic ethical system does not distinguish between public and private lives. Therefore, Islam influences the decision-making of its followers in every facet of their lives.

Discussion Questions

1. How does the business industry benefit from Islamic ethical system?
2. Discuss the linkage between Islamic ethics and corporate social responsibility (CSR)?
3. Explore how core principles of Islamic corporate social responsibility (CSR) are derived from al-Qur'ān and sunnah?
4. What is a concept of Tazkia, or growth and purification, is the idea of active contribution in the material world?

REFERENCES

Arsad, S., Ahmad, R., & Fisol, W. N. M., Said, R., & Othman, Y. H. (2015). Maqasid Shariah in Corporate Social Responsibility of Shari'ah Compliant Companies. *Research Journal of Finance and Accounting*, *6*(6), 239–247.

Dahlsrud, A. (2008). How Corporate Social Responsibility is Defined: An Analysis of 37 Definitions. *Corporate Social Responsibility and Environmental Management*, *15*(1), 1–13. doi:10.1002/csr.132

Daryabadi, A. M. (1998). *Tafseer-e-Majidi* (Vol. 1). Majlis-e-Nashriat-e-Qur'ān.

Dusuki, A. W. (n.d.). *Corporate Governance and Stakeholder Management: an Islamic Perspective*. Retrieved on July 03, 2019 from https://pdfs.semanticscholar.org/65c7/a867ce59799d12fae6562f8a50e5a57bc81b.pdf

Elasrag, H. (2015). *Corporate Social Responsibility: An Islamic Perspective*. MPRA Paper No. 67537. Available at https://mpra.ub.uni-muenchen.de/67537/

Ilyas, M. (2018). Islamic Work Ethics and Corporate Social Responsibility in Business Organisations: Issues and Challenges. *Academy of Accounting and Financial Studies Journal*, *22*, 1–6.

Jalil, A. (n.d.). *The Significances of Maslahah Concept and Doctrine of Maqasid (Objectives) al-Shari'ah in Project Evaluation*. Retrieved on July 03, 2019 from: http://ssrn.com/abstract=1785109

Khurshid, M. A., Al-Aali, A., Soliman, A. A., & Amin, S. M. (2014). Developing an Islamic corporate social responsibility model (ICSR). *Competitiveness Review*, *24*(4), 258–274. doi:10.1108/CR-01-2013-0004

Mir, U. R., Hassan, S. M., & Hassan, S. S. (n.d.). *Islamic Perspective of Corporate Social Responsibility*. Retrieved on June 30, 2019 from: http://pu.edu.pk/images/journal/szic/pdf_files/30_v31_No_46_16.pdf

Murphy, M. J., & Smolarski, J. M. (2017). Religion and CSR: An Islamic "Political" Model of Corporate Governance. *Business & Society*, *00*(0), 1–32.

Shaharuddin, A. (2010). Maslahah-Mafsadah Approach in Assessing the Shari'ah Compliance of Islamic Banking Products. *International Journal of Business and Social Science*, *1*(1), 129–136.

Zaman, R., Roudaki, J., & Nadeem, M. (2018). Religiosity and corporate social responsibility practices: Evidence from an emerging economy. *Social Responsibility Journal*, *14*(2), 368–395. doi:10.1108/SRJ-10-2017-0204

Chapter 10
Islamic Ethics and Conflict Management

ABSTRACT

Islamic ethics provides a compact infrastructure for conflict management. Islamic ethics mandates maintaining a shura (expert or advisory council) as a permanent feature of the society or an organisation to handle conflicts amicably. Appointment of a muslih (mediator) in case of a conflict must be a key feature of workplace according to Islamic ethics with responsibilities of (1) verifications and (2) nasihah (advice). The Qur'an gives precise guidance toward conflict management and resolution with prescribed hierarchy by directing believers to refer to the Qur'an and Prophetic traditions to settle disputes. This chapter discusses that the impact of religion and religiosity at the workplace cannot be ignored in almost all aspect of management; it takes even more importance when it comes to developing conflict management strategies.

INTRODUCTION

Islam as a religion is considered a holistic way of life (Dīn) for the believers providing guidelines for every facet of life while conflict management is not an exception. Religion when considered as a principle of life implies an integrated approach to life including both personal and work life through Islamic theology and faith (Imān). Religiosity by its very nature has always been a strong moderator of actions and behaviour from Protestant, Confucius

DOI: 10.4018/978-1-7998-5295-7.ch010

to Islamic work ethics. Although conflict management theories exist in every society, however, usually these focused on the causes, types, nature, and the temporal strategies to conflict management rather than the theological moderators for lasting conflict resolutions. Managers consider conflict as a negative issue that may lead to loss of in productivity if not resolved, which in many instances is true, but Islamic work ethics view conflict as positive and inherent to human makeup.

This chapter will focus on the holistic approach of Islamic work ethics for effective conflict management approaches ranging from parties in the conflict to others surrounding the situation to discharge their responsibilities according to the guiding principles of Islam. Therefore, in Islamic work ethics all disputes are to be filtered through the teachings of al-Qur'ān and Sunnah.

Islamic Work Ethics and Conflict

The concept of expert council, or Shura, in Islamic history is well established in politics and government. Shura is specifically encouraged for conflict management in all facets of a human life from day to day activities in home to exceptionally sensitive matters of running a government. Therefore, Islamic work ethics workplace is not an exception to establish a Shura for managing conflicts. Shura is described as an attribute of believers as described in a chapter of the Qur'ān entitled as al-Shura:

And those who have responded to their lord and established prayer and whose affair is [determined by] consultation among themselves, and from what We have provided them, they spend (al-Qur'ān, 11:118–199)

The term Shura is also used for the consultation. Shura (the consultation) is a proactive Islamic method of conflict resolution. Shura minimises conflict between stakeholders and leads to a positive atmosphere to resolve differences. Shura minimises conflict due to the acceptability of the concept in Islamic belief and its legislative authority even today in several Muslim societies. In early days of Islam Shura had a definitive role and power to establish policies and determine procedure for their implementation.

So, by mercy from Allah, [O Muhammad], you were lenient with them. And if you had been rude [in speech] and harsh in heart, they would have disbanded from about you. So, pardon them and ask forgiveness for them and consult them in the matter. And when you have decided, then rely upon Allah. Indeed, Allah loves those who rely [upon Him] (al-Qur'ān, 3:159).

Shura as a consultative group has decisive character to minimise disagreements among stakeholders and enables fostering an environment for a promising workplace. Muslih (the mediator) is an individual who facilitates reconciliation and mediation thus is highly regarded in Islam with promises of great rewards:

No good is there in much of their private conversation, except for those who enjoin charity or that which is right or conciliation between people. And whoever does that seeking means to the approval of Allah - then We are going to give him a great reward (al-Qur'ān, 4:114)

And if a woman fears from her husband contempt or evasion, there is no sin upon them if they make terms of settlement between them - and settlement is best. And present in [human] souls is stinginess. But if you do good and fear Allah - then indeed Allah is ever, with what you do, Acquainted (al-Qur'ān, 4:128)

The Prophetic tradition regards sulh (the reconciliation) as an act of charity and social responsibility (Cader, 2017). The function of a Muslih is to facilitate mediation through honest and empathetic communication between contending parties for compromise and settlement:

And if two factions among the believers should fight, then make settlement between the two. But if one of them oppresses the other, then fight against the one that oppresses until it returns to the ordinance of Allah. And if it returns, then make settlement between them in justice and act justly. Indeed, Allah loves those who act justly (al-Qur'ān, 49:9).

The primary duty of the muslih (mediator) is Tathabbut (verification). Mulish must verify all available information to reach to a conclusion to ensure justice between competing parties. Following two verses are giving comprehensive guidelines for mulish to perform duties of reconciliation with justice and verification of available information.

O you who have believed, if there comes to you a disobedient one with information, investigate, lest you harm a people out of ignorance and become, over what you have done, regretful (al-Qur'ān, 49:6).

O you who have believed, be persistently standing firm in justice, witnesses for Allah, even if it be against yourselves or parents and relatives. Whether one is rich or poor, Allah is more worthy of both. So, follow not [personal] inclination, lest you not be just. And if you distort [your testimony] or refuse [to give it], then indeed Allah is ever, with what you do, Acquainted (al-Qur'ān, 4:135).

Nasihah is often translated as ''giving sincere advice'', theoretically nasihah means much more than simply giving advice. It includes helping others in any way possible. It implies loving for your brother what you love for yourself. Teaching and helping people are also called nasihah, concealing their faults and commanding good and forbidding evil are also under the domain of nasihah; however, this should be done in private so as not to humiliate people (Helmy et al, 2014).

Those who listen attentively to what is said, then follow the best in it, it is they whom Allah has given guidance and it is they who have wisdom (al-Qur'ān, 39:18).

Islamic principles such as (1) ta'awun (cooperation), (2) sabr (patience), and (3) husn al-dhann (good assumptions) provide an amicable environment for conflict management (Cader, 2017).

'Ta'awun' means cooperation, which is essential for the conflict management, to promote healthy communication, reduce opposition, and eliminate hostility at the workplace. The Qur'ān encourages Muslims to promote ta'awun in the following verse for righteousness and piety:

..... And cooperate in righteousness and piety, but do not cooperate in sin and aggression. And fear Allah; indeed, Allah is severe in penalty (al-Qur'ān, 5:2)

Sabr (patience) is an important feature of Islamic ethics. Sabr has two dimensions; one is physical, which is enduring odd situations, harm and maintaining hard work to achieve set objectives, the other is non-physical, which is controlling carnal desires of the self (nafs) thus, raising the threshold of falling in conflict. Prophet Mohammad (PBUH) stated: "The believer is always in a good state, if when he receives, he is thankful, and when unfortunate he is patient which is good for him" (Helmy et al, 2014).

Husn al-dhann (good assumptions) means having positive and good opinion or thoughts about colleagues e.g. if a certain action of a colleague is not acceptable, others should have husn adh-dhan (good assumptions) considering that such a person may did it out of not knowing or his intention was not such. The Qur'ān educates as following:

O you who have believed, avoid much [negative] assumption. Indeed, some assumption is sin (al-Qur'ān, 49:12)

The Prophet Muhammad (PBUH) said, "Avoid suspicion, for suspicion is the gravest lie in talk and do not be inquisitive about one another and do not spy upon one another and do not feel envy with the other, and nurse no malice, and nurse no aversion and hostility against one another. And be fellow-brothers and servants of Allah" (Sahih Muslim 2563 a).

Fundamentals of Conflict Management

Conflict is divergence of interests or issues. Conflict is a disagreement or incompatibility that occurs between individuals or within organisations or teams. Conflict is a negative perception of an individual's actions or behaviour that causes harm (Cader, 2017). Expressed struggle and interference of parties with each other is also called conflict. Any situation in which

two or more social entities or 'parties' perceive that they possess mutually incompatible goals is a conflict (Abdalla, 2002). Interpersonal conflict refers to negative interactions, difference of opinions, and variation of perspectives with others in the workplace, which can range from momentary disagreements to heated arguments and even bullying. Interpersonal conflict can develop as a result of a competitive work environment, which may eventually lead to increase in overall productivity and rude or aggressive behaviour of co-workers, supervisors, and customers, which may sometimes has justified reasons but handled inappropriately leading to relational hostilities (Nixon et al., 2011).

Conflict is usually viewed as a negative phenomenon within organisations and is often sought to be avoided or eliminated. This notion of conflict has essentially resulted from the misconception that conflict is inherently distasteful, destructive and pathological to the attainment of organisational objectives. The modern organisation theorists have come to recognise that conflict is not only inevitable but can have useful or destructive effects depending on its management. There has been a growing need on the part of managers to learn the most effective strategies for managing conflicts.

Triangle of conflict includes the situation (e.g. norms, rules etc.), the behaviour and the attitude. Situational factors affect conflict behaviour and attitude. Islamic settings assume a great deal of social interdependence and community involvement even in interpersonal matters, which are more conducive to situational intrusions that allow for a deeper and wider analysis of conflict situations.

Conflict in Islamic work ethics is viewed as an inevitable and intentional state that can yield both positive &/ negative results depending on the approach of managing the conflict.

And if your Lord had willed, He could have made mankind one community; but they will not cease to differ, except whom your Lord has given mercy, and for that He created them (al-Qur'ān, 11:118–199)

O you who have believed, obey Allah and obey the Messenger and those in authority among you. And if you disagree over anything, refer it to Allah and the Messenger, if you should believe in Allah and the Last Day. That is the best [way] and best in result (al-Qur'ān, 4:59)

Islam outlines principles toward conflict management based on Islamic textual guidance (Vehapi, 2013). The Prophet Muhammad (PBUH) holds a high status in Islam (al-Qur'ān, 33:40) and is considered an example for Muslims to follow (al-Qur'ān, 3:31). The foremost principle to conflict management and resolution in Islam is to refer conflicts to fundamental sources of Islam i.e. the Qur'an and Sunnah:

But no, by your Lord! (O Muhammad) They cannot be believers until they make you judge in all disputes between them, and find in their souls no resistance against your decisions, but accept them with the fullest submission (al-Qur'ān, 4:65)

Financial Cost of Conflict Management

According to the research managers spend 13% to 25% of their time in resolving and mitigating conflict. In some severe cases, senior management may spend up to 80% of their time involved in conflict management and resolution **(Cader, 2017)**. Conflict remains one of the major sources of employee stress, while according to a study the annual costs of employee stress, including costs for missed wages due to absenteeism and reduced productivity and health care costs, have been estimated to be $200 to 350 billion in the United States, $64.8 to 66.1 billion in the United Kingdom, and $232 billion in Japan (Nixon et al., 2011)".

Besides direct monetary cost, conflict leads to following workplace issues thus significantly adds costs to the operations:

1. Loss of productivity
2. Absenteeism
3. Stress-related leave
4. Mediation
5. Health care

Organisations also bear cost of conflicts through physical symptoms such as headache, stomach disorder, musculoskeletal pain and backache of employees at the workplace which eventually deteriorates their job performance and productivity. Interpersonal conflicts are significantly related to such physical symptoms (Nixon et al, 2011). The conflict has several phases that take place within organisation and every type of conflict usually evolves following stages:

Potential Opposition or Incompatibility

The first step in the conflict process is the presence of conditions that create opportunities for conflict to develop. These causes or create opportunities for organisational conflict to rise. They need not lead directly to conflict, but one of these conditions is necessary if the conflict is to surface. These conditions are based on following three general categories.

1. Communication
2. Job Design and Job Structure
3. Personal Variables

Communication

Communication discrepancies are important cause of cultivating incompatibilities leading to the conflict. Communication gap, noise in the communication channels, lack of cultural awareness of communicating ends, insufficient exchange of information, use of connotations and phrases, issues related to the dialect all may lead to different perspectives in today's global workplace even for those who are sitting next to each other, thereby causing incompatibility and opposition leading to the conflict.

Job Structure and Job Design

Size of the organisation, the degree of specialisation required to perform assigned tasks by the group members, ambiguous span of control, members-goal compatibility, leadership styles, reward systems and the degree of dependence among groups are all influencing factors to avoid or cultivate opposition or incompatibility.

The size and specialisation act as forces to stimulate conflict. The larger the group and the more specialised its activities are, the greater is the likelihood of the conflict. Tenure and conflict have been found inversely related to each other. Age brackets of organisational members also have important influence on nurturing opposition or incompatibility. The potential for conflicts tends to be greatest when group members are younger and when turnover is high in the organisation. Job ambiguity is also one of the important factors of conflict at the workplace.

Personal Variables

Certain personality types e.g. individuals who are highly authoritarian and dogmatic are prone to create or face conflict quite often. Another reason for the conflict is the difference in value systems. Value differences are the best explanations of diverse issues such as prejudice disagreements over one's contribution to the group and rewards one deserves. Gender biases are also example of personal variables leading to conflict at the workplace. Group cohesion, mutual support, social relationships all belong to personal variables emerging from social backgrounds of people working together, inconsistency in these values lead to incompatibility and opposition.

1 Cognition and Personalisation

Conflict must be perceived by the parties; awareness of conflict and sense of personal involvement is the second stage in evolving the conflict to visibility. It is generally agreed that if relevant parties are not aware of the conflict then it does not exist.

If no one is aware of a conflict, then it is generally agreed that no conflict exists. On the other hand, if perceived conflict does not mean that is personalised, e.g. A may be aware that B and A are in serious disagreements, but it may not make A tense and it may have no effect whatsoever on A's affection towards B.

Stage two is the felt level when individuals become emotionally involved and parties experience anxiety, tension or hostility, here parties decide what the conflict is about and emotions play a major role in shaping perception.

2 Intentions

Stage three in the evolution of conflict is analysing intentions. Intensions are decisions to act in each way, intentions intervene between people's perception and emotions and their explicit behaviour. These intentions lead to future course of actions after perceiving and personalising the conflict.

3 Behaviour

Behaviour forms stage four in conflict evolution when conflict is visibly evident. While exhibiting specific behaviour towards the conflict statements are made, actions are taken, and reactions are recorded to register personal opinion about the conflict. These behaviours at this stage are usually open attempts to implement each party's intentions.

4. Outcome

There is always an outcome of a conflict either positive or negative. In case of functional outcome there is an improvement in the performance while dysfunctional outcome hinders group's performance.

Conflict is constructive when it improves the quality of decisions stimulates creativity and innovations encourage interest and curiosity among group members. Conflict is dysfunctional when breeds dissatisfaction which eventually leads to the destruction of the group.

Conflict Management Approaches

1. Competing (I Win, You Lose): Forcing

Human organisations offer ever changing environment for people around their operations. Dealing with day-to-day issues/problems exposes managers

Figure 1. illustrate the conflict stages
Source: *Adopted with permission from https://iedunote.com/5-stages-conflict-process Retrieved on September 08, 2019*

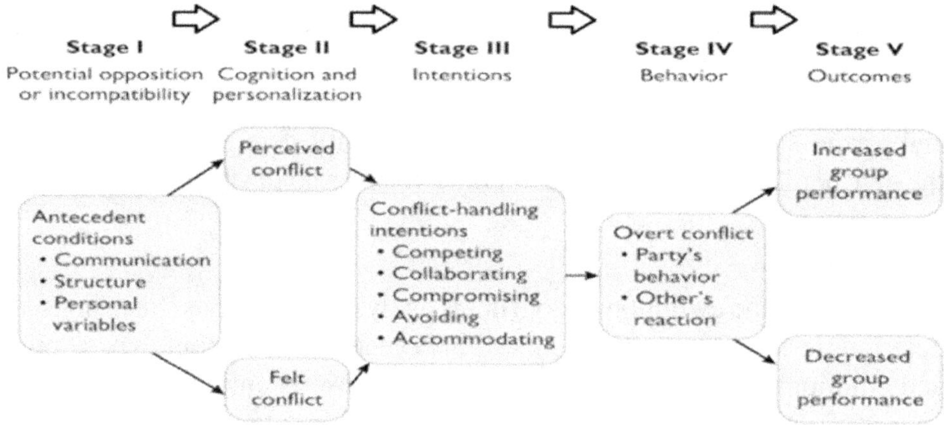

to variety of feelings and situations. If a conflict has vital implications for organisational operations, then managers must take decisive actions in a swift manner to save interest of entire organisation including those who are part of a conflict. However, in any case, it certainly seems forcing and may be considered unpopular measures.

This strategy usually leads where one party of the conflict loses while another seemingly wins, nevertheless, as managers one has to ensure collective success of the organisation and may resort to competing or forcing strategy for conflict resolution despite apparent assertive and authoritative behaviour.

During interpersonal management of conflicts, it will be indeed required to monitor the aggressor to avoid violation of rights of others and maintain justice on the workplace. Aggressors do exert pressures during the conflict through different means to attain what individual thinks is right. In such situations organisational environment must ensure that aggressor should remain reasonable. Therefore, providing opportunity to conflicting parties to deal with conflict with open mind is essential for productive outcome of conflicts.

2. Collaborating (I Win, You Win): Problem Solving

Conflicts do arise among people when both sides are determined to lead their organisations to achieve set objective but through different arrangements.

There are differences in conceptualising the issue in hand and may be likely outcome of existing procedures. Here parties are in conflict because of their differences in approaching the issue. These situations are generally a blessing for the workplace, however, if not handled appropriately these conflicts may lead to serious outcomes. Collaborating and problem-solving strategy help satisfy concerns of all parties by clarifying difference and join hands to attain collective objectives. A good communication among relevant parties is the key for the success of this strategy of conflict resolution. Once all parties are on-board, creative and pragmatic solutions are guaranteed for the organisation without compromising their own motivation and satisfaction.

3. Avoiding (No Winners, No Losers): Withdrawing

Avoiding minor deviations to accommodate human errors is probably a good approach subject to several considerations. There is perhaps nothing trivial in human life, sometimes apparently tiny matters can lead to disasters. Therefore, managers and subordinates all have to remain watchful for even minute issues emerging on daily basis on the workplace to avoid major disasters.

Situations where there is less opportunity to satisfy your concerns, still an important strategy would be to consult and exchange views with those who faced same situations earlier in the same setting.

It is indeed wise consideration in certain situations to let the people cool down to accommodate different perspective, nevertheless it may not always be appropriate.

Avoiding is best suited when conflicting parties are reasonably competent to resolve their issues amicably. However, it can be detrimental to avoid or withdraw once conflict is recognised as a threat and left unattended with the view that conflict will resolve itself. It is essential to keep a close eye on the conflict even conflicting parties are dependable, as long as conflict is settled.

In any case a manager / leader cannot avoid responsibility of negative outcomes of the conflict under all circumstances. This requires continuous vigilance about even a minor conflict as it appears on a surface.

4. Accommodating (I Lose, You Win): Smoothening

Accommodating others during the conflict is essentially a daunting task when apparently one intruding side. Still there are examples of selflessness and accommodating faults of others on the workplace, but such instances are quite rare.

Accommodating a problematic side to maintain peace at workplace usually leads to further disasters. There is always a need to come up with sound and creative solutions to the conflict. Building social credit through accommodating or smoothening may not be useful; however, it is indeed beneficial when an individual is on the wrong side of the conflict, which may be considered as conciliation.

5. Compromising (You Bend, I Bend): Resolution

If collective objectives take precedence, then conflicting parties do give up something for combined benefit. Compromising is about coming up with a resolution that would be acceptable to the parties involved. Thus, one party is willing to sacrifice their interest as long as the others will do the same.

Opponents of equal power with mutually exclusive objectives also compromise during conflicts. Sometimes short-term benefits, temporary settlements of complex issues and to arrive at expedient solutions also lead to compromising. Compromising is a last resort when collaboration and competition are unsuccessful.

Figure 2. highlights below compromising resolution
Source: Adopted with permission from https://iedunote.com/5-stages-conflict-process Retrieved on September 08, 2019

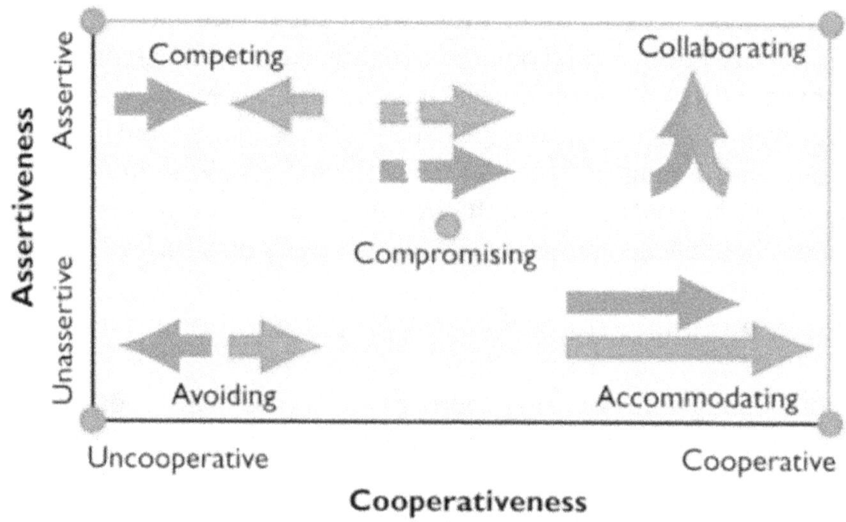

Causes of Conflict

There are several causes of conflict which may pop up sometimes absolutely out of the blue surprising relevant parties about the occurrence. However, there are some predictable causes of conflict as discussed below:

1. Incompatibility of beliefs or interests

Different beliefs and interests inherently carry conflicts while relevant ends look differently, act defensively and interpret according to their own point of view. If organisational

2. Incompatibility in personal preferences
3. Disparity in supply and demand
4. Beliefs, values, and skills that are perceived by others to be exclusive
5. Partially exclusive behaviours
6. Task interdependence

Islamic Principles for Conflict Management Models

An Islamic model for conflict management needs to reflect values, goals and processes as described in Islamic theory. The model also must respond to the specific needs and circumstances of the Muslim culture. The model should be guided by three principles (Abdalla, 2002).

1. Restoring to Islam its messages of justice, freedom and equality.
2. Engaging the community in the intervention and resolution processes.
3. Adjusting the intervention techniques according to the conflict situation, and its stages.

For the majority of Muslims, passionate sentiment attaches them to their Islamic heritage. The history of early Islam, as taught to the young at home, school, mosque and in the community, is rich with examples of self-sacrifice, courage, solidarity, love and compassion, justice and equality. Every Muslim seems to be able to identify with this heritage, and almost to feel a sense of ownership of this heritage.

It represents to Muslims the pure ideals of their religion. These ideals also represent a reality that once existed, of which any Muslim proudly feels that s/he is an integral part; that is, every Muslim owns this heritage, and this heritage is part of what every Muslim *is*. This "love" relationship with their Islamic religious heritage always provided continuity and momentum to Muslim societies, despite political and social institutions that strayed too far from that heritage.

Islamic ethics offers its followers a wide range of attitude and behaviour models applicable in different situations. *Islam, thus, is a process of modelling.* Righteousness is measured by one's ability to model all aspects of life after the ones prescribed in divine sources.

According to (Abdalla, 2002), the process of modelling attitudes and behaviours faces three obstacles. The first obstacle is the scholarly disagreement over the interpretation of several models for behaviour found in al-Qur'ān and *Sunnah.*

The second obstacle to the process of modelling is the intermixture of religious and traditional values, attitudes and behaviours.

The third obstacle to modelling process is perhaps a consequence of the first two factors. As we have seen, several schools of thought have different interpretations for various issues; and, institutions and practices persisted that were not consistent with Islamic principles.

Islamic theory and culture always emphasised a strong sense of community. Islamic culture and Islamic theory regard family as the basic unit (although individual accountability is strongly emphasised in al-Qur'ān). "The culture of relatedness refers to the family culture and inter-personal relational patterns characterised by dependent-interdependent relations with overlapping personal boundaries. Several Qur'anic verses advocated active involvement with community issues, standing up for justice (even against the interests of one's self and loved ones), and taking action in resolving disputes:

Righteousness is not that you turn your faces toward the east or the west, but [true] righteousness is [in] one who believes in Allah, the Last Day, the angels, the Book, and the prophets and gives wealth, in spite of love for it, to relatives, orphans, the needy, the traveller, those who ask [for help], and for freeing slaves; [and who] establishes prayer and gives zakah; [those who] fulfil their promise when they promise; and [those who] are patient in poverty and hardship and during battle. Those are the ones who have been true, and it is those who are the righteous (al-Qur'ān, 2:177)

Worship Allah and associate nothing with Him, and to parents do good, and to relatives, orphans, the needy, the near neighbour, the neighbour farther away, the companion at your side, the traveller, and those whom your right hands possess. Indeed, Allah does not like those who are self-deluding and boastful (al-Qur'ān, 4:36)

And what is [the matter] with you that you fight not in the cause of Allah and [for] the oppressed among men, women, and children who say, "Our Lord, take us out of this city of oppressive people and appoint for us from Yourself a protector and appoint for us from Yourself a helper? (al-Qur'ān, 4:75)

This strong sense of relatedness and community can be utilised to the benefit of conflict management in Islamic settings. The dynamics of conflict vary according to the stage of the conflict, which does not necessarily go through a linear progression; more than likely it goes through "ups and downs". In the Islamic theory, an intervention technique should best correspond to the stage of a conflict with the purpose of restoring justice and adhering to Islamic principles and values. For example, the Qur'ān, in a clear example of adjusting third party's intervention according to conflict stages, has promoted reconciliation as an intervention technique between two disputing factions. Yet, the Qur'ān mandated a more active role against one party if it transgresses. Once the transgression is brought under control, the third party returns to the reconciliation mode, with the purpose or restoring justice. The ultimate goal of third-party intervention, the Qur'ān has declared, is to reconcile members of the community (al-Qur'ān, 49:9-10.)

Islah (Reformation), Sulh (Settlement), Musalaha (Reconciliation) and Muslih (Reconciler or Mediator)

Semantically, the term Islah derives from the root word 'Sa La Ha', which means 'good' or righteous and antonym to the term 'Fa Sa Da' (mischief or destruction). Due to its original meaning of piety and good, Islah represents the permanent behaviour of transforming towards the direction of betterment and perfection. Islah also means the transformation from the state of bad to good, from good to better and from better to perfection. Therefore, its usage for 'mutual reconciliation' (Musalaha) involves mutually agreed consideration towards enhancement and to bring an end to fasaad (destruction or mischief).

Islah could best defined as 'a state of constant endeavour towards comprehensive excellence (ihsan) within the frameworks of innovative, constructive and reconstructive to attain falah according to Maqaasid al-Shari'ah'. This definition explicitly illustrated in al-Qur'ān:

And let there be [arising] from you a nation inviting to [all that is] good, enjoining what is right and forbidding what is wrong, and those will be the successful (al-Qur'ān, 3:104)

You are the best nation produced [as an example] for mankind. You enjoin what is right and forbid what is wrong and believe in Allah (al-Qur'ān, 3:110)

Sulh means peace in opposition to conflict. Establishment of peace (a situation of non-conflict) between groups, an agreement or truce or settlement between groups to halt and prevent further conflict or violence. Establishing communal unity and peace, often through a visible public action negotiated by mediators working with both groups is called sulh. The Prophetic tradition regards sulh as an act of charity and social responsibility. Sulh is considered contractual agreement in Islamic law, thereby binding the stakeholders to resolve and abide terms of the sulh (Cader, 2017).

Musalaha, the reconciliation between contending parties is extremely valuable act in Islamic ethics. The reconciliation is praised by the Almighty Allah (SWT) in the following verse of the Qur'ān:

No good is there in much of their private conversation, except for those who enjoin charity or that which is right or conciliation between people. And whoever does that seeking means to the approval of Allah - then We are going to give him a great reward (al-Qur'ān, 4:114)

The Muslih, or individual who facilitates reconciliation and mediation, is highly regarded in Islam with promises of great reward (al-Qur'ān, 4:114; 4:128)

The function of a Muslih is to facilitate mediation and discussion to achieve reconciliation between conflicting groups or individuals:

And if two factions among the believers should fight, then make settlement between the two (al-Qur'ān, 49:9)

The Prophet Muhammad encouraged individuals to facilitate reconciliation by likening it to acts of worship (Abu Dawud). Therefore, a Muslih suffices in the event of minor conflicts without the need to convene a Shura. The Muslih, essentially, is an arbitrator between two disputing parties. The Muslih also operates in a functional capacity and not solely as a facilitator. The main function of the Muslih is Tathabbut (verification). This is due to the commandment to verify information and news received in the event of conflict (Quran, 49:9).

Islamic Models of Conflict Management

SNT Model – Shura (Council), **Nasiha** (Advice) **and Ta'awun** (Cooperation)

SNT is one of the most popular Islamic models of conflict management. SNT means Shura (council), Nasīha (advice), and Ta'awun (mutual cooperation). SNT is not a linear-progression avoidance-based theory. The SNT model shifts away from the traditional paradigm of conflict management research in Islam. This shift is found in the integration of the Islamic principles of Nasīha and Ta'awun. SNT model is proactive and conducive to positive outcomes of conflict. This is due to the existence of Shura, an advisory & consultative council of experts on relevant subject matters. The nature of Shura is to consult with nonpartisan individuals alongside the stakeholders and parties involved in the conflict. Involved parties are given advice or feedback toward corrective measures, thereby increasing the probability of favourable outcomes. Based on consultation and advice, concerned parties are encouraged to cooperate (Ta'awun) with other upon good and moral activities. The purpose of cooperation is to create a positive atmosphere and reduce possible tension resulting from conflict (Cader, 2017).

The concept of expert council, or Shura, in Islamic history is well established in politics and government. However, Shura is encouraged as a resource for dispute management in all facets of a human life, including within the home, it is described as an attribute of a believer.

And those who have responded to their lord and established prayer and whose affair is [determined by] consultation among themselves (al-Qur'ān, 42:38)

Shura is a pre-emptive Islamic method of conflict resolution. Shura minimises conflict between stakeholders and leads to a positive atmosphere to resolve differences. Shura minimises conflict due to the acceptability of the concept in Islamic belief and its legislative authority (al-Qur'ān, 3:159).

Following are the attributes to establish shura:

1. Knowledge

In Islamic ethics knowledge is the foundation to select or elect a member of a shura. It is essential for a member of the shura to have sufficient knowledge of contemporary environment, Shariah and historic evolution of dynamics of human interactions.

O you who have believed, when you are told, "Space yourselves" in assemblies, then make space; Allah will make space for you. And when you are told, "Arise," then arise; Allah will raise those who have believed among you and those who were given knowledge, by degrees. And Allah is Acquainted with what you do (al-Qur'ān, 58:11)

2. Justice in Decision-Making

Justice is the cornerstone in every aspect of workplace life of human beings, however, it is even more important for the members of shura to ensure and establish justice in the decision-makings.

O you who have believed, be persistently standing firm for Allah, witnesses in justice, and do not let the hatred of a people prevent you from being just. Be just; that is nearer to righteousness. And fear Allah; indeed, Allah is Acquainted with what you do (al-Qur'ān, 5:8)

3. Reliability in Reporting Events and Passing Information

Reliability strengthens confidence of people on shura, recording and reporting events and utilising available information after sufficient verification makes the consultation process more effective and productive.

O you who have believed, if there comes to you a disobedient one with information, investigate, lest you harm a people out of ignorance and become, over what you have done, regretful (al-Qur'ān, 49:6)

4. Truthfulness

Truthfulness as always remains a key for the effectiveness of shura. Truthfulness in every aspect of dispensing resolutions of conflicts is required in Islamic ethics to ensure credibility of shura as an institution.

O you who have believed, fear Allah and be with those who are true (al-Qur'ān, 9:119)

5. Wisdom

While establishing shura it is important to assign this responsibility to those who have proven wisdom in dealing with both routine and complex conflicts at the workplace.

He gives wisdom to whom He wills, and whoever has been given wisdom has certainly been given much good. And none will remember except those of understanding (al-Qur'ān, 2:269)

6. Expertise

The Prophet (PBUH) and Abu Bakr employed a (pagan) man from the tribe of Bani Ad-Dail and the tribe of Bani 'Abu bin `Adi as a guide. He was an expert guide and he broke the oath contract which he had to abide by with the tribe of Al-`Asi bin Wail and he was on the religion of Quraish pagans. The Prophet (PBUH) and Abu Bakr had confidence in him and gave him their riding camels and told him to bring them to the Cave of Thaur after three days. So, he brought them their two riding camels after three days and both of them (The Prophet (PBUH) and Abu Bakr) set out accompanied by 'Amir bin Fuhaira and the Dili guide who guided them below Mecca along the road leading to the sea-shore (Sahih al-Bukhari 2263)

7. Sincerity

Sincerity remains a key for the resolution of conflicts. All those who are endowed with the responsibility of reconciliation have to remain deeply sincere with conflicting parties with the objective of resolving their dispute amicably.

And if you fear dissension between the two, send an arbitrator from his people and an arbitrator from her people. If they both desire reconciliation, Allah will cause it between them. Indeed, Allah is ever Knowing and Acquainted [with all things] (al-Qur'ān, 4:35)

Knowledge, expertise, and wisdom are key elements in the attributes of Shura. Members of Shura must be knowledgeable of the issues, organisation, and corporate environment in order to understand the issues that are raised in conflict. Professing a statement or deciding on a course of action without appropriate and relevant knowledge is reprehensible in Islam.

And do not pursue that of which you have no knowledge. Indeed, the hearing, the sight and the heart - about all those [one] will be questioned (al-Qur'ān, 17:36)

Prophet Muhammad (PBUH) said: Whoever is issued a ruling that is not based upon knowledge, the person who issued that ruling bears his sin.

Truthfulness, reliability, and sincerity are important characteristics of Shura.

O you who have believed, if there comes to you a disobedient one with information, investigate, lest you harm a people out of ignorance and become, over what you have done, regretful (al-Qur'ān, 49:6)

Truthfulness also plays a definitive role in Shura "And mention in the Book [the story of] Abraham. Indeed, he was a man of truth and a prophet. (al-Qur'ān, 19:41)". Prophet Muhammad (PBUH) said: Beware of lying, for indeed lying leads to corruption, and indeed corruption leads to the Fire. Surely a man will lie and persistently lies such that it written with Allah that he is a liar. Upon you is truthfulness, for surely truthfulness is piety, and piety leads to Heaven. Surely a man tells the truth and is persistently truthful such that it written with Allah that he is a truthful person.

It is imperative that members of Shura have the intention of reconciliation and do not merely act without sincerity.

He said, "O my people, have you considered: if I am upon clear evidence from my Lord and He has provided me with a good provision from Him...? And I do not intend to differ from you in that which I have forbidden you; I only intend reform as much as I am able. And my success is not but through Allah. Upon him I have relied, and to Him I return (al-Qur'ān, 11:88)

Nasīhah (sincere advice) and Ta'awun (mutual cooperation) are established within discussion of Islamic conflict management. A Muslim is highly encouraged to give sincere advice to his compatriots in the event of mistakes or disputes: The religion is sincere advice. (al-Bukhari)

Ta'awun (mutual cooperation) is a proactive behaviour mandated by Islam in all aspects of an individual's life. Ta'awun is required to foster a positive environment that prevents negative conflict. Ta'awun is a communication tool that reduces aggression in the workplace. Mutual cooperation upon righteousness and good is a behavioural norm in Islamic theology. Islamic texts specify Ta'awun to cooperation that leads to piety and good and forbids cooperation that leads to evils and negative outcomes: And cooperate in righteousness and piety, but do not cooperate in sin and aggression. (al-Qur'ān, 5:2)

This Ta'awun is an aspect of culture and not merely a tool for intervention. In a similar fashion, Sabr (patience) is a behavioural attribute that Islamic texts strongly encourage during times of difficulty, conflict, and even ease. The Muslih and Shura must emphasise and encourage patience in the conflict management and resolution process. Muslims are encouraged to remain patient when faced with hardships to success.

O you who have believed, persevere and endure and remain stationed and fear Allah that you may be successful (al-Qur'ān, 3:200)

In the Qur'ān, mankind is described as being in a state of loss, except for those believers who encourage others with correctness and with patience:

By time, (al-Qur'ān, 103:1)

Indeed, mankind is in loss, (al-Qur'ān, 103:2)

Except for those who have believed and done righteous deeds and advised each other to truth and advised each other to patience (al-Qur'ān, 103:3)

Prophet Muhammad encouraged his followers to remain steadfast in the face of conflict with leadership and when a person felt oppressed.

Salam Model: Islamic Conflict Resolution

The SALAM model of Islamic conflict resolution follows a linear progression through mediation. It begins with clearly stating the existence and nature of the conflict (S). Subsequently, the stakeholders within the conflict will agree that there is a conflict (A). Mediation begins with clear communication with both parties listening and learning from each other regarding the variables involved in the conflict (L). The result of this communication is advising each other (A). Finally, the resolution involves minimising disagreement to prevent further escalation of conflict (M). The SALAM model focuses on avoidance, however, if there is greater emphasis on the advice section that is strongly based on communication (L and A), there would be a greater probability toward a positive outcome. The SALAM model focuses on reaction to conflict rather than a proactive environment.

Tahkīm (Arbitration) Model

Moussalli (1997) proposed the Islamic concept of Tahkīm (arbitration) as a model of political conflict resolution. In this model, a third-party arbitrator is chosen to mitigate conflict between contending parties. Arbitration occurs after the conflict takes place, in many instances during escalation of the conflict. This model also suggests that the arbitrator must have attributes of justice, fairness, knowledge, and wisdom. Moussalli (1997) asserted that arbitration in the Islamic context is based on the al-Quran and Sunnah. Irani and Lebanon (1999) discussed the ritualistic nature of conflict management in Islam and postulated that the principles of sulh (settlement) and musalaha (reconcilement) are institutionalised forms of conflict management within Islam. They argued that some Islamic judicial systems revolve around control processes such as shura and sulh (the mediation or reconciliation). Sulh is considered as a contractual agreement in Islamic law, thereby binding the stakeholders to resolve their disputes. However, this approach is considered reactive strategy of conflict management.

Proactive Islamic Model of Conflict Management

Noor (2002) proposed a linear-progression model based on the leadership style of Prophet Muhammad (PBUH). Noor's model can be subdivided into three sections: (1) preliminary investigation, (2) response, and (3) maintenance. According to Noor (2002), the first step involves surveying the environment and approaching the concerned stakeholders to gain further understanding of the causes of conflict. Using this information, the manager or the mediator can diagnose the cause of the conflict and plan steps towards conflict resolution. It is imperative for the manager or the mediator to create a plan of action and a contingency plan at this stage to ensure conflict management and resolution. The manager/mediator should carry out the plan with the knowledge that variables may change and require arbitration. If the resolution is appraised, then the plan is institutionalised as an organisational norm. Alternatively, the manager/mediator must re-diagnose the issue to redesign conflict management/ resolution strategies.

Constructive–Proactive Conflict Management Model

Islamic texts clearly indicate that it is sinful to act and speak based on ignorance. Therefore, Muslims are instructed to refer to "people of knowledge" when they are in need of guidance in their affairs:

And We sent not before you, [O Muhammad], except men to whom We revealed [the message], so ask the people of the message if you do not know (al-Qur'ān, 21:7).

Wisdom is born out of the knowledge and experience. Islamic texts commend the use of wisdom in reconciliation to a high extent (al-Qur'ān, 2:269). Muslims are commanded to seek justice and act justly when reconciling between two conflicting parties:

And if it returns (the dispute), then make settlement between them in justice and act justly. Indeed, Allah loves those who act justly. (Quran, 49:9)

Conflicting parties are encouraged to practice Husn Al-Dhann (having good opinions of the other). To reduce or nullify the negative effect of conflict, stakeholders should assume the best intentions of their counterparts and avoid suspicion:

O you who believe, avoid negative assumption. Indeed, some assumption is sin. And do not spy or backbite each other. Would one of you like to eat the flesh of his brother when dead? You would detest it. And fear Allah; indeed, Allah is accepting of repentance and Merciful. (Quran, 49:12)

The Prophet Muhammad (PBUH) exemplified this organisational framework of brotherhood:

The similitude of believers regarding mutual love, affection, and sympathy is that of one body; when any limb of it aches, the whole-body aches, because of sleeplessness and fever (Muslim, 1996).

The believers are but brothers, reconcile between your brothers. (Quran, 49:10)

The Prophet Muhammad (PBUH) gave his followers directives to desire that their colleagues receive the same treatment and result as themselves (Al-Bukhari, 2001). In fact, he connected this proactive behaviour to soundness of one's belief and commended his followers who acted in the best interest of their counterparts.

CONCLUSION

This chapter has offered some inspired discussion on Islamic work ethics and conflict management approaches according to the principles of Islam. Islamic theology considers that conflict is a part of human nature and if managed properly can lead to achieve positive results. The conflict itself is neither negative nor positive but a natural state of human interactions. The religious interventions to be leveraged to create effective strategies for conflict management. However, if conflict is of unique nature then those who are in authority have to be followed for smooth functioning of the organisation with explicit instructions for those who are in authority to maintain justice as their topmost priority.

The Prophet Muhammad encouraged individuals to facilitate reconciliation by likening it to acts of worship (Abu Dawud). Therefore, a Muslih suffices in the event of minor conflicts without the need to convene a Shura. The Muslih, essentially, is an arbitrator between two disputing parties. The Muslih also operates in a functional capacity and not solely as a facilitator. The main function of the Muslih is Tathabbut (verification). This is due to the commandment to verify information and news received in the event of conflict (Quran, 49:9).

The primary concern of this chapter was to identify the organisation, in an Islamic perspective, as a unified body that requires employees to act according to the best interests and shared values rather than individually. The teaching of Prophet Muhammad has encouraged his followers to remain steadfast in the aspect of conflict with leadership and when a person felt oppressed.

Discussion Questions

1. Critically discuss Proactive Islamic Model of Conflict Management?
2. Analyse and evaluate the holistic approach of Islamic work ethics for effective conflict management approaches ranging from parties

in the conflict to others surrounding the situation to discharge their responsibilities according to the guiding principles of Islam?

3. What are the Islamic work ethics and conflict management approaches according to the principles of Islam?
4. What are the religious interventions to be leveraged to create effective strategies for conflict management?

REFERENCES

Abdalla, A. (2002). Principles of Islamic interpersonal conflict intervention: A search within Islam and western literature. *The Journal of Law and Religion*, *15*(151), 151–184.

Cader, A. A. (2017). Islamic principles of conflict management: A model for human resource management. *International Journal of Cross Cultural Management*, 1–19.

Helmy, S., Labib, A., & AbouKahf, A. (2014). The Impact of Islamic values on interpersonal relationship conflict management in Egyptian business organisations "an applied study". *Procedia: Social and Behavioral Sciences*, *143*, 1090–1110. doi:10.1016/j.sbspro.2014.07.561

Irani, G. E. (1999). Islamic Mediation Techniques for Middle East Conflicts. *Middle East Review of International Affairs*, *3*, 2.

Moussalli, A. S. (1997). An Islamic Model for Political Conflict Resolution: Tahkim. In Conflict Resolution in the Arab World. Academic Press.

Nixon, A. E., Mazzola, J. J., Bauer, J., Krueger, J. R., & Spector, P. E. (2011). Can work make you sick? A meta-analysis of the relationships between job stressors and physical symptoms. *Work and Stress*, *25*(1), 1–22. doi:10.1080/02678373.2011.569175

Noor, I. (2002). *Prophet Muhammads Leadership: The Paragon of Excellence Altruistic Management*. Utusan Publications.

Vehapi, F. (2013). *Conflict Resolution in Islam: Document Review of the Early Sources* (Doctoral Dissertation). Portland State University. (Dissertations and Theses. Paper 1446)

Chapter 11
Protection of Maqasid Al-Shari'ah

ABSTRACT

The Maqasid al-Shari'ah is central to Islamic ethics in protecting individuals against aggressive behaviour of those individuals who manage multinational companies, medium and small businesses, who are pursuing financial gains at the expense of community and the nation as a whole. Islamic ethics fundamentally drives to establish the Maqasid al-Shari'ah with the honest desire of the individual taking responsibility to develop clear and effective intent behind all the daily dealings in business. The purpose of this chapter is to develop an understanding of why the Maqasid al-Shari'ah should be established as key principle as a guide to key stakeholders in dealing with financial matters that ensure justice and contribute to develop the society.

INTRODUCTION

This chapter purpose is to provide an understanding of the Maqasid al-Shari'ah and discuss the essential objectives of Maqasid al-Shari'ah for whole society within Islamic al-Shari'ah. However, understanding the concept of the Maqasid al-Shari'ah is essential part of the faith. The justice and moral values of individuals are based on faith as a central point when dealing with people and society. Otherwise, Maqasid al-Shari'ah is not possible to accomplish and provide for each other.

DOI: 10.4018/978-1-7998-5295-7.ch011

Traditional classifications of maqasid al-Shari'ah divide them into three levels including a) necessities (darurāt), b) needs (hajiyāt), and c) luxuries (tahsiniyāt). Necessities are further classified into what 'preserves one's faith, soul, wealth, mind, and offspring.' Some jurists added 'the preservation of honour' to the above five widely popular necessities. These necessities were considered essential matters for human life itself.

There is also a general agreement that the preservation of these necessities is the 'objective behind any revealed law,' not just the Islamic law. Purposes at the level of needs are less essential for human life. Examples are marriage, trade, and means of transportation. Islam encourages and regulates these needs. However, the lack of any of these needs is not a matter of life and death, especially on an individual basis. Purposes at the level of luxuries are 'beautifying the life,' such as using perfume, stylish clothing, and beautiful homes. These are things that Islam encourages to obtain; however, also asserts how they should take a lower priority in one's life.

Maqasid Al-Shari'ah

The term 'maqsid' (plural: maqāsid) refers to a purpose, objective, principle, intent, goal, end, *telos* (Greek), *finalité* (French), or *Zweck* (German). Maqasid al-Shari'ah are the objectives/purposes/intents/ends/principles behind the Islamic principles. For a number of scholars, it is an alternative expression to people's 'interests' masālih (singular: maslahah). Al-Qarafi (1994) linked maslahah and maqasid by a 'fundamental rule' that stated: 'A purpose (maqsid) is not valid unless it leads to the fulfilment of some good (maslahah) or the avoidance of some mischief (mafsadah).' Therefore, a maqsid, purpose, objective, principle, intent, goal, end, or principle in the Islamic teachings is there for the 'interest of humanity.'

Maqasid al-Shari'ah (purposes of the Islamic law) are classified in various ways by Muslim scholars according to the dimensions of their interest and/or particular focus (Auda, 2008). Following are some of these dimensions for classification of Maqasid al-Shari'ah:

1. Levels of necessity, which is the traditional classification.
2. Scope of the rulings aiming to achieve purposes.
3. Scope of people included in purposes.
4. Level of universality of the purposes.

According to Auda (2008) Contemporary theorists criticised the above traditional classification of necessities for several reasons, including the following:

1. The scope of traditional maqasid is the entire Islamic law. However, they fall
2. short to include specific purposes for single scripts/rulings or groups of scripts
3. that cover certain topics or 'chapters' of Islamic law.
4. Traditional maqāsid are concerned with individuals rather than families, societies, and humans, in general.
5. The traditional maqasid classification did not include the most universal and
6. basic values, such as justice and freedom.
7. Traditional maqasid were deduced from the Islamic legal heritage itself, rather
8. than the original sources/scripts

To remedy the above shortcomings, modern scholarship introduced new conceptions and classifications of al-maqasid by considering new dimensions. First, considering the scope of rulings they cover, contemporary classifications divide maqasid al-Shari'ah into three levels:

1. General maqasid: These maqasid are observed throughout the entire body of
2. the Islamic law, such as the necessities and needs mentioned above and newly
3. proposed maqasid, such as 'justice' and 'facilitation.'
4. Specific maqāsid: These maqasid are observed throughout a certain 'chapter'
5. of the Islamic law, such as the welfare of children in family law, preventing
6. criminals in criminal law, and preventing monopoly in financial transactions
7. law.
8. Partial maqasid: These maqasid are the 'intents' behind specific scripts or
9. rulings, such as the intent of discovering the truth in seeking a certain number
10. of witnesses in certain court cases, the intent of alleviating difficulty in

11. allowing an ill and fasting person to break his/her fasting, and the intent of
12. feeding the poor in banning Muslims from storing meat during Eid/ festival
13. days.

In order to remedy the individuality drawback, the notion of maqasid has been expanded to include a wider scope of people – the community, nation, or humanity, in general. According to Auda (2008, p. 9) "Ibn Ashur (also introduced shortly), for example, gave maqasid that are concerned with the 'nation' (ummah) priority over maqasid that are concerned with individuals. Rashid Rida, for a second example, included 'reform' and 'women's rights' in his theory of maqasid. Yusuf al-Qaradawi, for a third example, included 'human dignity and rights' in his theory of maqasid".

Mohammad al-Ghazaly (d.1416 AH/ 1996 CE) called for 'learning lessons from the previous fourteen centuries of Islamic history,' and therefore, included 'justice and freedom' in maqasid at the necessities level. Al-Ghazali's prime contribution to the knowledge of maqasid was his critique on the literalist tendencies that many of today's scholars have.

Yusuf al-Qaradawi (1345 AH/ 1926 CE -) also surveyed the Quran and concluded the following universal maqasid: 'Preserving true faith, maintaining human dignity and rights, calling people to worship God, purifying the soul, restoring moral values, building good families, treating women fairly, building a strong Islamic nation, and calling for a cooperative world.' However, al-Qaradawi explains that proposing a theory in universal maqasid should only happen after developing a level of experience with detailed scripts.

Kamali (1999) stated that the Maqasid al-Shari'ah, or the goals and objectives of Islamic religious law, is essentially important but somewhat neglected area of research and developments in the studies of Shari'ah. The Shari'ah is predicated on the benefits of the individual and that of the community, and its laws are designed to protect these benefits and facilitate improvement and perfection of the conditions of human life on earth. The Qur'ān is expressive of this when it singles out the most important purpose of the Prophethood of Muhammad (peace be upon him) as:

And We have not sent you, [O Muhammad], except as a mercy to the worlds" (al-Qur'ān, 21: 107).

O mankind, there has to come to you instruction from your Lord and healing for what is in the breasts and guidance and mercy for the believers (al-Qur'ān,10: 57).

Fundamental objectives of compassion (rahmah) and guidance (huda) in the above mentioned verses are then validated by other provisions in the Qur'ān and the Sunnah that seek to establish justice, eliminate prejudice, and alleviate hardship. The laws of the Qur'ān and the Sunnah also seek to promote cooperation and mutual support within the family and the society at large. Justice itself is a manifestation of Allah's (SWT) mercy as well as an objective of the Shariah in its own right. Compassion (rahmah) is manifested in the realisation of benefit (maslahah) which the 'ulama' have generally considered to be the all-pervasive value and objective of the Shariah.

Development and education of people (tahdhib al-fard) is the most important objective of the Shariah so much so that it comes, in order of priority, even before justice and maslahah. Both of these are socially-oriented values which attain their sense in the background of communal relations, whereas tahdhib al-fard focuses to make each and every individual of the society a dependable component and advocate of core values of the Shariah, which can be achieved only through developing and educating the individual to realise most of social objectives of the Shariah.

The Qur'ān is explicitly expressive, at numerous occasions and with several contexts, of the rationale, purpose and benefit of its commandments which leads every instruction of the Qur'ān to a specific objective for the happiness and prosperity of human beings. Particularly this aspect of the Qur'anic teachings is common to its laws on dealings and other civil transactions (mu'āmalāt) as well as religious rituals ('ibadah). Thus, when the Qur'ān illustrates the formalities of ablution for prayer (wudu') it declares that:

Allah does not intend to make difficulty for you, but He intends to purify you and complete His favour upon you that you may be grateful (al-Qur'ān, 5: 6).

With regard to the prayer, the most important pillar of Islam, it is declared that

.... Indeed, prayer prohibits immorality and wrongdoing... (al-Qur'ān, 29: 45)

The Qur'ān proclaims the purpose of jihad in the following manner:

Permission [to fight] has been given to those who are being fought, because they were wronged. And indeed, Allah is competent to give them victory (al-Qur'ān, 22: 39).

It means the purpose of allowing jihad is to fight injustice (zulm) and the purpose of salāh remains to attain spiritual purity and fineness to be accomplished together with physical cleanliness through ablution before prayer.

Teachings of the Qur'ān about retaliation in kind (qisās) declare that

And there is for you in legal retribution [saving of] life, O you [people] of understanding... (al-Qur'ān, 2: 179)

The Qur'anic teachings categorically suggest the objective of Zakah, a mandatory almsgiving and the second most important pillar of Islam after namaz (prayer) in the following verse:

- so that it will not be a perpetual distribution among the rich from among you (al-Qur'ān, 59:7).

The Qur'anic teachings educate believers to lower their gaze in their encounter with females with following rationale:

Tell the believing men to reduce [some] of their vision and guard their private parts. That is purer for them. Indeed, Allah is Acquainted with what they do (al-Qur'ān, 24: 30).

The maqasid al-Shari'ah maintain central place in Islamic ethics. Attainment of maqasid al-Shari'ah remains crucial for contemporary workplace. According to Islamic ethics organisations should endure to protect maqasid al-Shari'ah for all relevant stakeholders. There are numerous classifications and components of maqasid al-Shari'ah according to the needs and requirements of the time. However central theme of maqasid al-Shari'ah stands the same as classical scholars suggested. Hierarchy of maqasid al-Shari'ah of Islamic ethics for contemporary workplace is presented in figure 1, where protection of life, faith, integrity and property take precedence over other objectives (maqasid) of al-Shari'ah.

Figure 1. Hierarchy of Maqasid

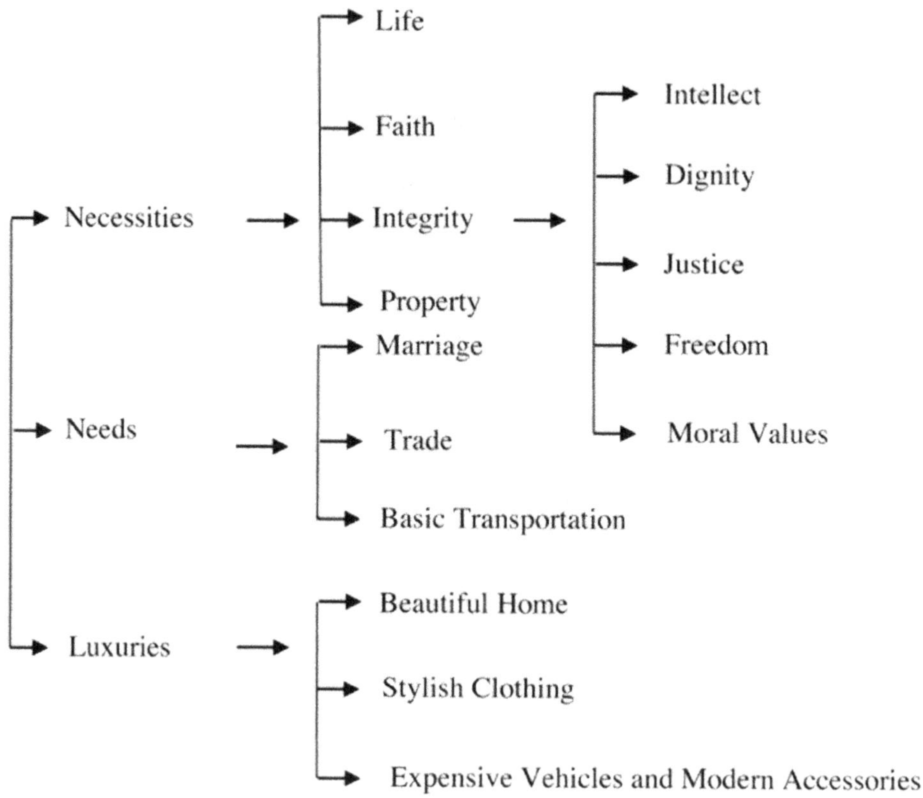

Human beings have always remained in search of protection. Objective of entire dynamism, scientific developments, social and political struggles on this planet is attaining durable protection for existence. Reliable protection inculcates confidence and satisfaction in people. Islamic teachings did not ignore this important aspect of life, al-Qur'ān says:

But Allah is your protector, and He is the best of helpers (al-Qur'ān 3:150)

There are different expressions of protection in al-Qur'ān to infuse reliance among people as mentioned in the following verses:

Allah is the protector of those who have faith: from the depths of darkness He will lead them forth into light. Of those who reject faith the patrons are the Evil Ones: from light they will lead them forth into the depths of darkness. They will be Companions of the Fire, to dwell therein (forever) (al-Qur'ān 2:257)

Say, "Never will we be struck except by what Allah has decreed for us; He is our protector". And upon Allah let the believers rely (al-Qur'ān 9:51)

Protection of Life

Islamic teachings explicitly support protection of life:

Nor take life -which Allah has made sacred- except for just cause (al - Qur'ān 17:33)

And remember We took your Covenant (to this effect): shed no blood amongst you, (al - Qur'ān 2:84)

On that account: We ordained for the Children of Israel that if anyone slew a person -unless it be for murder or for spreading mischief in the land- it would be as if he slew the whole people: and if any one saved a life, it would be as if he saved the life of the whole people (al-Qur'ān 5:32)

Modudi (2005a) explained that the existence of human life in the world depends on the fact that every individual respect the right of life of other individuals and help others in protecting the life (p. 464). A person, who unjustly takes the life of others, is not brutal to only one person, but he proves that he doesn't respect human life and he has no sympathy for human beings. Such characteristics can destroy entire humanity. Contrarily if a person helps protect the life, he is promoting humanity, because he has such quality as is vital for the existence of humanity. According to Human Events (2008) all life deserves to be protected and we should aspire to build a society where each one of us is welcomed in life.

Protection of human life is such an important concern in IVS as every member of organisation in general and leadership is responsible to contribute for the safety of human lives. This is the responsibility of leadership to provide safe working environment to employees to avoid any damage to human life. Islamic leadership must ensure on job safety in the organisation to avoid any human loss.

Protection of Faith

Islam gives liberty to everyone to practice his faith, thus ensures protection of every one's faith working in one organisation.

Allah (SWT) says that:

Let there be no compulsion in religion: Truth stands out clear from Error: whoever rejects Evil and believes in Allah hath grasped the most trustworthy hand-hold, that never breaks. And Allah heareth and knoweth all things (al - Qur'ān 2:256)

Modudi (2005a) explained that the meaning of this Verse is that no one can be forced to follow Islam's ideological, ethical and practical system of life (p. 196). Islamic teachings offer convincing paradigm for all people to follow the truth. There is no need to force people to follow Islam. Those who will follow will cherish peaceful and durable dynamics of social life and those who will not follow Islamic teachings will face consequences.

Umar (RA) Assurance

Assurance of safety given by Hazrat Umar bin al-Khattab (RA) to the people of Jerusalem in April 637 at the time of conquest is the prime example of protection of faith delineated by maqasid al-Shari'ah. This pact guaranteed protection of faith to all non-Muslims in following terms:

1. This is the assurance of safety [aman] which the servant of God Umar, the Commander of the Faithful, has given to the people of Jerusalem.
2. He has given them an assurance of safety for themselves, for their property, their churches, their crosses, the sick and healthy of the city and for all the rituals which belong to their religion.

It means Islamic work ethics for contemporary workplace can only facilitate protection of faith for every member of the organisation both Muslims and non-Muslims to practice their faith freely and independently as long as it does not impede peaceful coexistence, effective and efficient performance of all stakeholders of the organisation to achieve collective organisational objectives.

Protection of Integrity

Islamic attributes significant emphasis to protection of respect and integrity of all fellow human beings highlighted in figure 11.2. Modudi (2005b) mentioned that Islam declares all Muslims as universal family (p. 83).

The Believers are but a single Brotherhood: so, make peace and reconciliation between your two (contending) brothers (al - Qur'ān 49:10)

There is clear instruction for Islamic workforce to give new dimensions to management by ensuring protection of integrity of all organisational members. Allah (SWT) says in Qur'ān-e-Hakeem;

O ye who believe! let not some men among you laugh at others: it may be that the (latter) are better than the (former): nor let some women laugh at others: it may be that the (latter) are better than the (former): nor defame nor be sarcastic to each other, nor call each other by (offensive) nicknames: (al - Qur'ān 49:11)

Figure 2. LFIP Protection Model of Islamic Ethics

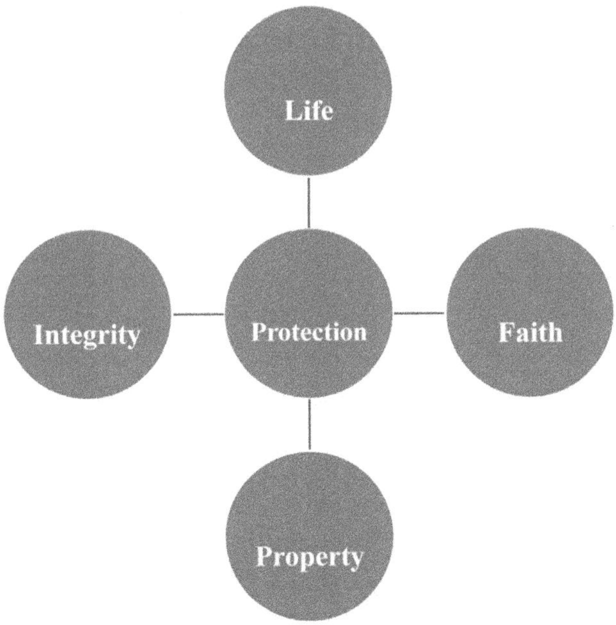

Islamic ethics give emphasis on the protection of integrity of every members of the organisation, as Allah (SWT) says:

nor speak ill of each other behind their backs (al - Qur'ān 49:12)

Speaking ill at the back of others manifests invading respect of others. Sayings of Prophet (PBUH) also strongly prohibit doing so.

Islamic value system starts with unity, as Allah SWT says in above mentioned Verse 49:10 that all Muslims are knitted with the relationship of brotherhood. This notion itself promotes the protection of integrity among all Muslims, as every brother is the guardian of integrity of other brother, in the same way all Muslims are the guardians of one another's integrity.

Islamic ethics addresses even minute aspects of interaction among people in their daily life. Islamic ethics doesn't allow anyone to laugh at others, to defame others, to be sarcastic and to call others by offensive nicknames as these are the means to invade integrity of others. The concept of 'do unto others as you would have others do unto you' is the value that makes the world a more decent and civilised place.

Islamic ethics give prime importance to individual respect and integrity, therefore speaking ill behind each other is strongly prohibited. On one side invading integrity is not allowed and on the other if someone is doing so, fellow beings have to stop him/her if they don't, they are equally guilty.

Following important aspects of integrity need special attention at contemporary workplaces:

(i) Intellect
(ii) Dignity
(iii) Justice
(iv) Freedom
(v) Moral values

Intellect

It has been narrated on the authority of Abi Ja'far al-Baqir (a.s.), God - Exalted is His Praise - created the Intellect. Then God ordered it to come forward, and it did. He then ordered it to go back, and it did. Then God stated, "I swear by My Majesty and Honor and I have not created any creatures dearer to me than you (referring to the Intellect) and would not perfect anyone's intellect unless I like him. I shall enjoin others to do good and admonish others against evil due to the Intellect. Reward and punishment is given by means of the Intellect" (Intellect, n.d.).

The Intellect is the most important thing which is the source of man's honor and virtue. The angels prostrate to man exactly due to the existence of the intellect in him. Man is the only creature from amongst all the creatures that has acquired this honor. Also, it is the most significant blessing which God the Blessed the Sublime has favored man with, so that he may distinguish the good from the evil, and the ugly from the beautiful by using it (Intellect, n.d.).

All this honour and virtues are due to the intellect. Al-Qur'ān stresses that one must think and use his/her intellect to progress, prosper and find solutions. This has been stressed many times in the Holy Quran such as:

..... perhaps you may use your intellect (al-Qur'ān 2:73)

Dignity

Human dignity is one of the most important aspects of Islamic teachings. There are valuable fundamentals of human dignity presented in al-Qur'ān and traditions of the Prophet Muhammad (PBUH). Human dignity, in contemporary legal and social literature, means that human being is inherently a venerated, esteemed and honoured creature. Although the term inherent dignity is not explicitly mentioned in al-Qur'ān, however human dignity in al-Qur'ān can be contemplated and investigated.

And We have certainly honoured the children of Adam and carried them on the land and sea and provided for them of the good things and preferred them over much of what We have created, with [definite] preference (al-Qur'ān 17:70)

The Messenger of Allah (PBUH) said: "When the words of Iqama are pronounced, none of you should run to it (to join the prayer) but walk with tranquillity and dignity, and pray what you are in time for and complete what has gone before (what the Imam has completed)" (Sahih Muslim 602 d).

Justice

The Prophet (PBUH) said: "If anyone seeks the office of judge among Muslims till he gets it and his justice prevails over his tyranny, he will go to Paradise;

but the man whose tyranny prevails over his justice will go to Hell" (Sunan Abi Dawud 3575).

The Prophet (PBUH) said: "The best fighting (jihad) in the path of Allah is (to speak) a word of justice to an oppressive ruler" (Sunan Abi Dawud 4344).

Freedom

According to Madani (2011) Allah (SWT) gave liberty of free choice between right and wrong. It is in the same reference that Allah (SWT) says in the Holy Qur'ān:

And inspired it [with discernment of] its wickedness and its righteousness, (al-Qur'ān 91:08)

This verse reflects that freedom is equally a shared goal of mankind, wherewith none violates freedom of other individuals.

The freedom in Islam is like allowance of movement to a horse tied with a rope. It is like authority which implies responsibility and accountability thus provides justification for the day of judgement. This is the clear message of Islam to whole mankind on earth and under the sun: There is no compulsion in religion.

All] sovereignty that Day is for Allah; He will judge between them. So, they who believed and did righteous deeds will be in the Gardens of Pleasure (al-Qur'ān 22:56)

Never did the Holy Prophet (peace be upon him) deny any human-being his right to freedom of expression. Both the believers of Islam and non-believers could freely speak their minds in front of him (Madani, 2011).

Moral Values

According to (Halstead, 2007) there are three main kinds of values in Islam:

a. akhlāq, which refers to the duties and responsibilities set out in the shari'ah and in Islamic teaching generally
b. aadab, which refers to the manners associated with good breeding
c. the qualities of character possessed by a good Muslim, following the example of the Prophet Muhammad (PBUH).

The inextricable link that exists in Islam between religion and morality is reflected in the many passages in al-Qur'ān that refer in the same breath to 'those who believe' and 'those who do good deeds'.

And give good tidings to those who believe and do righteous deeds that they will have gardens [in Paradise] beneath which rivers flow. Whenever they are provided with a provision of fruit therefrom, they will say, "This is what we were provided with before". And it is given to them in likeness. And they will have therein purified spouses, and they will abide therein eternally (al-Qur'ān 2:25)

Except for those who believe and do righteous deeds, for they will have a reward uninterrupted (al-Qur'ān 95:6)

Except for those who have believed and done righteous deeds and advised each other to truth and advised each other to patience (al-Qur'ān 103:3)

The implications seem to be that for Muslims faith and moral behaviour are two sides of the same coin, that moral behaviour presupposes faith and that faith is genuine only if it results in moral behaviour (Halstead, 2007).

Protection of Property (The Ownership)

Islamic ethics give attention to protect the property of every member of the organisation and prohibit everyone from illegal possession of property of others.

And do not eat up your property among yourselves for vanities, nor use it as bait for the judges, with intent that ye may eat up wrongfully and knowingly a little of (other) people's property (al-Qur'ān 2:188)

Modudi (2005a) explained that one interpretation of this Verse is that one should not take advantage by offering bribes to rulers (p. 148). Another meaning is that if one knows that the property belongs to other person, only because he doesn't have proof of his ownership; one should not take the case to court with the intention that one could eat his property.

To orphans restore their property (when they reach their age), nor substitute (your) worthless things for (their) good ones; and devour not their substance (by mixing it up) with your own. For this is indeed a great sin (al - Qur'ān 4:2)

Protection of every one's property is an important element in Islamic ethics. No one is allowed to use influence or money to occupy the property of other fellow beings. Divine laws of all ages assert same emphasis on protection of property of others as it is mentioned in Biblical privacy theme that "you shall not take someone else's property" (bcbsr.com). This brings satisfaction among all members of organisation that in a system under which they work or live takes the responsibility to protect their Life, Faith, Integrity and Property (LFIP).

To ensure protection of LFIP is the most sensitive and important responsibility of leadership in Islamic ethics. Leadership is responsible not only for the welfare of all stakeholders of organisation including business, employees, society and environment, but also for the protection of LFIP of all those who work with the organisation. Therefore, Islamic ethics paves the way for organisational environment that ensures welfare and protection of all stakeholders of the organisation.

CONCLUSION

This chapter provided insight to role of Maqasid al-Shari'ah plays in daily life of individual and how businesses should adopt key principles of Islamic values to ensure justice and contribute to development of whole society. Otherwise, Maqasid al-Shari'ah is not possible to accomplish and provide guideline for each other. However, Maqasid al-Shari'ah is essential part of the faith and set out clear goals for business community to follow when dealing with business transactions. The justice and moral values of individuals are based on faith as a central point when dealing with people and society. Protection of every one's property is an important element in Islamic ethics. Divine laws of all ages assert same emphasis on protection of property of others and bring satisfaction among all members of organisation and other key stakeholders.

The Maqasid al-Shari'ah play central role in Islamic ethics. Observation of Maqasid al-Shari'ah remains crucial for contemporary workplace. The Islamic ethics bear to protect Maqasid al-Shari'ah for all relevant stakeholders.

There are numerous classifications and components of Maqasid al-Shari'ah according to the needs and requirements of the time. Maqasid al-Shari'ah provides guideline to businesses and individuals to regulates their daily life according to teaching of Islamic ethics that benefit human beings, society and whole business environment. Maqasid al-Shari'ah system starts with unity and protection of integrity among all Muslims, as every brother is the guardian of integrity of other brother, in the same way all Muslims are the guardians of one another's integrity. Therefore, Islamic ethics paves the way for organisational environment that ensures welfare and protection of all stakeholders of the organisation.

Discussion Questions

1. Critically evaluate the principle of Maqasid al-Shari'ah for multinational companies?
2. Discuss the essential objectives of Maqasid al-Shari'ah for whole society within Islamic al-Shari'ah?
3. How Islamic ethics paves the way for organisational environment that ensures welfare and protection of all stakeholders of the organisation?
4. Discuss the importance of Islam attributes plays to protection of respect and integrity of all human beings?

REFERENCES

Auda, J. (2008). *Maqasid Al-Shariah an Introductory Guide*. IIIT. doi:10.2307/j.ctvkc67c6

Halstead, J. M. (2007). Islamic values: A distinctive framework for moral education? *Journal of Moral Education*, *36*(3), 283–296. doi:10.1080/03057240701643056

Intellect. (n.d.). *Chapter 1: On the Intellect*. Retrieved on May 23, 2019 from https://www.al-islam.org/bright-lights-guidance-muhammad-ali-khansary/chapter-1-intellect#f_0655a9a3_1

Kamali, M. H. (1999). Maqāṣid al-Sharī'ah: the objectives of Islamic law. *Islamic Studies*, *38*(2), 193–208.

Madni, A. H. (2011). Freedom and Its Concept in Islam. In *2nd International Conference on Humanities, Historical and Social Sciences IPEDR* (vol. 17). IACSIT Press.

Modudi, A. A. (2005). Tafheem-ul-Qur'ān, vol. 1. Idara-e-Tarjaman ul Qur'ān Lahore.

Chapter 12
Diversity, Liberty, and Virtue in Islam

ABSTRACT

Islamic teachings state that diversity is intended to encourage people to learn and understand each other rather than disharmony. It requires one to look at the mindset and the culture of an organisation and the different perspectives people bring to an organisation on account of their ethnicity, social background, professional values, styles, disabilities, or other differences. Diversity is 'otherness' or those human qualities that are different from our own and outside the groups to which we belong yet are present in other individuals and groups. Age, ethnicity, gender, physical abilities, race, and sexual orientation are considered primary dimensions, while education, place of residence, class, marital status, religious beliefs, occupational status, and life experiences are secondary dimensions of diversity. This chapter aims to analyse and discuss diversity management as an inclusive concept, encompassing a broader focus than employment equity.

INTRODUCTION

This chapter further focuses on diversity procedures, it is usually thought of in terms of obvious attributes – age differences, race, gender, physical ability, sexual orientation, religion and language. Diversity in terms of background professional experience, skills and specialisation, values and culture, as well as social class, is a prevailing pattern.

DOI: 10.4018/978-1-7998-5295-7.ch012

The last sermon of holy Prophet (PBUH) specifically addresses dimensions of human diversity while laying down basic principle of superiority i.e. righteousness does not race, ethnicity or any other aspect of otherness:

All mankind is from Adam and Eve, an Arab has no superiority over a non-Arab nor a non-Arab has any superiority over an Arab; also, a white has no superiority over a black nor does a black have any superiority over a white - except by piety and good action.

The concepts of diversity and multiculturalism can be easily found in several verses of the al-Qur'ān and the tradition (*Sunnah*) of holy Prophet (PBUH) (Muhtada, 2012).

Had Allah willed, He would have made you one nation [united in religion], but [He intended] to test you in what He has given you; (al-Qur'ān 5:48)

Even though humankinds are created in diversity, the concept of unity and brotherhood are crucial. The diversity of human beings should not lead to disharmony (Muhtada, 2012).

O mankind, fear your Lord, who created you from one soul and created from it its mate and dispersed from both of them many men and women (al-Qur'ān 4:1)

This verse reminds human beings that they have been created of a single sole, so that they should respect each other (Muhtada, 2012). The same message of brotherhood is repeated in following verse:

O mankind, indeed, We have created you from male and female and made you peoples and tribes that you may know one another (al-Qur'ān 49:13)

Gender equity is reflected through several verses that treat male and female equally (Muhtada, 2012).

And whoever does righteous deeds, whether male or female, while being a believer - those will enter Paradise and will not be wronged, [even as much as] the speck on a date seed (al-Qur'ān 4:124)

And their Lord responded to them, "Never will I allow to be lost the work of [any] worker among you, whether male or female;" (al-Qur'ān 3:195)

In Islamic ethics male and female have same opportunities to secure rewards of their deeds:

Whoever does righteousness, whether male or female, while he is a believer - We will surely cause him to live a good life, and We will surely give them their reward [in the Hereafter] according to the best of what they used to do (al-Qur'ān 16:97)

Indeed, the Muslim men and Muslim women, the believing men and believing women, the obedient men and obedient women, the truthful men and truthful women, the patient men and patient women, the humble men and humble women, the charitable men and charitable women, the fasting men and fasting women, the men who guard their private parts and the women who do so, and the men who remember Allah often and the women who do so - for them Allah has prepared forgiveness and a great reward (al-Qur'ān 33:35)

Islamic ethics establish common grounds among other religious communities to emphasise similarities instead of differences:

Say, "O People of the Scripture, come to a word that is equitable between us and you - that we will not worship except Allah and not associate anything with Him and not take one another as lords instead of Allah". But if they turn away, then say, "Bear witness that we are Muslims [submitting to Him]" (al-Qur'ān 3:64)

Islamic teaches respect for places of worship of other religions:

[They are] those who have been evicted from their homes without right - only because they say, "Our Lord is Allah ". And were it not that Allah checks the people, some by means of others, there would have been demolished monasteries, churches, synagogues, and mosques in which the name of Allah is much mentioned. And Allah will surely support those who support Him. Indeed, Allah is Powerful and Exalted in Might (al-Qur'ān 22:40)

Management of Diversity and Islamic Ethics

According to Muhtada (2012, p. 82) "Managing diversity is about valuing employees as individuals. It is about transforming organisational culture to recognise the heterogeneity of employees. It does not only embrace the range of individual characteristics that differentiate employees, but also implement policies and managerial skills that maximise every worker's contributions to the organisational purposes. It also means the planned and systematic commitment of organisations to recruit, retain, reward, and promote their heterogeneous employees"

The management of diversity is important for senior management to value the employees from different backgrounds. Diversity is considered fundamental principle for individual and business community to meets the challenges and benefits to meet the changing workforce of the world. Table 1 looks at the Challenges & Benefits of Diversity Management within organisation that faces key business managers on daily basis. In modern world diversity, democratic rule, religious liberty and freedom impression plays key role in the success of the business development in recruiting employees from diverse background.

Table 1. Challenges & Benefits of Diversity Management

Challenges	Benefits
Convincing all stakeholders that diversity is inevitable	Greater workforce unity and productivity
Marketing the benefits of diversity management, because, costs are easier to quantify than benefits	Widening the suite of performance indicators to include qualitative measures as well as purely financial
Existing employees may feel threatened or resentful and may perceive that recruitment and promotion opportunities have been reduced	Employment conditions can be developed to meet individual needs and aspirations (as opposed to one size fits all)

Hayes (1999) categorises six levels of organisation (from level 0 to 5) in dealing with workforce diversity. An organisation at level "zero" has thought about equitable employment status, but it does not have any diversity management policy. An organisation at level "one" performs equity policies just to avoid legal consequences. An organisation at level "two" has a desire to "lend a hand" to the disadvantaged employees because of a sense of altruism.

An organisation at level "three" implements diversity programs because of "business reasons" such as improving customer service or organisation performance. An organisation at level "four" is motivated to realise equity and takes steps to make it happen. It trains its employees to build a work environment that recognises diversity. Such an organisation is in transition to be one at level "five", which has created a culture that values heterogeneity and provided an inclusive work environment for all employees. Figure 1 outlines the equity groups.

Figure 1. The Equity Continuum
Level 0 = Think about equitable employment status; Level 1 = Legislative fairness
Level 2 = Altruism; Level 3 = Business reasons; Level 4 = Transition
Level 5 = Equitable employment status
Source: *Hayes, V. (1999), Beyond employment equity: the business case for diversity, Ivey Business Journal, 64(1), 45-46*

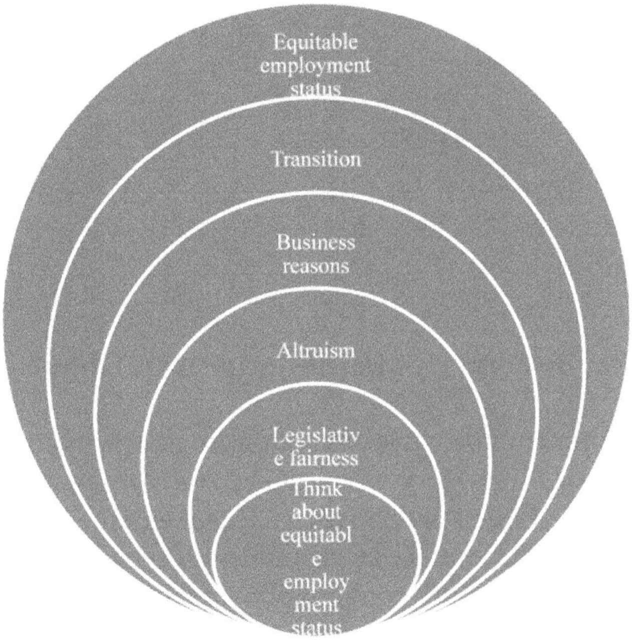

Friday and Friday (2003) indicate three potential states in dealing with diversity, namely acknowledging diversity, valuing diversity, and managing diversity. Acknowledging diversity refers to recognising the existence of individual differences. Valuing diversity refers to appreciating and respecting the significance of diversity. Managing diversity refers to a set of actions to manage individual differences such as planning, organising, and leading, which is intended to achieve the organisation's strategic purposes. The figure 2 highlights the managing diversity concept.

Figure 2. Managing Diversity Concept
Source: *Friday, E and Friday, S. S. (2003), Managing diversity using a strategic planned change approach, Journal of Management Development, 22, (10), 863-880*

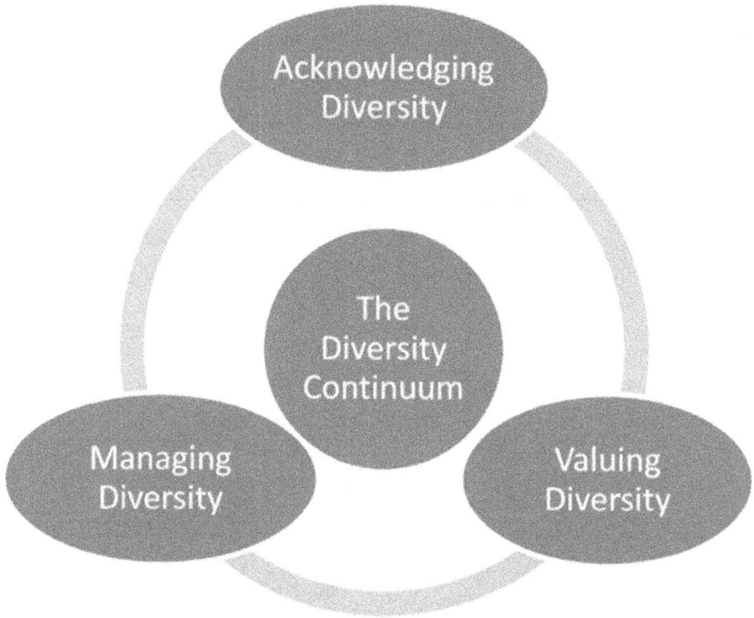

Qualities for Successful Management of Diversity

- **Leadership:** demonstrable commitment and support including the establishment of advisory groups and effective communication plans.
- **Valid and Reliable Performance Measurement:** pan-organisational assessments, benchmarking and comparative analysis.
- **Education:** awareness training complemented by advance training, development of in-house expertise.
- **Cultural and Management Change:** devising and implementing effective human resource management strategies.
- **Follow-up:** longitudinal evaluation, performance management system and knowledge management.

Liberty

Humans have always been in search of suitable framework of life. It is human instinct to spend life according to a doctrine. Constitutions, acts, regulations, policies and reports are all indicative of human endeavor to outline human life. Liberty as a concept has same dynamics with certain exceptions for every society. Islam provides significant space for liberty of choice. Islam desires lasting success and prosperity of an individual. There are detailed teachings about good and bad, sin and righteousness, rights and responsibilities in al-Qur'ān and Sunnah. An individual is then having complete liberty to choose any of the option. However, the basic philosophy of the Islam is to spread eternal peace and prosperity for human beings, therefore Islam has a complete support program to help an individual to avoid unjustifiable way of life. There are numerous verses of al-Qur'ān to advantages of virtuous path and disadvantages of sinful path. Islam provides liberty to the extent where others are not hurt. Nevertheless, in Islamic ethics individuals have independent persona with complete liberty of choice to shape up their destinies.

Dynamics of religiosity, liberty and plurality are significant for Muslim societies (Sambur, 2009) due to multifaceted interpretations and theological viewpoints settled in these societies over a few previous centuries. Muslims had vibrant societies accommodating several societies across the globe, eliminating racial and ethnic demarcations and joining hands with new strange cultures to learn and make them learn about their novel approach to life and religion. However, present-day Muslim societies are faced with the challenge of connecting to the heritage of their early times.

Over a few decades Muslims are resisting to keep their identity as historically unique, but this effort is intentionally or unintentionally heading to the circumstances where Muslims in their own selves are becoming case of marginalisation. The present and future of Muslim world largely depends on how Muslims see the nature of the relationship of religiosity, liberty and plurality. Muslims must develop a new perspective, which values liberty and pluralism as the highest values. Islam is indeed not the religion of fear, but a religion of freedom and pluralism where those who were not accepted by their own religious communities were welcomed by Islam and were given equal rights. If we start to ignore this inherent value of liberty and pluralism of Islam, tyranny and oppression would prevail and Muslim societies would be side-lined even further. Muslim societies should not forget that the idea of equality and freedom must grow in the hearts of all men and women before it can be killed at the hands of oppressors.

So-called traditional and literalist circles have resisted against free ideas in the name of defending religiosity and piety. These people have easily declared individuals, who think differently from them about Islamic issues, as apostates (kafir) and tried to oppress them (Sambur, 2009). Refusing freedom while maintain fundamental five pillars is not an Islamic attitude. Encouraging free debate and discussion is more Islamic attitude than oppressing various ideas to explore huge potential of this universe. The Qur'ān explicitly and repeatedly encourages people to think and reflect. It is not Islam, which promotes un-freedom and oppression. However, unfortunately it is Muslim attitudes, which put Islam in the side of fear and un-freedom. Religion easily could be turned into a totalitarian religion which such attitudes and practices. Islam itself is absolutely not a totalitarian way of life; it certainly promotes liberty and pluralism among Muslims in specific and among all human beings in general. Nevertheless, turning Islam to Islamism, from religion to religionism makes Islam hostile to freedom. Islamism, freedom and pluralism are incompatible, but Islam as natural religion promotes and encourages liberty and pluralism (Sambur, 2009).

According to Sir Muhammad Iqbal (1877-1938) "When enslaved, life is reduced to a small rivulet, in freedom, it is like a boundless ocean". He regards Islam as the universal religion of liberty and humanity as follows:

Liberty took roots from this message,
The sweet wine dripped from its grapes.
It never tolerated invidious distinctions,
Equality was implicit in its nature.
The modern age which has kindled a hundred lights,
Has opened its eyes in its lap.

Inner and outer life of humans is unique, they live, act, think and feel as unique being. Human action in outside world is the external manifestation of individual uniqueness. Humans shape their life according to unique aims, desires and ideals (Sambur, 2009).

Say, "Each works according to his manner, but your Lord is most knowing of who is best guided in way" (al-Qur'ān 17:84)

None can be forced to limit the freedom of choice. It is up to individuals to decide what is good or bad for them. Islam does not impose a choice on society and individuals. The Prophet Muhammad (PBUH) did not force people to accept the message of Islam.

And say, "The truth is from your Lord, so whoever wills - let him believe; and whoever wills - let him disbelieve" (al-Qur'ān 18:29)

It is evident from following verse of al-Qur'ān that plurality, not homogeneity, is the Divine plan of Allah (SWT) for the humanity.

And had your Lord willed, those on earth would have believed - all of them entirely. Then, [O Muhammad], would you compel the people in order that they become believers? (al-Qur'ān 10:99)

Islamic ethics suggest that anyone who wants to accept Islam should do this with complete freedom of choice; no one can be forced to accept Islam.

There shall be no compulsion in [acceptance of] the religion (al-Qur'ān 2:256)

Every individual has the right to have different believes. The Qur'ān expresses the right of individual to be different as follows:

For you is your religion, and for me is my religion (al-Qur'ān 109:6)

The Qur'ān recognises the diversity of human society and commands Muslims to be a part of this society (Sambur, 2009):

And We have revealed to you, [O Muhammad], the Book in truth, confirming that which preceded it of the Scripture and as a criterion over it. So, judge between them by what Allah has revealed and do not follow their inclinations away from what has come to you of the truth. To each of you We prescribed a law and a method. Had Allah willed, He would have made you one nation [united in religion], but [He intended] to test you in what He has given you; so race to [all that is] good. To Allah is your return all together, and He will [then] inform you concerning that over which you used to differ (al-Qur'ān 5:48)

Virtue

The development of good character in Islam is mostly a process of dealing with one's emotions. It helps to build and support positive or good emotions or virtues and to fight and suppress negative emotions. Character building would, therefore, have much to do with patience and perseverance in controlling emotions leading to negative aspects and reinforcement of emotions leading to positive ethics. Manipulation of emotions lead to good ethics would also guide one to have a spiritually and psychologically healthy life (Abdullah, 2014).

Virtues have recently become a significant topic of examination among organisational researchers who are exploring their role in creating more progressive, compassionate, and humane work environments. The current understanding of virtues and virtuousness in organisations is still 'adolescent' and not yet been fully developed. Little empirical research focuses on the diverse types of virtues in organisations. As organisations which have long been viewed as rational systems are considering making room for emotions, meaning, spirituality, and community. A large set of virtues have been discussed in organisational literature as enablers of organisational effectiveness including integrity, courage, fairness and justice, service to others, humility, and forgiveness (Karakas *et. al.*, 2017).

In the perspective of Islamic ethics following virtues needs to develop in the contemporary workplace to develop virtuous organisations to meet challenges of the modern days.

Think and Reflect

The most important virtue for contemporary workplace is to 'think and reflect' for innovations, improvements, developments and solutions. Allah (SWT) urged human beings at several occasions in al-Qur'ān to think and reflect to understand evident but complex dynamics of creatures and the creation of this universe. Purpose of this invitation to 'think and reflect' is that people can recognise and comprehend the existence of the Worthy Being. People are encouraged to 'think and reflect' upon their surroundings, cosmic dynamic, growing of crops, conversion of day & night, creation & reproduction of human beings and several other motivations to 'think and reflect'.

Then do they not reflect upon the Qur'an? If it had been from [any] other than Allah, they would have found within it much contradiction (al-Qur'ān 4:82)

Then do they not reflect upon the Qur'an, or are there locks upon [their] hearts? (al-Qur'ān 47:24)

The example of [this] worldly life is but like rain which We have sent down from the sky that the plants of the earth absorb - [those] from which men and livestock eat - until, when the earth has taken on its adornment and is beautified and its people suppose that they have capability over it, there comes to it Our command by night or by day, and We make it as a harvest, as if it had not flourished yesterday. Thus, do We explain in detail the signs for a people who give thought (al-Qur'ān 10:24)

Muslims were extremely fortunate that Allah (SWT) gave them fourteen hundred years ago numerous indications to think, reflect and pursue scientific developments to realise benefits of opportunities created by the Almighty available in and around this planet. However, Muslims considered these indications either as miracles or part of their belief system to trust without any doubt or pondering on relevant dimensions. Following are a few clues, just for examples to support our argument, which Muslims failed to capture thus remained unsuccessful to realise scientific developments and innovations which these indications could have manifested. Verses which outlined a huge depth of human creation are as follows;

Created man from a clinging substance (al-Qur'ān 96:2)

It is He who created you from dust, then from a sperm-drop, then from a clinging clot; then He brings you out as a child; then [He develops you] that you reach your [time of] maturity, then [further] that you become elders. And among you is he who is taken in death before [that], so that you reach a specified term; and perhaps you will use reason (al-Qur'ān 40:67)

Details of human development in the womb came to surface in recent times but Muslims had these indications in quite early centuries, but they couldn't dig these details only because they failed to 'think and reflect' on these verses.

The verse about rotation of day and night and weather dynamics was a blessing for human beings, however, those who were not aware of this verse worked on these areas and today we have precise information about these aspects.

Indeed, in the creation of the heavens and earth, and the alternation of the night and the day, and the [great] ships which sail through the sea with that which benefits people, and what Allah has sent down from the heavens of rain, giving life thereby to the earth after its lifelessness and dispersing therein every [kind of] moving creature, and [His] directing of the winds and the clouds controlled between the heaven and the earth are signs for a people who use reason (al-Qur'ān 2:164)

Flying of Hazrat Sulaiman (AS) was told to Muslims hundreds of years ago, except a few reported primitive attempts in Morocco we can't find serious attempts to develop an aero plane, probably because Muslims submitted to the fact that it was a miracle of a prophet.

And to Solomon [We subjected] the wind - its morning [journey was that of] a month - and its afternoon [journey was that of] a month, and We made flow for him a spring of [liquid] copper. And among the jinn were those who worked for him by the permission of his Lord. And whoever deviated among them from Our command - We will make him taste of the punishment of the Blaze (al-Qur'ān 34:12)

There are numerous indications in al-Qur'ān and a hadith to think and reflect to invent or find innovative and effective ways of performing in contemporary environments. Space scientists and physicists can still have significant opportunity of research on the route of the night journey of Prophet Muhammad (PBUH) to find most suitable corridor to access space.

Exalted is He who took His Servant by night from al-Masjid al-Haram to al-Masjid al- Aqsa, whose surroundings We have blessed, to show him of Our signs. Indeed, He is the Hearing, the Seeing (al-Qur'ān 17:1)

And he revealed to His Servant what he revealed. The heart did not lie [about] what it saw. So, will you dispute with him over what he saw? And he certainly saw him in another descent At the Lote Tree of the Utmost Boundary - Near it is the Garden of Refuge - When there covered the Lote Tree that which covered [it]. The sight [of the Prophet] did not swerve, nor did it transgress [its limit]. He certainly saw of the greatest signs of his Lord (al-Qur'ān 53:10-18)

Psychologists and experts in hormones still have to determine chemical, hormonal and psychological impact of Halal food upon human beings. Nowadays religiosity is at the center of investigations. A recently published Harvard study suggested that religious upbringing is better for kid's health and wellbeing (Justice, 2019). Study revealed that "those who went to religious services at least once a week as children were about 18 percent more likely to report higher levels of happiness as young adults between the ages of 23 and 30 than those who didn't. They were also shown to be 29 percent more likely to volunteer in their local communities and 33 percent less likely to engage in the use of illicit drugs.

Those who prayed or meditated at least once a day in their youth were shown to be 16 percent more likely to report higher levels of happiness as young adults and were 30 percent less likely to have become sexually active in their adolescence. These individuals were also 40 percent less likely to have contracted a sexually transmitted infection than those who never prayed or meditated".

The purpose of above discussion is that 'think and reflect' is the biggest virtue at contemporary workplace. As discussed in chapter three with the reference of earthquake that virtue is not only offering rituals with perfect regularity. Significant part of virtue is to attain the ability to facilitate and secure human lives through inventions, developments and research for modern, effective and efficient solutions.

Help and Support

Help and support is one of important virtues at the workplace. Islamic ethics provide guidelines where help is extended and where support is declined. There is huge research available around the globe on interpersonal interactions at the workplace. There are several structured frameworks are available for interventions to ensure interactions are coworkers remain beneficial for both the organisation and the individual. Somehow need for impeccable workplace environment is still there in every society.

Islamic ethics provide a concrete policy to 'help and support' in righteous deeds and do not extend 'help and support' in wickedness.

And cooperate in righteousness and piety, but do not cooperate in sin and aggression (al-Qur'ān 5:2)

Now righteousness includes every positive initiative which leads to the success of organisation, its employees and other stakeholders, while sin and transgression are violating rules, spoiling trust and avoiding justice at the workplace.

Preparedness

Islam expects that organisations including every member will remain well prepared to get benefit from any opportunity arising in day to day operations and remain prepared to handle any declared or concealed threat to the existence or operations of the organisation.

And prepare against them whatever you are able of power and of steeds of war by which you may terrify the enemy of Allah and your enemy and others besides them whom you do not know [but] whom Allah knows. And whatever you spend in the cause of Allah will be fully repaid to you, and you will not be wronged (al-Qur'ān 8:60)

This preparedness includes sharpening individual abilities as well as strengthening instrumental technologies and developing cutting-edge scientific and technological solutions with complete dedication to given assignments.

Wisdom

The word wisdom (*al-Hikmah*) has been used in more than a dozen times in al-Qur'ān suggesting its importance for human life. Allah (SWT) commanded the last Prophet Muhammad (PBUH) that:

Invite to the way of your Lord with wisdom and good instruction and argue with them in a way that is best. Indeed, your Lord is most knowing of who has strayed from His way, and He is most knowing of who is [rightly] guided (al-Qur'ān 16:125)

Human beings have to be grateful to the Creator for blessing the faculty of wisdom to the mankind:

And We had certainly given Luqman wisdom [and said], "Be grateful to Allah". And whoever is grateful is grateful for [the benefit of] himself. And whoever denies [His favor] - then indeed, Allah is Free of need and Praiseworthy (al-Qur'ān 31:12)

Wisdom has several manifestations in individual lives; however following verses indicate some important dimensions of wisdom from the perspective of Islamic work ethics.

Oneness of Allah (SWT)

Do not make [as equal] with Allah another deity and [thereby] become censured and forsaken (al-Qur'ān 17:22)

That is from what your Lord has revealed to you, [O Muhammad], of wisdom. And, [O mankind], do not make [as equal] with Allah another deity, lest you be thrown into Hell, blamed and banished (al-Qur'ān 17:39)

Care of Elderly Parents

And your Lord has decreed that you not worship except Him, and to parents, good treatment. Whether one or both of them reach old age [while] with you, say not to them [so much as], "uff," and do not repel them but speak to them a noble word (al-Qur'ān 17:23)

And lower to them the wing of humility out of mercy and say, "My Lord, have mercy upon them as they brought me up [when I was] small" (al-Qur'ān 17:24)

Allah (SWT) is Most Forgiving

Your Lord is most knowing of what is within yourselves. If you should be righteous [in intention] - then indeed He is ever, to the often returning [to Him], Forgiving (al-Qur'ān 17:25)

Rights of Fellow beings

And give the relative his right, and [also] the poor and the traveler, and do not spend wastefully (al-Qur'ān 17:26)

And if you [must] turn away from the needy awaiting mercy from your Lord which you expect, then speak to them a gentle word (al-Qur'ān 17:28)

Conserve Resources

Indeed, the wasteful are brothers of the devils, and ever has Satan been to his Lord ungrateful (al-Qur'ān 17:27)

Moderation

And do not make your hand [as] chained to your neck or extend it completely and [thereby] become blamed and insolvent (al-Qur'ān 17:29)

Gratefulness for the Blessings

Indeed, your Lord extends provision for whom He wills and restricts [it]. Indeed, He is ever, concerning His servants, Acquainted and Seeing (al-Qur'ān 17:30)

And do not kill your children for fear of poverty. We provide for them and for you. Indeed, their killing is ever a great sin (al-Qur'ān 17:31)

Prohibition of Extramarital Relations

And do not approach unlawful sexual intercourse. Indeed, it is ever an immorality and is evil as a way (al-Qur'ān 17:32)

Life is Sacred

And do not kill the soul which Allah has forbidden, except by right. And whoever is killed unjustly - We have given his heir authority but let him not exceed limits in [the matter of] taking life. Indeed, he has been supported [by the law] (al-Qur'ān 17:33)

And do not approach the property of an orphan, except in the way that is best, until he reaches maturity. And fulfill [every] commitment. Indeed, the commitment is ever [that about which one will be] questioned (al-Qur'ān 17:34)

Honesty

And give full measure when you measure, and weigh with an even balance. That is the best [way] and best in result (al-Qur'ān 17:35)

Avoid Distractions

And do not pursue that of which you have no knowledge. Indeed, the hearing, the sight and the heart - about all those [one] will be questioned (al-Qur'ān 17:36)

Humility

And do not walk upon the earth exultantly. Indeed, you will never tear the earth [apart], and you will never reach the mountains in height (al-Qur'ān 17:37)

Avoid Evil

All that - its evil is ever, in the sight of your Lord, detested (al-Qur'ān 17:38)

Affection

According to an HBR study of 3,201 employees in seven different industries from financial services to real estate, "Love is a not word you often hear uttered in office hallways or conference rooms. And yet, it has a strong influence on workplace outcomes. The more love co-workers feel at work, the more engaged they are. Here love means "companionate love" which is far less intense than romantic love. Companionate love is based on warmth, affection, and connection rather than passion. It may not be surprising that those who perceive greater affection and caring from their colleagues perform better, but few managers focus on building an emotional culture. That's a mistake. People who worked in a culture where they felt free to express affection, tenderness, caring, and compassion for one another were more satisfied with their jobs, committed to the organisation, and felt internally to be accountable for their performance. A warm smile, a kind note, a sympathetic ear that help create and maintain a strong culture of affection leads to employee satisfaction, productivity, and client satisfaction" (Barsade and O'Neill, 2014).

Islamic ethics did not ignore this important aspect of human organisations.

Indeed, those who have believed and done righteous deeds - the Most Merciful will appoint for them affection (al-Qur'ān 19:96)

Diligence

Researchers in organisational studies place greater emphasis on the role of individual diligence and attention, criticising excessive reliance on system measures, arguing that people on the frontline of health care or any other hazardous enterprise generally have little opportunity to bring about rapid system improvements. In every hands-on and very personal business, personal qualities do matter. One of the unintended consequences of a systems approach has been a lack of sufficient attention paid to the role of individual diligence in preventing the occurrence of adverse events. While this might be a very understandable counterbalance to the traditional approach of "blaming and shaming" individuals for errors which were facilitated by broader organisational issues of systems approaches to error which have tended to reduce individual responsibility for causing error. This might make them more acceptable but can also suggest that it is someone else's task to deal with the issues, which may be problematic if it is unclear whose responsibility it is to address complex system issues (Corbett *et al.*, 2011).

Islamic ethics emphasise individual diligence as Allah (SWT) said in al-Qur'ān:

And say, "Do [as you will], for Allah will see your deeds, and [so, will] His Messenger and the believers. And you will be returned to the Knower of the unseen and the witnessed, and He will inform you of what you used to do" (al-Qur'ān 9:105)

The Prophet (PBUH) educated in different ways on how to be diligent, "Nobody has ever eaten a better meal than that which one has earned by working with one's own hands. The Prophet (PBUH) of Allah, David used to eat from the earnings of his manual labor" (Sahih al-Bukhari 2072)

Abu Huraira reported Allah's Messenger (PBUH) as saying: "A strong believer is better and is more lovable to Allah than a weak believer, and there is good in everyone, (but) cherish that which gives you benefit (in the Hereafter) and seek help from Allah and do not lose heart, and if anything (in the form of trouble) comes to you, don't say: If I had not done that, it would not have happened so and so, but say: Allah did that what He had ordained to do and your" if" opens the (gate) for the Satan" (Sahih Muslim 2664)

Inspiration

Islamic ethics are based on extensive inspirations for both worlds. One can find numerous inspirational indicators to perform well in contemporary workplace. Inspiration is always good and positive while motivation can be positive or negative, productive or destructive. Inspiration focuses on people's deepest and noblest desires. Inspiration arises spontaneously without intention. Inspiration is also something extraordinary and often involve events clearly and awareness of new possibilities. Inspiration is an influence intended to make real change. Inspiration enables organisations to accumulate and share internal knowledge, gather and integrate external information, challenge the status quo and enables creativity (Indrawati, 2014).

Different aspects of inspiration for people in al-Qur'ān are given below for reflections:

Say, "O My servants who have transgressed against themselves [by sinning], do not despair of the mercy of Allah. Indeed, Allah forgives all sins. Indeed, it is He who is the Forgiving, the Merciful" (al-Qur'ān, 39:53)

For indeed, with hardship [will be] ease. Indeed, with hardship [will be] ease (al-Qur'ān, 94:5-6)

[Allah] said, "Fear not. Indeed, I am with you both; I hear and I see (al-Qur'ān, 20:46)

And whoever fears Allah - He will make for him of his matter ease (al-Qur'ān, 65:4)

Allah does not charge a soul except [with that within] its capacity. It will have [the consequence of] what [good] it has gained, and it will bear [the consequence of] what [evil] it has earned. "Our Lord, do not impose blame upon us if we have forgotten or erred. Our Lord, and lay not upon us a burden like that which You laid upon those before us. Our Lord, and burden us not with that which we have no ability to bear. And pardon us; and forgive us; and have mercy upon us. You are our protector, so give us victory over the disbelieving people. (al-Qur'ān, 2:286)

and He is with you wherever you are (al-Qur'ān, 57:4)

CONCLUSION

The increased demand in people movement from a various of religious beliefs, ethnicity and cultures. This chapter has developed logical argument how diversity through Islamic ethics can be achieved and management at modern contemporary workplace. Therefore, diversity in terms of background professional experience, skills and specialisation, values and culture, as well as social class, is a prevailing pattern. Within increasing trend and demand of globalisation having impact on multinational companies to consider age, ethnicity, gender, physical abilities, race and sexual orientation as an important factor in terms of background professional experience, skills and specialisation, values and culture, as well as social class, is a prevailing pattern. The management of diversity is important factor for senior management to consider employees backgrounds as a fundamental principle for individual and business community to overcome challenges facing modern workforce.

Moreover, Islamic ethics has developed Muslims thinking that they are extremely fortunate that Allah (SWT) gave them logical framework fourteen hundred years ago to think, reflect and pursue scientific developments to realise benefits of opportunities created by the Allah (SWT) available in and around this planet. There are numerous indications in al-Qur'ān and a hadith to think and reflect to invent or find innovative and effective ways of performing in contemporary business environments. Therefore, Islamic ethics are based on extensive inspirations for both worlds. One can find numerous inspirational indicators to perform well in contemporary workplace. Inspiration is always good and positive while motivation can be positive or negative, productive or destructive. Inspiration focuses on people's deepest and noblest desires. Islamic ethics value diversity as a key principle in development of human resources management and improve productivity modern workplace. Islamic ethics keep concept is to develop human organisations according to Qur'an.

Indeed, those who have believed and done righteous deeds - the Most Merciful will appoint for them affection (al-Qur'ān 19:96)

Discussion Questions

1. How diversity is implemented in the workplace?
2. Analyse and discuss diversity management from Islamic ethics point view?

3. Evaluate the concepts of diversity and multiculturalism according to verses of the al-Qur'ān and the Islamic tradition?
4. Critically discuss the qualities for successful management of diversity within Islamic and western societies?

REFERENCES

Abdullah, F. (2014). Virtues and Character Development in Islamic Ethics and Positive Psychology. *International Journal of Education and Social Science*, *1*(2), 69–77.

Barsade, S., & O'Neill, O. A. (2014). *Employees Who Feel Love Perform Better*. Retrieved on June 16, 2019 from: https://hbr.org/2014/01/employees-who-feel-love-perform-better

Clements, P., & Jones, J. (2006). *The diversity training handbook: a practical guide to understanding & changing attitudes*. Kogan Page.

Corbett, A., Travaglia, J., & Braithwaite, J. (2011). The role of individual diligence in improving safety. *Journal of Health Organization and Management*, *25*(3), 247–260. doi:10.1108/14777261111143518 PMID:21845981

Friday, E., & Friday, S. S. (2003). Managing diversity using a strategic planned change approach. *Journal of Management Development*, *22*(10), 863–880. doi:10.1108/02621710310505467

Hayes, V. (1999). Beyond employment equity: The business case for diversity. *Ivey Business Journal*, *64*(1), 45–46.

Indrawati, N. K. (2014). Management by Inspiration: Implementation of Transformational Leadership on Business at Pondok Pesantren Sunan Drajat. *Procedia: Social and Behavioral Sciences*, *115*, 79–90. doi:10.1016/j.sbspro.2014.02.417

Justice, T. (2019). *Harvard Study Reveals Religious Upbringing Better for Kids' Health, Well-Being*. Retrieved on June 15, 2019 from: https://stream.org/new-study-reveals-religious-upbringing-better-kids-health well/?fbclid=IwAR0fZhlJJX3yPGdGnl5gE8YzMjK1xPrG0PY_f_1wainjD0npnCWETciRicA&sfns=mo

Karakas, F., Sarigollu, E., & Uygur, S. (2017). Exploring the Diversity of Virtues Through the Lens of Moral Imagination: A Qualitative Inquiry into Organisational Virtues in the Turkish Context. *Journal of Business Ethics*, *141*(4), 731–744. doi:10.100710551-016-3150-6

Muhtada, D. (2012). Managing workforce diversity: An Islamic perspective. *Indonesian Journal of Islam and Muslim Societies*, *2*(1), 79–108. doi:10.18326/ijims.v2i1.78-108

Sambur, B. (2009). Islam, liberty and pluralism. *Al-Hikmat*, *29*, 35–58.

Appendix

SHARI'AH GOVERNANCE FRAMEWORK FOR ISLAMIC BANKING INSTITUTIONS

(updated till June 2018)

ISLAMIC BANKING DEPARTMENT
STATE BANK OF PAKISTAN

Table of Acronyms

AAOIFI	Accounting and Auditing Organization for Islamic Financial Institutions
AGM	Annual General Meeting
BAC	Board Audit Committee
BOD	Board of Directors
CEO	Chief Executive Officer
EM	Executive Management
FAPC	Fit and Proper Criteria (for appointment of Shari'ah Scholar members of Shari'ah Board of an IBI)
FAQs	Frequently Asked Questions
IAH	Investment Account Holder
IBD	Islamic Banking Department (of SBP)
IBI	Islamic Banking Institution (includes full-fledged Islamic bank, Islamic banking subsidiary, and Islamic banking division of a conventional bank)
ICAP	Institute of Chartered Accountants of Pakistan
IFI	Islamic Financial Institution (includes IBI, Takaful Company, Islamic Mutual Fund and Collective Investment Scheme, Modaraba, and any other institution declared or notified as such)
ISA	Internal Shari'ah Audit
ISAU	Internal Shari'ah Audit Unit
PD	Product Development
PLS	Profit and Loss Sharing
RSBM	Resident Shari'ah Board Member
SAC	Shari'ah Advisory Committee (of SBP)
SB	Shari'ah Board (of IBI)
SBP	State Bank of Pakistan
SCD	Shari'ah Compliance Department (of IBI)
SECP	Securities and Exchange Commission of Pakistan
SGF	Shari'ah Governance Framework
SOP	Standard Operating Procedure
TOR	Terms of Reference

Table of Contents

SHARI'AH GOVERNANCE FRAMEWORK FOR ISLAMIC BANKING INSTITUTIONS

Introduction

Complying with the principles of Shari'ah as enshrined in the Holy Quran and the Sunnah of the Prophet (peace be upon him) is the essence and raison d'être of Islamic banking industry. A sound and effective Shari'ah compliance framework is thus critically important to give confidence to the general public about Shari'ah conformity of Islamic Banking Institutions' (IBIs') products and services. State Bank of Pakistan (SBP) endeavors to ensure that the operations of IBIs remain in conformity with the rules and principles of Shari'ah. Accordingly, it has been issuing regulations, instructions and guidelines on Shari'ah compliance since the re-launch of Islamic banking in 2001.

In 2008, SBP issued detailed set of instructions and guidelines for Shari'ah compliance vide IBD Circular No. 2 of 2008. However, keeping in view the developments taking place in the Islamic banking industry over the recent years, some of the instructions and guidelines have been revisited and a comprehensive Shari'ah Governance Framework ('SGF or Framework') was developed in 2015, which has now been further reviewed. The Framework shall be applicable to all IBIs i.e. full-fledged Islamic banks, Islamic banking subsidiaries and Islamic banking divisions of conventional banks. The primary objective of the Framework is to strengthen the overall Shari'ah compliance environment of IBIs and explicitly define the roles and responsibilities of various organs of IBIs including the Board of Directors (BOD), Executive Management (EM), Shari'ah Board (SB), Shari'ah Compliance Department

(SCD), Product Development (PD), internal auditors and external auditors towards Shari'ah compliance.

The SGF of an IBI shall, at the minimum, covers the following:

i. An effective mechanism for the BOD's oversight of the IBI's Shari'ah compliance environment.
ii. Accountability of management and staff of the IBI in implementation of the Framework.
iii. An independent and effective SB appointed as per Fit and Proper Criteria (FAPC) set out in Annexure-A of this Framework, with one of its Shari'ah scholar members working as Resident Shari'ah Board Member (RSBM) to oversee the procedures and processes to be adopted for implementation of the SB's fatawa, resolutions and guidelines and provide clarification thereon.
iv. A SCD to assist SB and to serve as a conduit between the SB and the management of an IBI.
v. Shari'ah compliance review mechanism to assess operative effectiveness of Shari'ah governance and compliance framework devised by the SB and BOD of the IBI.
vi. An independent Internal Shari'ah Audit Unit (ISAU) which may be a part of internal audit department or an independent unit depending on the size of the IBI.
vii. A product development (PD) department / unit responsible for development of new and innovative products and services.
viii. External Shari'ah Audit to be undertaken along with the annual audit of the IBI.

1. Role of Board of Directors (BOD

i. The BOD shall be ultimately responsible and accountable for ensuring full conformity of the IBI's operations with Shari'ah principles. Like other risks faced by an IBI, the BOD needs to be fully cognizant of the risk of Shari'ah non-compliance and its potential implications on the reputation and business of the IBI. Towards this end, the BOD shall introduce an effective mechanism including diligent oversight on functioning of the Framework and compliance with the fatawa, instructions, and guidelines of the SB.
ii. The BOD should also be fully aware of its fiduciary responsibility, particularly, towards Investment Account Holders (IAHs) /Profit and Loss

Sharing depositors (PLS depositors) who accept risks that are almost similar to those of the shareholders but without having any voting rights and fora like Annual General Meetings (AGMs) to express their concerns on the IBI's performance. The IAHs expect IBIs to not only exercise prudence in deployment of their funds in different avenues but to also ensure Shari'ah conformity of returns to be earned and distributed to them. The BOD is thus expected to introduce the necessary mechanisms and risk management systems to safeguard the interests of IAHs/PLS depositors.

iii. The BOD shall appoint a SB to perform such functions as stipulated under Para 3(B) of this Framework and shall cause to take appropriate measures for introducing and implementing an effective Shari'ah compliance framework. It shall also approve the Terms of Reference (TOR) of the SB and fix remuneration of the SB members. In case of foreign banks having Islamic Banking Branches, the appointing authority shall be the Country Manager/CEO in Pakistan.

iv. The BOD shall meet the SB at least on a half yearly basis to a) have a detailed briefing on the Shari'ah compliance environment, the issues/weaknesses (if any), and recommendations to improve Shari'ah compliance environment, and b) ensure timely and effective enforcement of the SB's decisions, fatawa, observations and recommendations. However, one of the meetings between the SB and BOD, during a calendar year, may be held through video conferencing.

v. The deliberations of the meeting between SB and BOD shall be properly recoded and duly confirmed by the BOD. A copy of the same shall be submitted to IBD-SBP within 15 days of the confirmation.

2. Role of Executive Management (EM)

i. The EM of an IBI shall be responsible for implementation of the Framework. Every concerned executive and staff shall ensure that all procedure manuals, product programs and structures, process flows, related agreements and contracts, etc. as approved by the SB are made available to and understood by everyone working in his/her group or functional area. Moreover, every executive shall be responsible for arranging adequate training to his/her group employees in coordination with Training Department and SCD of the IBI.

ii. Every group head and executive shall also be accountable and responsible for implementation of decisions, rulings, fatawa and guidelines given by SB relating to his/her group or functional area. The EM needs to show zero tolerance on Shari'ah non-compliance and take appropriate action against employees who have failed to ensure compliance with the Shari'ah rules and principles in their respective areas of responsibility. Instances of Shari'ah non-compliance shall also have a strong bearing on their performance appraisals, promotions, increments, bonuses, etc.
iii. Whenever the management refers a matter to the SB for a decision, ruling or fatwa it shall ensure that complete and relevant information is submitted to the SB for its proper understanding of proposal(s) and product(s).
iv. The decisions, rulings, fatawa of the SB shall be binding on the IBI.
v. The EM shall take appropriate measures to address the operational and human resource issues that may result in Shari'ah non-compliance risk.
vi. IBIs should arrange trainings and/or orientation programs on Islamic banking and finance for the members of the BOD and appropriate training programs for senior executives to improve their understanding and general acumen in Islamic finance.
vii. The management is also expected to arrange programs on a regular basis for orienting and sensitizing the BOD and key executives about the business utility and importance of an enabling Shari'ah compliance environment and the key distinguishing features of Islamic finance products vis- à -vis conventional banking products.
viii. IBI shall provide exposure to the SB members with regard to domestic and international developments in Islamic banking and finance. A yearly statement on the actions taken by the IBI shall be submitted to IBD-SBP by 15th of January every following year.

3. Shari'ah Board (SB)

A. Constitution of the SB and Appointment of SB Members

i. Every IBI shall have a SB comprising at least three Shari'ah scholars appointed by the BOD as per the FAPC prescribed in Annexure-A of this Framework.

ii. The appointment of the SB members shall be subject to prior written clearance of SBP. The IBI shall apply for SBP's clearance after obtaining BOD's approval.
iii. IBIs may, in consultation with the SB, also seek services of or engage lawyers, accountants, economists and such other professionals to assist and advise the SB on banking, legal, financial, economic and other relevant matters. The engagement of such members shall however be of advisory nature and they shall not have any voting rights in the meetings of SB.
iv. The SB members shall be appointed for a term of three (3) years. The SB members shall be eligible for reappointment with the approval of SBP. The three (3) years term of SB shall commence from the date of SBP's clearance for appointment / reappointment.
v. Up to three (3) years i.e. June 2021, the SB members, except RSBM, may serve on the SBs of up to three IBIs in Pakistan.
vi. IBIs shall include a confidentiality clause in the contract or terms of appointment of SB members for maintaining secrecy and confidentiality of IBI's non-public information and matters.
vii. At least two months prior to the expiry of the term of the SB, members (including the Chairperson) of SB may be reappointed as a member of SB for another term by the BOD, subject to afresh prior written clearance of SBP and pursuant to FAPC.
viii. If an IBI decides not to offer another term to any member(s) of the SB, it shall also inform Islamic Banking Department (IBD), SBP about its decision, along with the rationale, at least three months before the expiry of the term.
ix. No member of a SB shall be terminated before the expiry of his/her term except under any of the circumstances or on any of the grounds stipulated in paragraphs 3 to 6 of the FAPC given in Annexure-A of this Framework. The IBI shall submit detailed rationale to the SBP along with documentary evidence, if any, to support its decision. The decision to terminate any member of SB shall be subject to prior approval from IBD-SBP on sufficient cause being shown by the IBI and upon giving such member due opportunity of being heard by the BOD of the IBI.
x. In case any SB member resigns before the expiry of his/her term, such member shall submit the resignation, together with reasons thereof, to the BOD in case of domestic banks and Country Manager in case of foreign banks along with a copy to IBD-SBP.

xi. A casual vacancy arising on the SB caused by resignation, removal or termination or death of a member shall be filled by the BOD within three months from the date on which such vacancy was caused. However, the SB member appointed on casual vacancy shall hold the office until the expiry of the existing term of the SB.

B. Role of Shari'ah Board

i. The SB shall be empowered to consider, decide and supervise all Shari'ah related matters of the IBI. All decisions, rulings, fatawa of the SB shall be binding on the IBI whereas SB shall be responsible and accountable for all its Shari'ah related decisions.
ii. The SB shall cause to develop a comprehensive Shari'ah compliance framework for all areas of operations of the IBI. All products or services to be offered and/or launched by the IBI shall have prior approval of the SB.
iii. The SB shall review and approve all the procedure manuals, product programs/ structures, process flows, related agreements, marketing advertisements, sales illustrations and brochures so that they are in conformity with the rules and principles of Shari'ah. The EM while seeking the SB's decision on any proposal shall ensure provision of all necessary information, details and documents so as to enable the SB to have proper understanding of the product, its process flows, business and economic outcomes and Shari'ah permissibility or impermissibility.
iv. The SB shall have at all reasonable times unhindered access to all books of accounts, records, documents and information from all sources including professional advisors and IBI's employees in the due discharge of its duties.
v. Considering the importance and binding nature of decisions, rulings and fatawa given by SB, it shall rigorously deliberate on the issue placed before it for consideration before giving any decision/fatwa. All such deliberations and rationale for allowing or disallowing a particular product or service shall be duly recorded and documented.
vi. All reports of internal Shari'ah audit, external Shari'ah audit, Shari'ah compliance reviews and SBP Shari'ah compliance inspection shall be submitted to the SB for consideration and prescribing appropriate enforcement action. The report of Internal

Shari'ah Audit shall be finalized by the Internal Shari'ah Audit Unit/ department (ISAU) and the final report shall be submitted to SB for prescribing appropriate enforcement/ corrective actions. The SB shall take up the unresolved issues with management and shall include all significant outstanding issues in its annual report on the Shari'ah compliance environment of the IBI. Moreover, the Head of SCD and RSBM shall discuss both the significant and unresolved issues with SBP inspection team during their on-site inspection.

vii. The SB shall also specify the process/procedures to be adopted for changing, modifying or revisiting fatawa, rulings and guidelines already issued by it.
viii. The SB shall not delegate any of its roles and responsibilities prescribed in this framework to any other person or any of its members.

Notwithstanding anything contained herein, all decisions and rulings of the SB of the IBI shall be in conformity with the directives, regulations, instructions and guidelines issued by SBP in accordance with the rulings of Shari'ah Advisory Committee of SBP.

C. Shari'ah Board Meetings, Quorum, Minutes

i. The SB shall, in addition to its meetings with the BOD, pursuant to paragraph 1(iv) of this Framework, meet at least on a quarterly basis and each member of the SB shall attend at least two thirds of the meetings held during a calendar year. Further, in addition to the mandatory quarterly meeting, the Chairperson of the SB may convene SB's meetings as and when he deems it necessary.
ii. The quorum of the SB meetings, including that with BOD of the IBI, shall be at least two thirds of Shari'ah scholar members.
iii. The SB decisions should preferably be made through consensus of the Shari'ah scholar members; however, in case of difference of opinion, the decisions may be made by a majority vote of the Shari'ah scholar members. In the event of equality of votes, the Chairperson shall have a second or casting vote.
iv. All meetings shall be chaired by the Chairperson of the SB and in his absence one of the Shari'ah scholar members, other than the RSBM, shall be elected as the acting Chairperson to preside over the meeting.

v. The agenda of the SB meeting along with sufficient details and documents shall be sent to SB members well in advance enabling them to come prepared to the meeting; the specific timelines for submission of the agenda shall be set by the SB itself.
vi. The meetings of the SB shall be held by physical presence of the members. However, in appropriate circumstances to be determined by the Chairman of the SB, meeting(s) may be held through video conferencing subject to recording of proper minutes of the meeting.
vii. All SB approvals taken through circulation shall be placed for ratification of the SB at its next meeting. A resolution in writing signed by all SB members for the time being and shall be as valid and effective as if it had been ratified at a SB meeting. Proper documentary evidence of the SB approvals taken through circulation must be kept in record for audit & inspection.
viii. The SB shall ensure to cause that minutes of its meetings are properly recorded incorporating necessary details of all deliberations, decisions, rulings and fatawa issued along with the rationale and difference of opinion or dissenting note, if any. Further, the minutes shall be signed by all the SB members who attended the meeting and a copy thereof be provided to each member of the SB.
ix. For implementation of the decisions of SB meeting prior to the confirmation of the minutes of the meeting, the approval / confirmation of the relevant resolution / decision for the specific agenda must be obtained from SB through written consent duly singed by the SB members or through email by the SB members. However, the same shall be ratified in the subsequent meeting of SB.
x. The approved / confirmed minutes of meetings of the SB shall be submitted to IBD-SBP within 15 days of its approval / confirmation for information and record. Further, the minutes shall be made available to the BOD, SBP inspection teams, internal auditors and external auditors on request, enabling them to appreciate and understand the rationale and background of the SB rulings, decisions and fatawa.

D. Independence of Shari'ah Board (SB)

The SB shall discharge its duties independently and objectively. The members of the SB shall continuously assess their relationships with their respective IBIs to identify any situation where any issue related to independence may actually or potentially arise or can reasonably be inferred. The BOD shall ensure that the SB is not subject to any undue influence or pressure from the management and/or its own members. The IBI shall inter alia comply with the following:

i. The appointment letter of each SB member shall clearly state the role and responsibilities of the SB and shall be duly accepted by him/her.
ii. The members of SB shall neither involve nor be responsible in any manner for the operational activities or management function of the IBI.
iii. SBP Prudential Regulation G-2 shall also be applicable on the members of the SB. However, the BOD of the IBI may approve employee related facilities for the SB members and the same shall be stipulated in their appointment letter.

E. Report of Shari'ah Board

The SB shall, based on the findings and reports of internal Shari'ah audit and external Shari'ah audit and Shari'ah compliance review, prepare a report on the IBI's Shari'ah compliance environment and conditions. The minimum requirements for the report are given in Annexure – B of this Framework. The report shall be signed by all the members of the SB. Further, the report shall also be placed before the BOD meeting for discussion and shall be published in English with Urdu translation in the IBI's annual report.

4. Resident Shari'ah Board Member (RSBM)

The SB of an IBI shall, in consultation with the management, designate one of the SB members other than the Chairperson as RSBM. The RSBM shall oversee the procedures to be adopted for implementation of the resolutions, pronouncements and fatawa of the SB and provide guidance thereon. In principle, RSBM shall be appointed on a full time basis; however, SB having regard to specific circumstances of the IBI may, at its own discretion, allow RSBM to devote some time to academic activities related to the Shari'ah.

Further, RSBM of an IBI shall not serve in any capacity whatsoever in any other IBI in Pakistan. However, he may with prior approval of the SB of IBI serve as a member of Shari'ah Board of a maximum two other IFIs.

Moreover, RSBM shall not hold any administrative and/or full time position with any organization / institution other than the IBI where he is appointed as RSBM. SB shall ensure that engagements of the RSBM other than the IBI shall not be hinder his activities at the IBI. Without prejudice to the generality of the aforesaid provision, the RSBM will have the following role:

i. Provide explanation/clarification to management and staff of IBI on products, documents, process flows and on other operational Shari'ah related matters, in the light of decisions, rulings, fatawa already issued by the SB.
ii. The management while seeking explanation/clarification from RSBM on any matter shall ensure provision of all necessary information, details and documents so as to enable him/her to have proper understanding of the product, its process flows, business and economic outcomes and Shari'ah permissibility or impermissibility.
iii. Guide the SCD in conducting Shari'ah compliance reviews of key business areas on a test check basis.
iv. Review responses to Shari'ah related queries of IBI's clients regarding IBI's products and services as submitted by SCD.
v. Facilitate the SCD and Training Department in designing and conducting training activities.
vi. Submit at least a quarterly report to the SB, for ratification, of all the material explanations/clarifications provided by him/her on products, services, documents, process flows and other operational Shari'ah related issues, in the light of decisions, rulings, and fatawa already issued by SB.

The explanation or clarification given by RSBM shall be binding on IBI.

5. Shari'ah Compliance Department (SCD)

Every IBI shall have a SCD which may be headed by a RSBM or a suitably qualified, trained and experienced officer recommended by the SB. The SCD shall have dedicated and adequate staff as per the advice of the SB, so as to enable it to discharge its due responsibilities in a proper and timely manner. The SCD shall have at least one qualified

Shari'ah expert (other than RSBM) who shall meet the criteria of "Academic Qualifications" as prescribed in Annexure-A of this Framework. Moreover, IBI's are encouraged to depute individuals with expertise and/or qualification in Shari'ah, Risk Management, Legal and Accounting to strengthen its Shari'ah compliance function.

The SCD shall work under the overall guidance and supervision of the SB and its Head shall functionally report to the SB and his/her performance appraisal shall be finalized by SB. However, administrative reporting of Head SCD shall be to the Chief Executive Officer of Islamic Bank and Chief Compliance Officer in case of Islamic Banking Branches of Conventional Bank. The SCD shall be responsible for the following:

i. Secretariat of Shari'ah Board

It shall serve as the Secretariat to the SB with the responsibility to provide all the necessary secretarial support to the SB including timely provision of meetings' agenda, proposals, and working papers. It shall also maintain proper record of agenda items, minutes of the SB meetings and fatawa issued by the SB along with their rationale.

ii. Conduit Between Management and the Shari'ah Board

The SCD shall act as conduit between the SB and management of the IBI. It shall review all the product proposals and related agreements, contracts, manuals, process flows, checklists submitted by management before presenting these to the SB for approval. The RSBM will also help and advise the SCD in its review of the proposals to be submitted to the SB.

i. The SCD shall not involve in any operational / business related functions / activity including product development.
ii. The SCD shall perform research and analysis on Shari'ah issues under the guidance of the RSBM/SB.
iii. The SCD shall be responsible to verify distribution of profit and loss to the depositors prior to its disbursement.
iv. The SCD shall prepare responses to Shari'ah related queries of IBI's clients regarding IBI's products and services after discussion with the relevant stakeholders and submit the same to RSBM for his advice/ review / confirmation.

iii. Shari'ah Compliance Review

The SCD shall keep a continuous watch on the IBI's Shari'ah compliance environment and shall ensure that all organs of Shari'ah Governance including the BOD oversight mechanism, internal Shari'ah audit, and enforcement of the SB's directives by EM are operative and are effectively discharging their respective functions and responsibilities as defined in the Framework. In order to monitor and ensure compliance of IBI's operations on an ongoing basis with the rules and principles of Shari'ah, the SCD under the supervision of RSBM shall, on sample basis, conduct an internal Shari'ah control review of the IBI's business units, branches, and other Head Office departments.

The Shari'ah compliance review shall be conducted to ensure that the IBI's operations are in conformity with fatawa/guidelines issued by SB of the IBI and directives, regulation, instructions and guidelines issued by SBP in accordance with the rulings of Shari'ah Advisory Committee of SBP. Based on these reviews and other mechanisms as may be introduced by the SCD for assessing conformity of the IBI's operations with the principles and rules of the Shari'ah, the Head SCD shall periodically submit a report to the SB on the overall Shari'ah compliance environment of the IBI, the ownership and commitment of the BOD and EM in building the necessary infrastructure for Shari'ah compliance together with identifying key areas of improvement. The frequency of this report shall be decided by the SB.

iv. Enforcement of Shari'ah Audit Reports

All the reports of internal Shari'ah audit, external Shari'ah audit, internal Shari'ah review, and SBP Shari'ah compliance inspection shall be sent to SB for information and for determining appropriate corrective actions. The Board Audit Committee (BAC) shall ensure compliance of the corrective actions determined by SB on the reports of 'internal Shari'ah audit' and 'external Shari'ah audit'. The SCD shall, however, be responsible for enforcement of corrective actions directed by the SB on the reports of 'internal Shari'ah review' and 'SBP Shari'ah compliance inspection'. The BAC and SCD shall also keep record of all unresolved issues requiring compliance and shall apprise the SB of their status at least on a half yearly basis. The SB shall take up the unresolved issues with the management and shall include all significant outstanding issues in its annual Shari'ah Report to be published in the Annual Report of the IBI. Moreover, SB/Head of SCD shall discuss all the significant and unresolved issues with SBP inspection team during their on-site inspection.

v. Training on Shari'ah Compliance

The SCD shall facilitate Training Unit of Human Resources Department of IBI to develop training material and to organize Shari'ah training activities as per training plan approved by the management and the SB. Moreover, the SCD shall be responsible for ensuring that necessary training has been imparted to all the Islamic banking staff and that periodic refresher courses are also organized by HRD to keep the staff abreast with the latest developments in the field. The management shall provide all required facilities for this purpose and the SCD shall report its concerns, if any, in this regard to the SB.

vi. Other Functions

a. The SCD shall prepare a comprehensive procedure manual including checklists and standard operating procedures (SOPs) to assist its staff in discharging their duties.
b. The SCD shall ensure that the IBI's website gives a brief introduction of the SB members, disclosures required by SBP, key features of all the products offered and their difference with conventional products, frequently asked questions (FAQs) and the contact details of the SCD personnel.

6. Product Development

Every IBI shall have a Product Development (PD) Department / Unit which may be part of the Business units or an independent department / unit. PD shall be responsible for research and development of new and innovative products and services keeping in view the business needs of the IBI and considering international developments / practices.

The IBI shall ensure providing of adequate qualified and trained staff to PD to perform its duties. The IBI shall be encouraged to engage at least two individuals, who shall meet the criteria of "Academic Qualifications" as prescribed in Annexure-A of this Framework. Thus the PD shall be able to seek guidance and support on Shari'ah aspects of new products / ideas during the product development process.

7. Internal Shari'ah Audit

i. Every IBI shall have an Internal Shari'ah Audit Unit (ISAU) which may be a part of the internal audit department or an independent unit, depending on the size of the IBI. Moreover, Head of ISAU shall report to Head of Internal Audit in case it is part of Internal Audit Department, whereas in cases where ISAU is independent, it shall report directly to Board Audit Committee (BAC).
ii. The Internal Audit Department or ISAU shall have dedicated and adequate staff as per the advice of the SB keeping in view the size of operations of the IBI, so as to enable it to discharge its due responsibilities in a proper and timely manner. The IBI shall ensure that staff of ISAU are adequately qualified (preferably having Shari'ah qualification) and trained to perform their duties. Internal Shari'ah audit staff shall be dedicated to Shari'ah audit only; however, Internal Shari'ah audit and regular audit of a branch or a function can be performed simultaneously. The IBI shall be encouraged to engage at least one individual in the Internal Audit Department or ISAU, who shall meet the criteria of "Academic Qualification" as prescribed in Annexure-A of this Framework.
iii. The scope, methodology, Internal Shari'ah audit manual and format of Internal Shari'ah audit report shall be reviewed and approved by the SB. Furthermore, the SB shall review the methodology and Internal Shari'ah audit manual at regular intervals.
iv. The Internal Audit Department or ISAU, as the case may be, shall prepare Internal Shari'ah audit plan which, after review by the SB, shall be approved by the BAC.
v. The Internal Audit Department or ISAU of the IBI shall conduct a post disbursement audit on quarterly basis. The report of internal Shari'ah audit on profit and loss distribution shall be submitted to SB of the IBI.
vi. The final Internal Shari'ah audit report shall be submitted to SB for consideration and for determining appropriate corrective action(s).
vii. The final report along with the enforcement/corrective actions determined by the SB shall be sent to the BAC for information and ensuring compliance with the SB directives on the report. The SCD shall submit a report regarding the status of compliance of audit observations to the SB for information on a periodic basis.

8. External Shari'ah Audit

In order to have an independent assessment of the Shari'ah governance and compliance environment of an IBI, the scope of external audit of IBIs shall also include an independent and objective assessment of the conformity of IBI's operations with Shari'ah rules and principles. The audit firms would need to take appropriate measures to have the capacity in relation to resources and methodology to conduct the Shari'ah audit of an IBI.

For the purposes of this Framework, the scope of external Shari'ah audit shall be limited to assessing compliance of an IBI's financial arrangements, contracts, and transactions with Shari'ah rules and principles. The Shari'ah rules and principles for the purpose of the external Shari'ah audit shall mean the following, in the sequence provided below:

i. Essentials, Regulations, Instructions and Guidelines issued by the State Bank of Pakistan (SBP) including the Shari'ah Standards issued by Accounting and Auditing Organization for Islamic Financial Institutions (AAOIFI), as adopted by SBP with suitable modifications, if any;
ii. The rulings of Shari'ah Board of SBP as notified by SBP;
iii. Requirements of the applicable Islamic Financial Accounting Standards as notified by the Securities and Exchange Commission of Pakistan (SECP) and as circulated by SBP;
iv. Approvals and rulings given by the SB of an IBI in line with the SBP directives, regulations, instructions and guidelines issued in accordance with the rulings of Shari'ah Advisory Committee of SBP.

The external auditors shall prepare a report for the BOD giving their opinion on the above and shall also report on a) the overall Shari'ah compliance environment, b) the risks associated with Shari'ah non-compliance, c) the capacity and quality of the risk management system to measure, manage and mitigate these risks, d) the level of awareness and sensitization of the EM and the BOD in addressing the said risks and e) any other issues deemed significant by the external auditors.

The following instructions shall be adhered to while conducting external Shari'ah audit of the IBIs:

i. SB members of IBI shall not be allowed to be engaged with any external audit firms.

ii. It will be the responsibility of the external Audit firms to take measures for capacity building of their staff for conducting Shari'ah audit and provide them with appropriate trainings. Moreover, external Audit firms shall prescribe a FAPC for

Shari'ah scholars to be engaged for external Shari'ah audit of IBIs. In this regard, FAPC for SB members as prescribed in Annexure-A of this Framework may be used as a guiding principle for engagement of Shari'ah auditor.

iii. External Audit shall also include review and provide opinion on bank's pool management practices & IT based system; specially computation and distribution of profit & loss to the depositors, tagging and movement of assets and allocation of income & expenses, etc.
iv. The format of external Shari'ah audit report for submission to BOD of an IBI and to State Bank of Pakistan (SBP) is enclosed as Annexure-C.
v. Institute of Chartered Accountants of Pakistan (ICAP) may develop comprehensive guidelines to conduct external Shari'ah Audit in consultation with external Audit firms.
vi. A copy of external Shari'ah audit report shall be submitted to IBD-SBP within 45 days of the date of finalization of IBIs Audited Accounts. The IBIs shall not publish the External Shari'ah Audit report till further instructions.

9. Conflict Resolution

i. In case of any difference of opinion between an IBI and the SBP inspection team or any other department of SBP regarding Shari'ah conformity of IBI's products, services, contracts and transactions, the matter shall be referred to IBD-SBP. If deemed appropriate by IBD-SBP it may escalate the case to Shari'ah Advisory Committee of SBP for consideration and decision.
ii. Similarly, in case of a difference of opinion between IBD-SBP and IBI on Shari'ah conformity of IBI's products, services, contracts and transactions, IBD-SBP shall refer the case to Shari'ah Advisory Committee of SBP for consideration and decision on the issue of Shari'ah permissibility of such matters.
iii. The SB of the IBI may also refer Shari'ah issues to SBP for seeking opinion of its Shari'ah

Advisory Committee. The case shall be sent to SBP along with all relevant documents and the related Shari'ah arguments. The Shari'ah Advisory Committee of SBP shall consider and give its decision or provide guidance, as the case may be, on such issues at its earliest convenience.

10. Competence of the Organs Dealing With Shari'ah Governance Framework

i. The BOD and EM of an IBI are expected to have a reasonable knowledge of Shari'ah principles and their broad application in the context of the Islamic finance. It shall be ensured that the members of the BOD and the EM are provided orientation sessions/training in Islamic banking on a regular basis which, apart from their professional development, would also facilitate an effective implementation of this Framework.
ii. Similarly, members of the SB of an IBI shall also be required to undergo and attend training sessions and orientation programs related to the applicable legal and regulatory framework, banking, finance, treasury operations etc. to improve their understanding of such matters in the context of an IBI. The IBI shall take appropriate measures to ensure that SB members are abreast with the developments internationally. For the said purpose, IBI's are encouraged to provide opportunity to SB members to attend / participate in domestic and international forums.
iii. An IBI shall also ensure that all its key executives including heads of credit, marketing, operations, treasury and risk management, branch managers, relationship managers and other front line staff have adequate understanding of Islamic banking and finance and are able to appreciate and understand inherent and reputational risks of Shari'ah non-compliance. The IBIs shall also ensure to require such officials to undergo and attend various training sessions, seminars, and workshops for their continuing professional development. This would provide confidence to the public that the IBI they are dealing with is manned by professionals having adequate experience and expertise in Islamic banking.

x...x...x

ANNEXURE - A

Fit and Proper Criteria for the Appointment of Shari'ah Scholar Member of Shari'ah Board of an IBI

1. Academic Qualification

Shahadat ul Aalamiyyah (شهادة العالمية) Degree (*Dars e Nizami*) from any recognized Board of Madaris with minimum 70% marks and Bachelor's Degree with a minimum of 2nd Class

OR

Post Graduate Degree in Kuliyyatush Shari'ah (كلية الشريعة) or Kuliyyah Usooluddin (كلية اصول الدين), L.L.M. (Shari'ah) with a minimum GPA of 3.0 or equivalent from any recognized University.

2. Experience and Exposure

i. The Shari'ah scholar members must have at least four (4) years' experience of giving Shari'ah rulings including the period of *Takhassus fil Ifta*; or at least five (5) years post qualification experience in teaching or Research and Development in Islamic Banking and Finance. Preference will be given to those who have certificate in *Takhassus fil Fiqh/Takhassus fil Ifta*.

ii. Majority of Shari'ah scholar members of Shari'ah Board of an IBI, including RSBM, shall have at least three (3) years' experience as Shari'ah Advisor or Member of Shari'ah

Board (SB) of an Islamic Financial Institution (IFI) or deputy to a Shari'ah Advisor or member of the Shari'ah team of an IFI.

iii. Each Shari'ah scholar member of the SB must be able to demonstrate:
   a) Adequate understanding of banking and finance in general and Islamic finance in particular;
   b) Strong skills in Islamic jurisprudence (*Usul Al-Fiqh*), as he must know the appropriate *Fiqh* methodologies for deriving juristic opinion

c) Good comprehension of Arabic language
d) Good communication skills in English Language

On a sufficient cause being shown by an IBI and an application made by it to the effect, the SBP may, at its discretion, allow relaxation from one or more of the aforesaid requirements of the FAPC, for such period and on such condition(s), as the SBP may deem appropriate in the specific circumstances of each case.

3. Track Record

Each member of Shari'ah Board must have an impeccable track record of professional conduct and in social, economic and financial dealings.

4. Solvency and Financial Integrity

Each member of the Shari'ah Board shall, at the time of acceptance of his appointment thereon, declare in writing that he:

i. has not been associated with any illegal activity.
ii. has not been in default of payment of dues owed to any financial institution and/or default in payment of any taxes in an individual capacity or as a proprietary concern or as a partner of any partnership firm or as a director or CEO or major shareholder of a company or any other corporate body in Pakistan or aboard.

5. Integrity, Honesty and Reputation

Each member of the Shari'ah Board shall, at the time of acceptance of his appointment thereon, declare in writing that he:

i. has not been convicted of any criminal offence involving financial impropriety or moral turpitude.
ii. has not been subject to any adverse findings or any settlement in civil or criminal proceedings with regard to investments, financial or business misconduct or fraud.
iii. has not contravened any of the requirements and standards of financial, banking or corporate regulatory regime.

6. Conflict of Interest

i. The Resident Shari'ah Board Member (RSBM) of an Islamic Banking Institution (IBI) shall not work or be employed in any other IBI in any capacity whatsoever. He may, however, with prior approval of the SB of IBI serve as a member of the Shari'ah Board of a maximum two other IFIs. Further, RSBM shall not hold any administrative and/or permanent position with any organization / institution other than the IBI where he is appointed as RSBM.

ii. Upto three (3) years i.e. June, 2021, the SB members, except the RSBM, can serve as a member on the SBs of up to three IBIs in Pakistan.

iii. Members of a Shari'ah Board shall neither own nor have any direct or beneficial equity or proprietary interest in the business of: (a) the IFI in which they are being appointed/working as member Shari'ah Board, (b) Exchange Company (c) Member of Stock Exchange, and (d) Corporate Brokerage House nor he should be an employee of any of the aforementioned entities. Any person, on being appointed as a member of Shari'ah Board of an IBI and is exposed to any of the aforesaid restriction(s), shall within sixty (60) days of assuming his office as a member, divest himself from ownership or holding of equity or proprietorial interest in any of the companies or undertakings stipulated above. Failure to do so shall, ipso facto, render such person as disqualified from being a member of the Shari'ah Board.

iv. Each SB member (including RSBM) shall provide statement of changes in his engagements to Secretary of the IBI's Shari'ah Board on half yearly basis. In case of no change in engagement NIL statement shall be provided.

7. Declaration of Fidelity and Secrecy as per Section 33A of BCO 1962

Each member of the Shari'ah Board shall sign a declaration of fidelity and secrecy, before assuming office, as per provisions of Sub-section (2) of Section 33A of the Banking Companies Ordinance 1962 or any other statutory modification thereof, the format of which is provided as set out below. The Declaration shall be kept in safe custody by the IBI.

x...x...x

Proforma: Particulars of Shari'ah Board Members to be Submitted by Islamic Banking Institution

1. Full name: ______________________________(2 x 2.5 cm Photo)
2. Father's name: ______________________________
3. Date of Birth: (dd/mm/yyyy)
   Place of Birth: ______________________
4. Religion: ___________________________
   Nationality(ies):______________________
5. C.N.I.C. Number/Passport No.: _______________
   N.T.N.__________________________
6. Present residential address in full:

   ____
7. Permanent residential address in full:

   ____
8. Present job/Status:

   ____

   Institution/ Official address:

   ____
9. Contact Details:
   Residential Phone No. _______________
   Office Phone No.____________________
   Mobile Phone No. ___________________
   E-mail:____________________________
10. Education:
    a) Details of Shahadat-ul-Aalamiyyah/Post Graduate Degree

S.No.	Degree Name	Board/ University	Date of Passing	Percentage Marks	Grade/GPA

    b) Major Subjects studied in Bachelors/Masters degree:
       i) ______________________________________
       ii) ______________________________________
       iii) ______________________________________
       iv) ______________________________________
    c) Courses/ Trainings attended related to Banking and Finance, if any:
       i) ______________________________________
       ii) ______________________________________
       iii) ______________________________________

d) Language Skills in English and Arabic (Excellent/Good/Fair/Poor)

Proficiency in...	English	Arabic
Writing		
Reading		
Speaking		

e) Courses/ Certifications in English/ Arabic, if any:
   i) ______________________________
   ii) ______________________________
   iii) ______________________________

f) Computer Knowledge (Courses/ certifications or skills acquired)
   i) ______________________________
   ii) ______________________________
   ii) ______________________________

11. Experience/Appointments/Positions held during the last five years:
   a) Fatwa Experience:
      i) Experience of giving Shari'ah rulings

S.No.	Name of Institution	Field(s) of Fatwa	From (dd/mm/yyyy)	To (dd/mm/yyyy)

      ii) No. of Fatawa Issued

S.No.	Name of Institution	Field(s) of Fatwa	No. of Fatwa

      iii) No. of Fatawa Published

S.No.	Name of Publication	Subject	Publisher Name	Year of Publication

   b) Research Experience: __ Years
      i) Total No. of Publications/Articles Published in Research Journals

S.No.	Subject of Publication/Article	Name of Journal/Magazine	Date of Publication

      ii) No. of Books Authored/Compiled: _______

S.No.	Name of Book	Subject	Publisher Name	Year of Publication

c) Teaching Experience

S.No.	Name of Institution	Subjects and Books Taught	Level of Teaching: (under graduation/graduation/ post graduation)	From (dd/mm/yyyy)	To (dd/mm/yyyy)

d) Banking Experience (including current positions held)

S.No.	Name of Institution	Designation	From (dd/mm/yyyy)	To (dd/mm/yyyy)

e) Financial Institutions (excluding Banks) / Other Institutions Experience (including current positions held)

S.No.	Name of Institution	Designation	From (dd/mm/yyyy)	To (dd/mm/yyyy)

12. Name(s) & designation(s) of the supervisor (one grade up) under whom Shari'ah scholar member of Shari'ah Board has served during the last five years

S.No.	Name of Supervisor	Designation of Supervisor	Name of Institution

13. Has he ever been terminated or dismissed in the capacity of employee director/chairman from any institution, firm or a company?
Yes______ No______ (If yes, provide details in the following format)

S.No.	Year	Designation	Name of Institution	Reason of Termination/ Dismissal

14. Has he ever been convicted of any offence?
Yes______ No______ (If yes, provide details in the following format)

S.No.	Year	Nature of Offence	Authority by Whom Convicted	Penalty/Sentence Imposed

15. Has he ever been censured and/or penalized by any financial/tax authority (local or foreign)?
Yes_____ No_____ (If yes, provide details in the following format)

S.No.	Year	Nature of Findings	Authority by Whom Penalized	Penalty Imposed

16. Has he ever been dismissed from employment?
Yes _____ No_____ (If yes, provide details in the following format)

S.No.	Year	Employer by Whom Dismissed	Reason for Dismissal

17. Does he hold/has held any executive/non-executive position in any other financial institution?
    Yes_____ No_____ (If yes, provide details in the following format)

S.No.	Designation and Nature of Position	Name of Financial Institution	From (dd/mm/yyyy)	To (dd/mm/yyyy)

18. Does he hold any direct or beneficial equity or proprietary interest in the business of: (a) the IFI in which he is being appointed as member Shari'ah Board, (b) Exchange Company (c) Member of Stock Exchange, and (d) Corporate Brokerage House or he is employee of any of the aforementioned entities.
    Yes_____ No_____
    If having equity or proprietory interest, provide details in the following format

S.No.	Name of Institution	Percentage Interest Held	From (dd/mm/yyyy)	To (dd/mm/yyyy)

If employee of any of the aforementioned entities, provide details in the following format

S.No.	Name of Institution	Designation	From (dd/mm/yyyy)	To (dd/mm/yyyy)

19. Shareholding in the IBI
    Number of shares held as of _________
20. Does he hold any direct or beneficial equity interest in the business of any other Islamic banking or Islamic financial institution? If yes, provide details in the following format

S.No.	Name of Institution	Percentage Interest Held	From (dd/mm/yyyy)	To (dd/mm/yyyy)

21. Names & addresses of three respectable persons (not relatives) who have been closely acquainted with the member Shari'ah Board of the IBI during the last five years

S.No.	Name	Address	Contact No.

____

(Signature of the proposed member of Shari'ah Board of the IBI)

Affidavit

(On Non-Judicial Stamp Paper)

I,____________________ son/daughter/wife of________________________ adult, resident of ____ ______________________________ and holding CNIC No./Passport No. ______________________________ do hereby state on solemn affirmation as under:

a. that the deponent hereby confirms that the statements made and the information provided in the attached proforma and the answers thereof are correct and that there are no other facts that are relevant for "Fit and Proper Criteria" which I have not disclosed;
b. that the deponent undertakes that the State Bank of Pakistan may seek additional information from any third party it deems necessary in view of assessing "Fit and Proper Criteria"
c. that the deponent undertakes to bring to the attention of the State Bank of Pakistan any matter which may potentially affect my status of eligibility as being someone fit and proper as and when it arises; and
d. that whatever is stated above is true and correct to the best of my knowledge and belief and nothing has been concealed therefrom.

Deponent

The Deponent is identified by me

Signature ____________________

Advocate

(Name and Seal)

Solemnly affirmed before me on this ______ day of ____________ at ____________ by the Deponent above named who is identified to me by ______________, Advocate, who is known to me personally.

Signature______________________

OATH COMMISSIONER FOR TAKING AFFIDAVIT

(Name and Seal)

Declaration of Fidelity and Secrecy

(To be signed by the Shari'ah Board Member)

In terms of Clause 7 of Fit and Proper Criteria for the appointment as a Shari'ah Board Member, I, (insert name) on becoming Shari'ah Board Member of the (insert name of bank), in terms of Section 33-A of the Banking Companies Ordinance, 1962 do hereby solemnly & sincerely confirm/declare that I shall observe strict fidelity, secrecy and usage customary among bankers and all matters relating thereto and in particular shall not divulge or communicate any information relating to the affairs of its customers, which may come to my knowledge in discharging my duties directly or indirectly, except in circumstances in which it is in accordance with law, practice and usage customary among bankers.

Dated: __________________ Signature: ______________________

Stamp: ____________________

ANNEXURE - B

Report of Shari'ah Board

(Period)

In the name of Allah, the Beneficent, the Merciful

1. While the Board of Directors and Executive Management are solely responsible to ensure that the operations of (*name of the bank*) are conducted in a manner that comply with Shari'ah principles at all times, we are required to submit a report on the overall Shari'ah compliance environment of
(*name of the bank*).
2. To form our opinion as expressed in this report, the Shari'ah Compliance Department of the bank carried out reviews, on test check basis, of each class of transactions, the relevant documentation and process flows. Further, we have also reviewed the reports of the internal Shari'ah audit and external Shari'ah audit. Based on above, we are of the view that:
(SB's opinion at least on the following may be given)
    i. Whether or not IBI has complied with Shari'ah rules and principles in the light of fatawa, rulings and guidelines issued by its Shari'ah Board
    ii. Whether or not IBI has complied with directives, regulations, instructions and guidelines related to Shari'ah compliance issued by SBP in accordance with the rulings of SBP's Shari'ah Board.
    iii. Whether or not the bank has a comprehensive mechanism in place to ensure Shari'ah compliance in their overall operations.
    iv. Whether or not the bank has a well-defined system in place which is sound enough to ensure that any earnings realized from sources or by means prohibited by Shari'ah have been credited to charity account and are being properly utilized.
    v. Whether or not the bank has complied with the SBP instructions on profit and loss distribution and pool management.
    vi. The level of awareness, capacity and sensitization of the staff, management and the BOD in appreciating the importance of Shari'ah compliance in the products and processes of the bank.
    vii. Whether or not the Shari'ah Board has been provided adequate resources enabling it to discharge its duties effectively.

3. Further, the following are the significant Shari'ah related issues of the bank which have been taken up with its management; however, these are still outstanding.

Signature
Name
Chairman Shari'ah Board

Signature
Name
Member Shari'ah Board

Signature
Name
Member Shari'ah Board

Date of Report: _______________

ANNEXURE-C

Draft Sample

Independent Assurance Report on Compliance with the Shari'ah Rules and Principles To the Board of Directors of [____________ / ___________ - Islamic Banking Institution]

1. Introduction

We have undertaken a reasonable assurance engagement that the State Bank of Pakistan has required in terms of its Shari'ah Governance Framework – External Shari'ah Audit of [____________ / ______________– [IBI] (the Islamic Banking Institution) for assessing compliance of the IBI's financial arrangements, contracts, and transactions having Shari'ah implications with Shari'ah rules and principles for the year ended__________. This engagement was conducted by a multidisciplinary team including assurance practitioners and independent Shari'ah scholar(s).

2. Applicable Criteria

The criteria for the assurance engagement, against which the underlying subject matter (financial arrangements, contracts, and transactions having Shari'ah implications for the year ended ____________) is assessed, comprise of the Shari'ah rules and principles that for the purpose of External Shari'ah Audit, mean the following, in the sequence provided below:

i) Essentials, Regulations, Instructions and Guidelines issued by the State Bank of Pakistan (SBP) including the Shari'ah Standards issued by Accounting and Auditing Organization for Islamic Financial Institutions (AAOIFI), as adopted by SBP with modifications, if any;
ii) The rulings of SBP's Shari'ah Board as notified by SBP;
iii) Requirements of the applicable Islamic Financial Accounting Standards as notified by the Securities and Exchange Commission of Pakistan (SECP) and as circulated by SBP;
iv) Approvals and rulings given by the SB of the IBI in line with the SBP directives, regulations, instructions and guidelines issued in accordance with the rulings of SBP's Shari'ah Board.

The above criteria were evaluated for their implications on the financial statements of IBI for the year ended ____________, which are annexed.

3. Management's Responsibility for Shari'ah Compliance

IBI's management is responsible to ensure that the financial arrangements, contracts and transactions having Shari'ah implications, entered into by the IBI with its customers, other financial institutions and stakeholders and related policies and procedures are, in substance and in their legal form, in compliance with the requirements of Shari'ah rules and principles. The management is also responsible for design, implementation and maintenance of appropriate internal control procedures with respect to such compliance and maintenance of relevant accounting records.

4. Our Independence and Quality Control

We have complied with the independence and other ethical requirements of the Code of Ethics for Chartered Accountants issued by the Institute of Chartered Accountants of Pakistan, which is founded on fundamental principles of integrity, objectivity, professional competence and due care, confidentiality and professional behavior.

The firm applies International Standard on Quality Control 1 "Quality Control for Firms That Perform Audits and Reviews of Historical Financial Information, And Other Assurance and Related Services Engagements" and accordingly maintains a comprehensive system of quality control including documented policies and procedures regarding compliance with ethical requirements, professional standards and applicable legal and regulatory requirements.

5. Our Responsibility and Summary of the Work Performed

Our responsibility in connection with this engagement is to express an opinion on compliance of the IBI's financial arrangements, contracts, and transactions having Shari'ah implications with Shari'ah rules and principles, in all material respects, for the year ended __________ based on the evidence we have obtained. We conducted our

reasonable assurance engagement in accordance with International Standard on Assurance Engagements 3000, 'Assurance Engagements other than audits or reviews of historical financial statements', issued by the International Auditing and Assurance Standards Board. That standard requires that we plan and perform this engagement to obtain reasonable assurance about whether the compliance of the IBI's financial arrangements, contracts, and transactions having Shari'ah implications with Shari'ah rules and principles is free from material misstatement.

The procedures selected by us for the engagement depended on our judgement, including the assessment of the risks of material non-compliance with the Shari'ah rules and principles. In making those risk assessments, we considered and tested the internal control relevant to the IBI's compliance with the Shari'ah rules and principles in order to design procedures that are appropriate in the circumstances, but not for the purpose of expressing an opinion on the effectiveness of the IBI's internal control. In this connection, we have also reviewed the work carried out by the Internal Shari'ah Audit

Department and the Shari'ah reviews carried out by the Shari'ah Compliance Department. We have designed and performed necessary verification procedures on various financial arrangements, contracts, classes of transactions and related policies and procedures based on judgmental and systematic samples with regard to the compliance with Shari'ah rules and principles. In performing our audit procedures necessary guidance on Shari'ah matters was provided by independent Shari'ah scholar(s) referred above.

We believe that the evidences we have obtained through performing our procedures were sufficient and appropriate to provide a basis for our opinion [or modified opinion].

6. Description of the Matter(s) Giving Rise to the Modified Conclusion (if any)

a) ______________________________;
b) ______________________________;
[insert material modifications to report, if any]

7. Conclusion

Based on our reasonable assurance engagement, we report that in our opinion, [except for the effect of the matters reported in paragraph(s) a) to x) above], the IBI's financial arrangements, contracts and transactions for the year ended __________ are in compliance with the Shari'ah rules and principles, in all material respects.

A long form report highlighting key matters noted during the course of engagement is issued separately to the Board of Director of IBI of date.

Date: __________
Name of firm Chartered Accountants __________________
[Place / City] __________________________
Name of Engagement Partner ______________________________

Long Form Report

The long form auditors' report under the SBP Shari'ah Governance Framework will include the following aspects, as a minimum:

Objective and scope of the engagement

The report will include key findings including those related to the following:

a) the overall Shari'ah compliance environment,
b) the risks associated with Shari'ah non-compliance,
c) the capacity and quality of the risk management system to measure, manage and mitigate these risks,
d) the level of awareness and sensitization of the EM and the BOD in addressing the said risks,
e) pool management practices and IT based system specifically computation and distribution of profit & loss to the depositors, tagging and movement of assets and allocation of income & expenses, etc. and,
f) any other issues deemed significant by the external auditors.

Management's and auditors' responsibilities and other important terms of engagement

Description of the procedures performed

Limitations with respect to the engagement involving performance of the procedures Detailed description of the factual findings resulting from the auditors' work identifying the gap/ issue identified and the recommendation to address the same

Statement that the procedures performed do not constitute either an audit or a review under the applicable standards and, as such, no assurance is expressed

To give the name of the Shari'ah Consultant appointed by the firm for the said engagement.

x...x...x

About the Authors

Abdus Sattar Abbasi has a vast experience of both the corporate sector and the academia. He remained posted in four countries, other than the homeland - including Kazakhstan, Tajikistan, Uzbekistan and Azerbaijan - during this journey of more than two and a half decades. He is Associate Professor and Head CIF, COMSATS University Islamabad, Lahore Campus, Pakistan. He is the founding editor of COMSATS Journal of Islamic Finance (CJIF). He also founded GFIF and IFEA. He travelled to several countries to attend conferences and training courses including China, England, Turkey, Thailand, Sri Lanka, Malaysia, Singapore and Dubai; besides he also visited Saudi Arabia, Afghanistan and Iran.

Razaq Raj is an internationally renowned academic with over 18 years' higher education experience of teaching and research in the UK, Malta, Portugal, Spain, Italy, Germany, China and South Korea. He is Principal Lecturer for Research and Enterprise and Visiting Professor at the Kedge Business School, France and University of Vitez, Bosnia. He has substantial external examining and curriculum development experience of both undergraduate and postgraduate degrees in business management, events and tourism. He is Co- founding editor of the International Journal of Religious Tourism and Pilgrimage and Series Co-Editor for CABI's Religious Tourism and Pilgrimage Series (with Kevin Griffin).

Index

www.ingramcontent.com/pod-product-compliance
Lightning Source LLC
LaVergne TN
LVHW061538290926
849162LV00004B/834